A Journal of the American Civil War

Managing Editor:

Mark A. Snell

Director, George Tyler Moore Center for the Study of the Civil War

Shepherd College, Shepherdstown, West Virginia

VOLUME FIVE

NUMBER THREE

Published quarterly by Savas Publishing Company

Subscription and General Information

Civil War Regiments is published quarterly by Savas Publishing Company, 1475 South Bascom Avenue, Suite 204, Campbell, CA 95008. Executive Editor Theodore P. Savas, 408.879.9073 (voice); 408.879.9327; (fax); MHBooks@aol.com (e-mail). Managing Editor Mark A. Snell may be contacted at the George Tyler Moore Center for the Study of the Civil War, 136 W. German Street, Shepherdstown, WV 25443. 304.876.5429 (voice); 304.876.5079 (fax).

Trade distribution is handled by Peter Rossi at Stackpole Books, 5067 Ritter Road, Mechanicsburg, PA 17055-6921. Voice: 1-800-732-3669; Fax: 1-717-976-0412.

SUBSCRIPTIONS: $29.95/year, ppd (four books), individual and institutional. Back issues may be ordered from the publisher. Write to: Back Issues: CWR, 1475 South Bascom, Suite 204, Campbell, CA 95008, or call 1-800-848-6585, for pricing information, contents and availability. Please specify the volume and issue number when placing your order. Prepayment with check, money order, or MC/V is required. Two hundred and fifty signed and numbered four-issue Collector's Sets for the premier volume were printed. Cost is $40.00ppd. Inquire as to availability. FOREIGN ORDERS: Subscriptions: $35.95/year, including surface delivery. Payment in United States currency only or MC/V. Allow eight to twelve weeks for delivery.

MANUSCRIPTS AND CORRESPONDENCE: We welcome manuscript inquiries. For author's guidelines, send a self-addressed, double-stamped business envelope to: Editor, *Civil War Regiments*, 136 W. German Street, Shepherdstown, WV 25443. Include a brief description of your proposed topic and the sources to be utilized. No unsolicited submissions will be returned without proper postage. Book review inquiries should be directed to Dr. Archie McDonald, Book Review Editor, Stephen F. Austin University, Department of History, P.O. Box 6223, SFA Station, Nacogdoches, Texas 75962-6223. (409) 568-2407. Enclose a SASE if requesting a reply.

Thanks to your support, *Civil War Regiments* has been able to make a number of donations to Civil War-related preservation organizations. Some of the recipients of these donations are listed below:

(LIFE MEMBER) ASSOCIATION FOR THE PRESERVATION OF CIVIL WAR SITES

RICHARD B. GARNETT MEMORIAL, HOLLYWOOD CEMETERY

HERITAGEPAC / CIVIL WAR ROUND TABLE ASSOCIATES

SAVE HISTORIC ANTIETAM FOUNDATION / TURNER ASHBY HOUSE,
PORT REPUBLIC, VA

THE COKER HOUSE RESTORATION PROJECT, JACKSON, MS CWRT

AMERICAN BLUE & GRAY ASSOCIATION

APCWS 1993 MALVERN HILL/GLENDALE CAMPAIGN

Civil War Regiments, Vol. 5, No. 3, Copyright 1997

by Savas Publishing Company

ISBN 1-882810-53-8

CONTRIBUTORS:

Wilbur Jones is a retired naval officer and former assistant to President Gerald Ford. He is the author of *Giants in the Cornfield* (Shippensburg, 1997), a regimental history of the 27th Indiana Infantry.

D. Scott Hartwig is a Ranger-Historian at Gettysburg National Military Park. He has published widely on the Civil War and currently is working on a history of the Maryland Campaign.

Tom Clemens is an associate professor of history at Hagerstown Junior College. He is the president of Save Historic Antietam Foundation, Inc. (SHAF)

George E. Otott, a geologist for Thums Long Beach Company in Southern California, has spent several years researching the 1st Texas Infantry, which is the subject of his Master's Thesis.

David Mellott is a trial attorney in Cleveland, OH. He is working on a book-length regimental history of the 7th West Virginia Infantry. "A Dear Bought Name" is his first published article on the Civil War.

A Journal of the American Civil War

Table of Contents

Introduction

Theodore P. Savas

On the crest of a tidal wave of Southern victories, Robert E. Lee and the Army of Northern Virginia launched their first raid across the Potomac River in September 1862. "The present seems to be the most propitious time since the commencement of the war for the Confederate Army to enter Maryland," Lee wrote President Jefferson Davis on the 3rd day of September.[1] As usual, Lee was right.

After assuming command of the army just three months earlier, Lee had thrown back George McClellan's numerically superior Army of the Potomac from the outskirts of Richmond during the Seven Days Battles. This blistering offensive was followed with the thrashing of John Pope at Second Manassas. Concurrently, two Confederate armies in the Western Theater under Braxton Bragg and Kirby Smith were preparing to march into Kentucky. Europe was taking a second look at the South as a viable candidate for recognition. It looked as though the Confederacy's hour was at hand.

Lee faced two options after Manassas: either revert to the strategic defensive by covering his capital at Richmond and resting his army in the process, or move north across the Potomac and strike a disorganized and demoralized enemy. Characteristically, Lee retained the initiative by taking the bold course of action and crossing the Potomac. It was a decision he hoped would render decisive results.

Unfortunately for the Confederates, the real opportunity that autumn lay with the Federals. Lee badly underestimated McClellan's ability to revitalize John Pope's disorganized regiments, and within days the Army of the Potomac marched to meet its foe. Quickly the tables were turned. With the Army of Northern Virginia now badly weakened by casualties and wholesale straggling, its position on the north bank of the Potomac risked total destruction. This was especially so once Special Orders No. 191, detailing the exact disposition of the various segments of Lee's army, fell into McClellan's lap. President Abraham Lincoln appreciated Lee's precarious position and urged full-scale offensive operations. "Destroy the rebel army, if possible," commanded Lincoln just two days before Antietam. Porter Alexander, James Longstreet's brilliant artillerist and wisdom-filled scribe, clearly digested the situation. "Not twice in a lifetime does such a chance come to any general. Lee for once has made a mistake. . . ." Historian Gary Gallagher agrees. "When Lee decided to stay north of the Potomac and offer battle, he gave McClellan the most incredible military opportunity of the conflict."2

Indeed, in September of 1862 Lee's game involved great risks, and McClellan's, great opportunities.

The articles in this compendium offer a variety of historical slices of the Maryland Campaign. The lead essay, "Who Lost Lee's Lost Orders? Stonewall Jackson, His Courier, and Special Orders No. 191," by Wilbur D. Jones, Jr., purportedly unmasks, for the first time, the identity of the culprit who misplaced the "Lost Dispatch." Jones methodically sifts through a considerable body of evidence (much of it readily available and yet long overlooked or ignored) in an attempt to weed out the possible suspects. In the end, his historical piece of detective work points to only one man who could have lost the orders. The author concludes his stimulating brief by asking, "If the culprit was not – – – – , then who remains in contention?" Wherever he is, D. H. Hill, long the slippery fingered scapegoat, must be smiling.

The crucial battles for the South Mountain passes are usually glossed over in a sentence or two by historians and writers who should know better. The bitter fighting on the wooded hillsides, which set the stage for the bloodiest day in American history just seventy-two hours later, could have been catastrophic for Lee. D. Scott Hartwig, a ranger-historian at Gettysburg National Military Park, offers a compelling account of the struggle for one of those passes in "'My God! Be Careful!' Morning Battle at Fox's Gap." Students of the campaign will find Scott's well researched and smoothly written examination of the tactics of the battle and its ramifications both enlightening and thought-provoking.

Antietam was fought by veterans and neophytes. One of the latter was Col. Walter Phelps, Jr., who assumed command of a brigade of New York regiments in the streets of Frederick, Maryland on September 14. His new command, thinned out by casualties, disease and vigorous marching, totaled but 500 men.

In "A Brigade Commander's First Fight: The Letters of Colonel Walter Phelps, Jr. during the Maryland Campaign," editor Tom Clemens presents a telling and personal portrait of a man preparing to face the trial of his life, as told largely through letters written to his wife Eliza. "It is possible I may have an opportunity to distinguish myself as a brigade commander," he wrote home on September 13. He could not have known how prophetic his words would be.

Some of the most well-known acreage in American history was planted in corn on September 17, 1862. One of the myriad of units that fought, marched and died amongst the green stalks of the Miller farm was the 1st Texas Infantry. While the tribulations suffered by the Texans are generally known—they lost at Antietam probably the highest casualty rate (over 82%) of any regiment in any Civil War battle—no one has deeply researched the regiment in an attempt to offer a definitive account of its service north of the Potomac River. "Clash in the Cornfield: The 1st Texas Volunteer Infantry in the Maryland Campaign," by George E. Otott, is a splendidly presented monograph brimming with firsthand entries, solid analysis and enough tactical minutiae to satisfy the most hardened student of the Civil War. Based upon years of research and supported by a half dozen outstanding cartographic plates, Otott's article, which clarifies and redefines the fighting on the Miller farm, increases our understanding and appreciation of what took place during those confused minutes early that morning.

Rounding out this collection is another stellar tactical entry, "A Dear Bought Name: The 7th West Virginia Infantry's Assault on Bloody Lane," by David W. Mellott. Despite having carved out one of the finest combat records of any Federal regiment, the 7th West Virginia has been shunned by chroniclers of the war. Mellott, a trial attorney deeply interested in West Virginia's role in the Civil War, has greatly added to our knowledge of both this extraordinary unit and the confused and bloody fighting along the sunken road at Antietam that claimed so many of the regiment's souls.

Despite the availability of several excellent books on this campaign, these essays prove once again that there is still room for quality research and writing—even on fields that have been deeply plowed by prior historians. We have received so many outstanding articles that we have decided to publish two separate books on the fighting in Maryland. Look for the second installment early in Volume Six. If your interest in the mammoth Lee–McClellan encounter grows as a result of reading these articles, our task was successful.

New Editor

Finding someone who has a deep interest in the Civil War is hardly difficult. Locating someone with that interest *and* the ability to work with authors, research, write and edit—*and* understand what a deadline means—is something else altogether. We believe we have found such a person in Mark A. Snell, and I am pleased to introduce him to you as our new managing editor.

Mark received his Master's Degree in United States History from Rutger's University and performed his undergraduate work at York College of Pennsylvania. He is a retired U.S. Army major and previously served as an assistant professor of history at West Point. He currently is the Director of The George Tyler Moore Center for the Study of the Civil War, Shepherd College, Shepherdstown, WV. The primary mission of the Center is to develop a database that includes military, socio-economic and medical data on Union and Confederate servicemen. The Center serves a very worthwhile purpose, and I urge all of our readers to support its endeavors in any way they can. Make sure and visit personally if you are in the area. The setting, nestled up against the scenic Potomac, is lovely.

All of us associated with *Civil War Regiments* are excited by the wide variety of interesting and refreshing topics Mark is planning to see through into print. We look forward to a long and fruitful relationship with Mark and his staff, and as always, strive to bring to you the finest in Civil War history.

And now, as Edwin C. Bearss, Chief Historian Emeritus for the National Park Service, is fond of exclaiming: "On to the Maryland Campaign!"

Notes

1. *The Papers of Jefferson Davis, 1862* , edited by Lynda Lasswell Crist (Baton Rouge, 1996), vol. 8, p. 373.

2. *Antietam: Essays on the 1862 Maryland Campaign*, edited by Gary Gallagher (Kent, 1989), p. 12. This little gem of a book offers some of the most thought-provoking analysis of the campaign to be found on the subject.

"The facts were undoubtedly suppressed by those who were cognizant of them. . . ."

WHO LOST THE LOST ORDERS?
Stonewall Jackson, His Courier, and Special Orders No. 191

Wilbur D. Jones, Jr.

The Union Army's discovery of a copy of Confederate Gen. Robert E. Lee's Special Orders No. 191 near Frederick, Maryland, on September 13, 1862, outlining the disposition of his thin and widespread Army of Northern Virginia, precipitated the Battle of Antietam four days later. The revelations of the orders, called the "Lost Order" in the North and the "Lost Dispatch" in the South, prompted Union commander Maj. Gen. George B. McClellan to pursue Lee's divided army and force that fateful clash from which the South never fully recovered.

The results of the Union victory at Antietam reaped political consequences exceeding this bloody battlefield of the Civil War. President Abraham Lincoln used the military success to sign the Emancipation Proclamation, injecting slavery as an emotional and moral war issue. Powerful European nations eventually refused political recognition of the Confederacy and its military and economic benefits. Lee withdrew his battered forces back into Virginia, his first foray into the North a strategic failure. Antietam thus redirected the course of the war and ultimately led to the downfall of the Confederacy.

How No. 191 was lost, and who caused it to be lost, has remained one of the war's enduring mysteries. The copy of No. 191 found wrapped around three cigars in a clover field two miles south of Frederick by members of the 27th Indiana Infantry, addressed to Maj. Gen. D. H. Hill, was either intentionally placed or carelessly dropped. The act assured the Hoosier regiment a place in history, but its loser has avoided disgrace.

The act of losing S. O. 191 has evoked only passing interest from modern historians. Most have discussed the finding and what occurred later: when Lee knew about its disappearance, the battle itself, Lee's disastrous Maryland Campaign and the repercussions.[1] The mystery has been treated as either beyond solution or too sensitive. This article scrutinizes a possible circumstance and those suspected of perpetuating it, and concludes, through circumstantial evidence, what man allegedly lost it and how.

In order to determine just who lost S. O. 191, we shall begin with an examination of how Lee's orders to his field commanders were written, recorded and delivered, and the principals involved. A key Lee staff officer, Capt. Charles Marshall, described Lee's correspondence control system: "The staff took Lee's instructions, wrote them down, entered one copy in the 'confidential book' or held it to be copied later into the general order book, and sent another copy by orderly to the commander addressed. Sometimes the orderly was told to bring back a receipt."[2] That normal procedure failed to operate properly on September 9, 1862, the date No. 191 was issued. Colonel Robert Hall Chilton, Lee's chief administrative officer, signed the orders. Lee staff officers Marshall, Maj. Charles S. Venable and Maj. Walter H. Taylor also knew the system.

Marshall said Lee's general orders were frequently transmitted directly to each division commander.[3] Taylor said the custom was to send confidential orders to the wing and division commanders only, and that Hill, as a division commander unincorporated with either wing, received a copy of No. 191 as normal course. Venable said headquarters sent Hill a copy directly, and that Hill received another copy in the handwriting of Lt. Gen. Thomas J. Jackson.[4] The question of receipts arose. Chilton said couriers were told to return the delivery envelopes with written evidence of delivery. "This order was so important that violation of this rule would have been noticed, & I think I should certainly recollect if delivery had been omitted. . . ."[5] Chilton kept no journal (only file copies of correspondence) or "memoranda in consequence of being constantly otherwise occupied."[6] Lee would say later he could not believe a courier lost No. 191 "as couriers were always required to bring receipt to show that written orders were safely and surely delivered."[7]

Once deciding to split his army into two parts—Jackson's wing to Harpers Ferry, Virginia, and Lt. Gen. James Longstreet's to Hagerstown, Maryland—Lee wanted to quickly proceed. Chilton felt pressure to write the original, receive Lee's approval, then write the other copies and dispatch them to each commander assigned an objective and route, letting the administrative system catch up. It never did. He dispatched several couriers, with or without instructions to bring receipts. Most couriers had not returned when, as an afterthought, he penciled a copy to Hill. Harried, he pressed into courier service any available officer he saw in the headquarters.

Chilton did not write about the order during the war and answered few inquiries later. In 1874, he responded to Confederate President Jefferson Davis about the system: "That omission to deliver in his [the courier's] case so important an order w'd have been recollected as entailing the duty to advise its loss, to guard against its consequences, and to act as required. . . .But I could not of course say positively that I had sent any particular courier to him [Hill] after such a lapse of time."[8] The envelope in which No. 191 was found was blank, but because D. H. Hill was the addressee, a logical conclusion was that Hill lost it. If not Hill, then it was his staff. Daniel Harvey became the South's scapegoat and, despite his vehement denials, historians continued to speculate on his culpability.

This line of reasoning stemmed from the organization of Lee's army when the order was issued. Hill brought his division directly from Richmond to join Lee in early September. Hill was one of the first commanders to enter Maryland and immediately reported to Jackson, who until Lee arrived was ranking commander of all Confederate forces there. En route, Hill's Division had been an independent force. The army was not formally organized into corps, but each unit fell under either Jackson's or Longstreet's command. Jackson recognized Hill's arrival and began issuing his subordinate orders in the usual fashion.[9] Both generals agreed that Hill would come under the command of Jackson.

No. 191 defined Hill's new role. As the rear guard, he was independent again. Chilton thus correctly issued a copy directly to Hill, but he failed to determine if Jackson had ordered Hill, or so intended. Chilton wrongly assumed that Jackson would recognize Hill's independent role and that Lee would subsequently send the appropriate order to Hill. Although Lee was confident it was sent directly to Hill, the copy never reached him and became the "Lost Order." Lee also supposed Jackson sent a copy to Hill, so Hill would thus know he was no longer under Jackson.[10] Lee's comments were wishful hindsight: Chilton had acted on his own.

Jackson knew Hill had a separate assignment, but because he regarded Hill as still reporting to him when Lee issued the order, he felt obligated to inform Hill. In his own handwriting, Jackson penned a copy for Hill, minus the first two paragraphs, and dispatched it to him that afternoon via his trusted courier, Capt. Henry Kyd Douglas. Major J. W. Ratchford, Hill's top aide, received the copy from Douglas and gave it to Hill.[11] Hill insisted the Jackson link was proper: "I went into Maryland under Jackson's command. I was under his command when Lee's order was issued. It was proper that I should receive that order through Jackson and not through Lee."[12] Having received all other orders from Jackson, it was "utterly incomprehensible that all orders should come through officials channel except this one, the most important of all."[13] Hill never expected a direct order from Lee. He did not file Jackson's copy with his office papers, but sewed it into the lining of his coat and later sent it home.

In June 1863, Hill first heard of the Lost Order and his association with it. McClellan disclosed the discovery during his testimony before the Congressional Committee on the Conduct of the War. Hill heard about it again in September, and wrote his wife to save the copy he had sent home earlier.[14]

After the war, there was a strong bias in the Southern mind against Hill. In 1868 he repudiated his loudest early antagonist, the wartime editor of the Richmond *Examiner*: "The harsh epithets which he applies to me are unworthy of the dignity of the historian, and prove a prejudiced state of mind. Second, if I petulantly threw down the order [as was claimed], I deserve not merely to be cashiered, but to be shot to death with musketry. General Lee, who ought to have known the facts. . .never brought me to trial for it." He cited his later nomination for promotion by Davis and corps command at Chickamauga as evidence of his innocence.[15] Lee said "he did not know that General Hill had himself lost the dispatch and in consequence he had no grounds upon which to act, but that General Stuart and other officers in the army were very indignant about the matter."[16]

Hill devoted years clearing his name but never crusaded to find the guilty. In 1867, Ratchford affirmed that "no order came to the division from General Lee."[17] In the end, historians, rather than comrades, indicted Hill or his staff, but because of Hill's avid self defense, the lack of proof, and Ratchford's honorable service, contemporaries tactfully accepted Hill's word: it was someone else's carelessness, and the truth would not be known. Yet accusations still focused on the North Carolinian Hill and away from "The Virginians" (Lee, Jackson, Chilton, Taylor, et al.).

As Confederate veterans spoke out, they laid blame for many failures, including the Maryland invasion. In 1885, Hill wrote Longstreet, "[t]he Virginians in order to glorify Lee assume that he should have conquered a peace, but for my carelessness. . . .The vanity of the Virginians has made them glorify their own prowess and deify Lee. They made me the scapegoat for Maryland and you for [Gettysburg] Pennsylvania. . .[in] an effort to prove Lee's infallibility."[18]

Other historians charged Hill had left the copy on a table in Frederick, or that it was found on a street where Hill and his staff had been. "There are many still living who know that I occupied a tent, not a house, outside of Frederick," the fiery Hill responded.[19] Hill asked Chilton whether a courier could have dropped another general's copy in Hill's camp. Chilton wrote that "I should have supposed so important an order as constituting an important part of the history of the war would have been preserved amongst your papers if ever received."[20] Then Chilton hid behind a "very defective memory," thinking the orders had been issued in Leesburg, Virginia.[21]

In 1868, Capt. Joseph G. Morrison, a Jackson staff member (and brother-in-law of both Jackson and Hill), verified Jackson's handwriting was on the copy Hill saved, which Morrison already had written on that copy.[22] Hill speculated the loser was a traitor in the ranks—but by staff position, not name. Some Union generals thought the order was found in the camp of Maj. Gen. A. P. Hill, as if inferring the wrong Hill was blamed. D. H. accused no one and, partly in deference to A. P. who was later killed, never mentioned this.[23]

Hill rebuffed the statement by 27th Indiana Colonel Silas Colgrove in an 1886 *Century Magazine* article that the order was found in Hill's own campsite.[24] By 1885, Hill believed he had "exposed the unfairness of attributing to me the loss of a paper, solely on the ground that it was directed to me." He almost had the answer. "The explanation of the mystery may be that a copy was prepared by General Lee's adjutant for me but never forwarded," Hill speculated.[25]

The matter was unresolved in Hill's lifetime, and it bothered his family into the 1930s. Hill and Jackson had married sisters Isabella and Mary Anna Morrison of North Carolina, but the brothers-in-law were not close. The Hill side was jealous over the one-sided adulation given Jackson and the scant attention paid to their general. For instance, the Hills were rankled by an incident during the 1862 Seven Days battles, when D. H. was accused of losing a Jackson order. Hill recovered it before Union eyes saw it, however, and Jackson himself resolved the situation before it got out of hand.[26]

About January 1864, Mrs. Hill told her uncle, William A. Graham, that she had the copy of the order "in our dear Brother Jackson's own handwriting and filed away with his [D. H.'s] most important papers."[27] In 1931, Hill's daughter Eugenia wrote cousin Charles [believed Graham] who had located Hill's copy of the Jackson order:

Hurrah for you for finding the "Lost Dispatch." Mr. A. [Thomas Jackson Arnold, her husband] recognized it when I read your letter to him, & then I got

"Lt. Genl. T. J. Jackson & Staff"
Clockwise from 1 o'clock: R .L. Dabney, W. Allan, A. S. Pendleton, J. G. Morrison, D. B. Bridge-
ford, H. K. Douglas, J. P. Smith, H. McGuire, J. Hotchkiss, and W. J. Hawks
Miller's *Photographic History of the Civil War*

my father's account published in *The Land We Love* & verified it verbatim. I knew of course it was in his war papers. . . .As there <u>has been</u> so much <u>controversy over</u> it, for both of our fathers' sake we should clear it up as much as possible in our time.[28]

Eugenia suggested Charles write an article for *Confederate Veteran* magazine "& tell your part of it." Most importantly, she asked if he ever saw her husband's article in the August 1922 issue based on an 1897 address by Confederate Maj. Gen. Thomas Lafayette Rosser on the Lost Dispatch, "which I heard & wrote him of it the next day."[29] The *Confederate Veteran* article, written by Thomas Jackson Arnold but ignored by historians, follows:

The Lost Dispatch—A War Mystery

As is well known, General Hill received his own copy of the order, written in General Jackson's own handwriting, placed it in his files, and which is this day among his official papers. Why should there have been a duplicate of this order addressed to General Hill? A solution is here given, which would seem to clear up the mystery.

General Thomas L. Rosser, in an address delivered by him at Raleigh, N. C., on May 10, 1897, in referring to this lost dispatch, stated that the man who lost the dispatch had suffered enough humiliation from it for him (Rosser) not to mention his name. That it was one of Jackson's staff, who was a smoker; that when it was handed to him to deliver, he said, "O, we have that order," and so, carelessly, wrapped it around his cigars, placed it in his pocket, and lost it in that shape; and that he (Rosser) hoped this man would tell all his connection with it before he died. As the only member of Jackson's staff now living [1922] was not connected with his staff until after this event occurred, it is very evident that the staff officer referred to by General Rosser did not disclose the fact in his lifetime, and as General Rosser is not now living, the name of the staff officer may never be known. . . .

It is quite evident that the staff officer who wrote the second copy of the order was not present when General Jackson copied it and handed it to the official for delivery to General Hill. It is likewise evident that General Jackson was not present when the staff officer wrote the second copy and handed it to the official for delivery, and received the reply as quoted by General Rosser, "O, we have that order," and wrapped his cigars in the useless copy, placing the package in his pocket, and later lost it. . . .Imagine the chagrin of the staff officer upon learning the result of his carelessness; and what of the prospective interview between himself and General Jackson should the fact of his carelessness become known to the latter?

Evidently it never did, for the careless official's connection with headquarters would have ceased at that moment. Such gross carelessness would not have been excused. The facts were undoubtedly suppressed by those who were cognizant of them, and hence the mystery was never revealed. The quotation from General Rosser was written down the day following his address, and I have had this written statement in my possession ever since.[30]

A Jackson staff officer? If true, Rosser's assertions not only finally absolved Hill, but profoundly jeopardized the judgment, performance and credibility of the venerable Jackson team.[31] Historians have not speculated on any link between the Lost Order and Lee or Jackson. Here they, and Chilton, are not impervious to second guessing or criticism, and Jackson is held accountable for a grave lapse of judgment within his inner circle.

What about the "accuser"? Rosser, two weeks shy of graduating in 1861 from the U. S. Military Academy, resigned to join the Confederacy where he compiled a meritorious service record. Later he was a dynamic, popular speaker on the war and Americanism, who skillfully avoided defending the "Lost Cause" or imposing love of Union. In the 1890s, he was one of the most prominent living veterans.

Why did Southerners attack only D. H. Hill? Why was the mistake not handled in the army's judicial system? Why did it eventually just wash away? Who actually lost the Special Orders 191, and how?

First, neither Hill nor his staff lost something they never received. Guilt cannot be ascribed simply because Hill was the addressee. Involvement by a traitor or spy is a plot for parlor room fantasy or fiction writers, because of where the order was found and how long it had been there. The perpetrator was a Confederate soldier, because no one else could have touched that paper. Who are the suspect perpetrators?

1. First, Chilton: a mistake in perhaps his biggest service to Lee was something he wished to forget. He knew who took the copy for Hill—because he gave it to him—and thereby who lost it. Because he did not demand proper accounting, he is an accomplice of that man.

2. Venable, Taylor, Marshall: none were couriers except in emergencies. For one, Taylor was away meeting with President Davis. Lee's enlisted couriers: using enlisted men for such a major confidential delivery was unlikely. Because delivery was close to headquarters and contact with Federals was not unexpected, escorts were not needed.

3. Lieutenant Colonel Alexander Swift Pendleton, Jackson's Chief of Staff: he had left home for the front on September 9th after an illness and arrived the 13th.

4. Major Elisha F. Paxton, acting in Pendleton's absence: brand new, his job was to "mind the store" at Jackson's headquarters.

5. Lieutenant James Power Smith, Jackson's Aide-de-Camp: he was newly commissioned, had just joined the staff and had not earned his confidence. Morrison, Aide-de-Camp: trusted by Jackson, he could have been the courier, but no evidence indicates that it was him.

6. The principal non-line officers, Lt. Col. William Allan, Surgeon Hunter Holmes McGuire, Capt. J. K. Boswell, and Capt. Jedediah Hotchkiss: using them as couriers was unlikely for such a delivery.[32]

Of any other possible suspects, Henry Kyd Douglas comes closest to fitting the circumstantial evidence: he was in a position to act for Jackson; Jackson let him operate independently; he was Jackson's trusted courier; he smoked cigars; and his subsequent behavior raises a level of suspicion. Douglas lived until 1903, and could have been the Jackson staff member Rosser had referred to in 1897. Other potential couriers, except Smith, had died by 1897. Smith was still alive in 1922.

A detailed analysis of the evidence sheds further light on the alleged culprit. First, Douglas was in a position to act for Jackson. Had Pendleton been present the incident might not have happened. Douglas claimed postwar that he was the acting aide-de-camp in Maryland, a position of stature closer to Jackson than assistant inspector general.[33] Could the freewheeling Douglas have filled the vacuum during Pendleton's absence?

Second, Jackson had warmed to Douglas as a soldier despite the young Marylander's flair and egocentrism. Somewhere Jackson failed to counsel him, and the so-called "young Adonis" might have become Jackson's Achilles heel. Yet a Confederate general commenting on the Maryland Campaign said Douglas occupied "peculiarly confidential relations to him [Jackson]" and "probably knew as much of General Jackson's intentions as any man living."[34] Did Jackson let Douglas get too close and give him too much leash? If so, the young officer's self importance now casts a dark shadow over the judgment of both. If Douglas saw Chilton's copy for Hill, did informality override Douglas' normal meticulousness, moving him to abort Lee's correspondence system? At this momentous occasion, why would Douglas let down his fellow Virginians?

Third, Douglas was a valued courier for Jackson and other generals. In the Shenandoah Valley, Jackson sent him on a successful overnight round-trip mission.[35] At Second Manassas he carried Jackson's request to Longstreet for a division.[36] At Chancellorsville, Jackson directed him to remain at the front with Gen. Fitz Lee to bring any urgent message to Jackson.[37] At Gettysburg, Maj. Gen. Edward Johnson sent Douglas to tell the corps commander he could take Culp's Hill.[38]

Fourth, Douglas was an admitted cigar smoker and even received cigars from a friend while imprisoned at Johnson's Island, Ohio, after his capture at Gettysburg.[39] Taken alone, this circumstantial evidence is not enough to convict Kyd Douglas. Collectively, the pieces of evidence fit together and allow us to solve the puzzle.

Some exact events on September 9, 1862 and thereafter are known, others unknown. By September 6, Lee's army of about 40,000 had camped south of Frederick from the Monocacy River and Baltimore and Ohio Railroad track, west to the Buckeystown Road. Lee, Longstreet and Jackson established headquarters near each other around Best's Grove on the Truit farm.[40]

The whereabouts of D. H. Hill's camp is unknown. There is speculation that it was near the Markell house on Buckeystown Road, on the Thomas farm south of the Monocacy River near the Georgetown turnpike, or in the area where the Lost Order actually was found—in a triangle between the turnpike, the Frederick railroad spur and the main line, and the river.[41] On whose campground it was discovered is irrelevant. After nearly five days, the soldiers had created a cesspool of trash and filth, a deterrent to scavengers seeking valuables who mostly left the site undisturbed. From this point, a plausible scenario can be constructed describing how the perpetrator easily could have lost the orders.

September 9th—Early afternoon. After his meeting with Longstreet and Jackson, Lee directed Chilton to write the orders. Lee approved them and Chilton dispatched officer couriers to Jackson, Longstreet, Maj. Gen. Jeb Stuart, Maj. Gen. Lafayette McLaws, Maj. Gen. John G. Walker, and Taylor.[42] Douglas receipted for Jackson's copy, read it and delivered it.

Mid-Afternoon. Jackson wrote a modified copy for Hill which Douglas carried to Ratchford without requesting a receipt. On his return Douglas likely stopped by Lee's headquarters. Chilton had since written the modified copy for Hill but it was undelivered. He needed a courier and spotted Douglas, or some other officer, and asked him to take it to Hill. The courier just pressed into service said, "O, we have that order," but took it anyway.[43] Chilton did not ask him to sign its envelope as a receipt and considered the chore finished.

The courier took three cigars from a pocket, stuck them in the envelope containing the order to keep them dry from perspiration, and tied it with string.

He placed the envelope inside his coat and kept it on. But before returning to his own camp, he forgot the message he was carrying.

Late afternoon. Having provided the plan, Lee then notified his commanders of the march times for the 10th. Chilton dispatched couriers with verbal orders to Jackson and the other principals. Jackson in turn likely sent Douglas to inform his subordinate commanders verbally.

Early Evening. By late in the day, Douglas would have been beside himself. Tired and dirty, surely he hastened through his courier duties as darkness closed around the vast encampment. Shortly he could relax and contemplate tomorrow's move and the women of Boonsboro, where he who soldiered with the famous Jackson was known and appreciated.

Douglas would deliver Lee's marching orders to each of Jackson's generals except Hill. Douglas knew Hill already had the plan but not the departure hour. But there was no hurry; Hill was departing last. Still, this message meant Douglas disdainfully would have to see the crotchety man again that afternoon.

Alone, with no enemy about and while looking for Hill, Douglas easily could have ridden along the Baltimore and Ohio Railroad spur from Frederick down to the Monocacy River. He had been in the saddle all day (except for his curiosity stop at Lee's headquarters, where Chilton engaged him) performing the duty of trusted courier for Stonewall. Such duty was an important assignment that he relished for the attention it generated. But nature sought attention, too, and he possibly dismounted near a small grove in a clover field to respond. It meant tying his horse, flinging his coat over the saddle, and doing his business. Probably stretching longingly and thinking of Boonsboro, he could not wait to get going in eight hours. Focusing only on the approaching night, he would have mounted his horse and ridden off to return to camp. He would tell Hill first thing the next day. Might he have failed to notice a bulky envelope lying on the ground under the animal's hoofs?[44]

Later. A courier, searching his coat pocket for a cigar, by then would have realized the envelope was missing. But how? when? where? In Douglas' case, he was in so many places. Surely some comrade had found it and turned it in, maybe to Hill, for his was the only name in it, he probably thought. By reveille on the 10th, as thousands broke camp to march to their destinations, no one in authority had noted the missing envelope and its extremely sensitive contents. On the other hand, who would have claimed an innocuous piece of paper amongst all the waste? The Confederate camp proceeded as if all was normal.

History offers three versions of when Lee discovered that McClellan had the order in his possession. One is that a civilian Southern sympathizer who was in

McClellan's tent when the order was read got through to Stuart, and Stuart informed Lee the night of the 13th. Other versions are that Lee did not know until McClellan testified before Congress in 1863, or when he read McClellan's postwar report. (After the war, Lee waffled on "when.") Using Stuart's plausible information, plus intelligence reports the Federals were moving westward from Frederick, Lee began drawing his diverse units toward the most convenient defensive position: the Antietam Creek.

Preoccupied with his campaign's precariousness, Lee did not investigate Stuart's account. Only after retreating into Virginia did he likely tell Jackson, if at all. And then all they knew was the paper in question had to be No. 191. But whose copy was it?

Did Jackson, mindful of Douglas' role, discuss it with his captain? If so, Douglas, obviously fearful for his career, would verify only that he had delivered Jackson's handwritten copy to Hill. History does not indicate Chilton knew the second Hill copy of No. 191 was missing, and the courier certainly did not confess. Whatever Lee knew, he did nothing about it.

Ten days after Antietam, Douglas wrote, "When I think how callous I have become & how insensible to nearly all the finer feelings of human nature & how I see the horrors of mortality all around me day by day without a single feeling of emotion, I cannot but shudder at the thought & wonder to what an illimitable depth of dependency it is possible for a soldier to descend."[45] He obviously was aghast over the carnage left on the battlefield, but was he also touched by uncertainty, even guilt, over his error? The Confederate army was long gone, and the Frederick clover field would divulge no clues.

By October, the battle's consequences had stymied the Southern cause. The eastern army was weakened, and the western army had been pushed out of Kentucky. In early 1863, a New York newspaper had mentioned a dispatch found before the battle, but the potential humiliation kept that issue submerged in the South. The Confederacy needed no military scandals, and Lee desired no public retribution.

Once Lee's entourage found out about the Lost Orders, exactly what might Douglas eventually have told Jackson about the Chilton copy for Hill? It had to be the one McClellan saw. If Jackson believed Douglas had lost it, he would not bring charges because no proof of a crime existed. If he disciplined Douglas, he would have only Douglas' self incrimination. A tribunal would be no cover. The Richmond and Charleston papers would find out and embarrass the army. Morale would suffer. He and Lee would be subject to severe political risk.

Maj. Henry Kyd Douglas, C.S.A.

From the John M. Bracken Collection

This much we do know. Within weeks after Antietam, Jackson decided to send Douglas back to his regiment, the 2nd Virginia Infantry. Was it a routine transfer—or retribution? After all, he was detailed to the staff and could be terminated at any time. By the end of October Douglas was back with the 2nd Virginia.[46]

Their mutual affection soured. During the Winter of 1862-63, Jackson disapproved Douglas' furlough request. Douglas wrote his close friend, Helen McComb ("Tippie") Boteler:

> Man (or rather soldier) proposes, Maj. Genl. Jackson disposes, testo. . . .If ever Genl. Jackson & I change places, I will send him to do duty in the summer time in Mississippi. . .by forbidding him to visit his wife (which after all might not be much of a punishment), and if that don't satisfy, I shall issue a peremptory military order that he take the yellow fever, which he will understand martial discipline enough to obey. . . .The words may be somewhat emphatic, but they are decidedly expressive of the truth.[47]

Aware of how his words could haunt him—the Virginia Botelers knew Jackson well—Douglas took a chance. But Jackson died in May 1863, prior to the McClellan testimony and likely without saying a word about the Lost Dispatch. Lee probably never knew of the courier's implication. Chilton died in 1879 knowing the trail went cold after the fateful courier took the copy. Had it been passed to Hill? Chilton never cared to speculate. Did the Richmond rumor mill on the Lost Dispatch have any bearing on the April 11, 1863, refusal of the Confederate Senate to confirm Chilton to the rank of brigadier general?[48]

After the war, Douglas' activities and personality contained further traces of suspicion. By joining those who exalted the memory of Jackson, he buried any hint of their wartime estrangement. If he were culpable, he distanced himself from any hint and sought instead visibility, success and importance. Finally, might he have told Rosser? Hotchkiss, a wartime associate, said, "A fellow Marylander made an amusing remark about Douglas. He asked me if I knew General Douglas on whose staff General Stonewall Jackson served."[49]

Douglas had joined the 2nd Virginia in May 1861 and rose to lieutenant. He was detailed to Jackson's brigade staff in November 1861, becoming the assistant inspector general, a post of limited responsibility. Ingratiating himself to Jackson, he rose as Jackson rose. Ultimately promoted to colonel before Lee's surrender, he briefly commanded the brigade once led by generals Jubal A. Early and A. P. Hill. In the late 19th Century, he spent most of his life in Hagerstown. "Colonel" was his business and social rank of choice until a brief appointment in 1892 as Maryland Adjutant General with major general rank. He died December 18, 1903 and is buried in his birthplace, Shepherdstown, West Virginia. His war diaries were edited into the popular 1940 book, *I Rode with Stonewall.*

Douglas overplayed the "Stonewall card," agitating comrades of the 1862 staff including Hotchkiss and McGuire, to whom Douglas was an enigma. Contemporaries did not dislike Douglas but questioned, even discredited, his playing loose with facts. McGuire even wrote Hotchkiss disputing some of Douglas' accounts and advised Jackson biographer G. F. R. Henderson "to cut out all of Douglas' statement that does not agree with the one I have given."[50] Hotchkiss wrote Henderson, "Pardon me for again warning you about quoting from Douglas. He shoots with a long bow and generally misses the mark. . . ." He cited Douglas' "dramatic yarn" about A. P. Hill seeking release from arrest in Maryland. "I called Douglas' attention to this and he stoutly contended as usual that he knew what he was talking about."[51]

Some questioned whether Douglas was officially *part of* Jackson's staff, or Early's in 1864, as claimed. Early was unaware he was on his own staff: "From what I have heard about Kyd Douglas he is one of those men who is disposed to claim a great deal for himself."[52]

Douglas' inflated self esteem made him invincible in his own mind, and he dared initiate comment on the Lost Order: Jackson had entrusted him with the information early on September 10 while deceptively inquiring in Frederick for maps and roads to Pennsylvania. "I did not know then of Lee's order," Douglas said. Jackson then asked Douglas about his home Washington County roads and Potomac River fords. Finally, Douglas wrote that [o]n [the 13th] General McClellan came into possession, by carelessness or accident, of General Lee's order of the 9th. . . ."[53] The order was lost, he surmised, "by an accident never yet explained."[54]

Douglas participated heavily in veterans' activities, including those of Union veterans. He led the effort which re-interred Confederate Antietam dead to Hagerstown in 1877, and even invited McClellan to speak to Hagerstown's Grand Army of the Republic post. Douglas succeeded at law but was unsuccessful in other meaningful ventures, such as love, where two visible love affairs ended tragically, including one with Tippie Boteler. Politics was another failure for him. As his local popularity waned, he lost elections for both the Maryland Senate and U.S. Congress.

Douglas has been little studied. He certainly was an enigma. His comrade, Major Taylor, writing about whether the order was lost through the interposition of Providence against the Confederate cause, or by outright carelessness, may have had the courier in mind when he wrote, "This contention will never be settled until the line is established that marks where Divine Sovereignty ends and human free-agency begins."[55]

If the culprit was not Douglas, Jackson's quintessential free agent, then who remains in contention?[56]

Versions of How The Lost Order was Lost

DHH = Daniel Harvey Hill; TJJ = Thomas J. Jackson
REL = Robert E. Lee; (C) = Civil War Contemporary

Source	Loser	Conditions
Allan (C)[57]	Someone other than DHH	Carelessness; believed DHH when he said he never got it
Allan (C)[58]	Would not say	Lost in Frederick Sept. 10; picked up in front of store where DHH and staff sat on horses as their troops departed
Bridges[59]	Likely a spy	Supports DHH and Ratchford
Catton[60]	A Confederate General	Used it to wrap cigars, placed in breast pocket and it dropped out
Catton[61]	Some Confederate officer	
Chilton (C)[62]	Never said	
Conf. Mil. Hist.[63]	Did not assign fault	Blamed REL's HQ for not knowing
Cooke (C)[64]	DHH	Left it on table in Frederick
Davis[65]	Someone on DHH's staff	Concluded copy from REL received previously was valueless and threw it away; wrapped cigars, carelessly thrust from pocket

DHH (C)[66]	A traitor in the ranks	
Douglas (C)[67]	Some DHH staff officer	Wrapped cigars, put in pocket; DHH received both Lee and TJJ copies in that order
Dowdey[68]	Unknown DHH staff officer	Officer must have enjoyed self liberally in Frederick; left it behind when army departed; DHH got orders through TJJ; said copy from REL never reached DHH
Foote[69]	DHH's staff officer	Wrapped cigars, put in pocket
"Foreigner"(C)[70]	DHH	Contents did not please DHH; indignantly flung it to the ground after reading
Freeman[71]	Some DHH staff officer	Wrapped cigars; the costliest covering for such as purpose
Henderson[72]	Did not say	Picked up in Frederick streets
Henry[73]	Some careless courier	Used as wrapping paper; never reached DHH
Lee[74]	Did not know	

Marshall[75]	DHH	Remembered DHH accused of losing important order Seven Days battles; later said it might have occurred in many ways
Maurice[76]	An orderly	
McClellan(C)[77]	Did not know	The copy was addressed to DHH; found on ground vacated by REL
Murfin[78]	No opinion	Dismisses spy theory
Palfrey(C)[79]	Someone in DHH's camp	Carelessly left
Paris(C)[80]	DHH	Left on corner of table in DHH's Frederick HQ house; by a fatal negligence
Pollard(C)[81]	DHH	"This vain and petulant officer, in a moment of passion, had thrown the paper on the ground"
Sears[82]	Courier or someone on DHH's staff	Likeliest explanation
Williams(C)[83]	DHH or Lee's HQ	Found on DHH campgrounds; DHH carelessness or REL's HQ inadequate procedures responsible

SPECIAL ORDERS, HDQRS. ARMY OF NORTHERN VIRGINIA
Numbers 191.}   September 9, 1862.

I. The citizens of Fredericktown being unwilling, while overrun by members of this army, to pen their stores, in order to give them confidence, and to secure to officers and men purchasing supplies for benefit of this command, all officers and men of this army are strictly prohibited from visiting Fredericktown except on business, in which case they will bear evidence of this in writing from division commanders. The provost-marshal in Fredericktown will see that his guard rigidly enforces this order.

II. Major Taylor will proceed to Leesburg, Va., and arrange for transportation of the sick and those unable to walk to Winchester, securing the transportation of the country for this purpose. The route between this and Culpeper Court-House east of the mountains being unsafe will no longer be traveled. Those on the way to this army already across the river will move up promptly; all others will proceed to Winchester collectively and under command of officers, at which point, being the general depot of this army, its movements will be known and instructions given by commanding officer regulating further movements.

III. The army will resume its march to-morrow, taking the Hagerstown road. General Jackson's command will from the advance, and, after passing Middletown, with such portion as he may select, take the route toward Sharpsburg, cross the Potomac at the most convenient point, and by Friday morning take possession of the Baltimore and Ohio Railroad, capture such of them as may be at Martinsburg, and intercept such as may attempt to escape from Harper's Ferry.

IV. General Longstreet's command will pursue the main road as far as Boonsborough, where it will halt, with reserve, supply, and baggage trains of the army.

V. General McLaws, with his own division and that of General R. H. Anderson, will follow General Longstreet. On reaching Middletown will take the route to Harper's Ferry, and by Friday morning possess himself of the Maryland Heights and endeavor to capture the enemy at harper's Ferry and vicinity.

VI. *General Walker, with his division, after accomplishing the object in which he is now engaged, will cross the Potomac at Cheek's Ford, ascend its right bank to Lovettsville, take possession of Loudoun Heights, if practicable, by Friday morning, Keys' Ford on his left, and the road between the end of the mountain and the Potomac on his right. He will, as far as practicable, co-operate with Generals McLaws and Jackson, and intercept retreat of the enemy.*

VII. *General D. H. Hill's division will form the rear guard of the army, pursing the road taken by the main body. The reserve artillery, ordnance, and supply trains, &c., will precede General Hill.*

VIII. *General Stuart will detach a squadron of cavalry to accompany the commands of Generals Longstreet, Jackson, and McLaws, and, with the main body of the cavalry, will cover the route of the army, bringing up all stragglers that may have been left behind.*

IX. *The commands of Generals Jackson, McLaws, and Walker, after accomplishing the objects for which they have been detached, will join the main body of the army at Boonsborough or Hagerstown.*

X. *Each regiment on the march will habitually carry its axes in the regimental ordnance wagons, for use of the men at their encampments, to procure wood, &c.*

By command of General R. E. Lee:

R. H. CHILTON,
Assistant Adjutant-General.

Notes

1. Exceptions are authors Stephen W. Sears and James V. Murfin in their extensive studies of Antietam, and Hal Bridges, biographer of Major General D. H. Hill, to whom the Lost Order was addressed. Their discussions of the Lost Order are hardly exhaustive and hesitate to finger the guilty. In his book *Giants in the Cornfield: The 27th Indiana Infantry* (Shippensburg, Pa., 1997), Wilbur D. Jones, Jr., reveals precise, new details about the finding of the Lost Order and its subsequent routing to McClellan.

2. Charles Marshall to D. H. Hill, November 11, 1867. Daniel Harvey Hill Papers, Virginia State Archives.

3. Ibid.

4. A. L. Long, *Memoirs of Robert E. Lee* (New York, 1886), p. 213; Walter H. Taylor in *Confederate Veteran* 30, September 1922, p. 345.

5. Robert Hall Chilton to D. H. Hill, June 22, 1867. Daniel Harvey Hill Papers, North Carolina State Archives.

6. Chilton to Hill, January 11, 1868. Hill Papers, Virginia State Archives.

7. Robert E. Lee quoted in E. C. Gordon to William Allan, November 18, 1886. Copy in draft of *Lee's Lieutenants*. Douglas Southall Freeman Papers, Box 148, Manuscripts Division, Library of Congress.

8. Chilton quoted In Stephen W. Sears, *Landscape Turned Red* (New York, 1983), p. 349.

9. D. H. Hill writing about the Lost Dispatch in *The Land We Love* 4, February 1868 (Charlotte, N.C.,1868), p. 274.

10. Lee quoted in Gordon to Allan.

11. Hill's copy of No. 191 is in the North Carolina State Archives. The Lost Order copy found by the 27th Indiana and presented to McClellan is in the George B. McClellan Papers, Manuscripts Division, Library of Congress.

12. Hill in *The Land We Love* 4, November-April 1867-68 (Charlotte, N.C., 1868), 275; *Battles and Leaders of the Civil War* 2, pp. 570, 579.

13. *The Land We Love* 4, February 1868, 274; Hill to James Longstreet, February 11, 1885. James Longstreet Papers, Perkins Library, Duke University.

14. *The Land We Love* 4, February 1868, p. 275.

15. Other Southerners had trouble with editor Edward A. Pollard's reporting. See G. Wilson McPhail to Hill, February 17, 1868, and Henry A. Wise to Hill, October 3, 1869. Hill Papers, North Carolina State Archives; *The Land We Love* 4, February 1868, pp. 273-74.

16. Lee quoted in Gordon to Allan.

17. *The Land We Love* 4, February 1868, 275; also D. H. Hill to J. William Jones, *Southern Historical Society Papers* 13, January-December 1885, pp. 420-21.

18. Hill to Longstreet, February 11, 1885; see also Hill to Longstreet, May 21, 1885, and June 5, 1885, Perkins Library.

19. Hill in *Southern Historical Society Papers* 13, January-December 1885, p. 421.

20. Chilton to Hill, July 21, 1867. Hill Papers, North Carolina State Archives.

21. *Ibid.*, June 22, 1867.

22. Affidavit of Joseph G. Morrison, March 17, 1868. Hill Papers, North Carolina State Archives.

23. Randolph B. Marcy to S. W. Crawford, May 5, 1868, and Crawford to Hill, August 22, 1868. Hill Papers, Virginia State Archives.

24. Hal Bridges, *Lee's Maverick General* (New York, 1961), p. 97.

25. "The Lost Dispatch" essay, author [believed to be Hill] and date unknown. Hill Papers, North Carolina State Archives.

26. Mary Anna Jackson, *Memoirs of Stonewall Jackson*. (Reprint: Dayton, O., 1976), 304.Jackson married Mary Anna Morrison of Lincoln County, N.C., in 1857. She died in 1915. Hill married her sister, Isabella Morrison. Jackson's only sister, Laura Jackson, married Jonathon Arnold of Beverly, W.Va., in 1844. She died in 1911. Their son, Thomas Jackson Arnold of Elkins, W.Va., married Hill's daughter, Mary Eugenia Hill, in 1876. He died in 1933. She was born in Lexington, Va., but raised in Charlotte, N.C.. She died in 1934. Sources: Nancy Ann Jackson (fourth cousin descendant of Jackson), Clarksburg, W.Va., unpublished (with Linda Brake Myers) Jackson Family genealogy, 1995 (used with permission); A. S. Bosworth, *A History of Randolph County, West Virginia*. (Reprint: Parsons, W.Va., 1975. A surviving Arnold descendant in Elkins, a great granddaughter of both Jackson and Hill, Becky Arnold Vilseck, lives in a retirement home there. The author talked with her on April 22, 1995, but she offered no information.

27. Eugenia Morrison Hill to William A. Graham, January [believed 1864]. Hill Papers, North Carolina State Archives. Graham was brother of Mary Graham, mother of Isabella and Mary Anna Morrison.

28. Eugenia Hill Arnold to Cousin Charles [believed Graham], October 10, 1931. Daniel Harvey Hill Collection, Southern Historical Collection, University of North Carolina.

29. Ibid.

30. Thomas Jackson Arnold in *Confederate Veteran* 30, August 1922, p. 317. Arnold, the son of Jackson's sister Laura, wrote about history. Other works included the book *Early Life and Letters of General Thomas J. Jackson* (New York, 1916), and the monograph *Beverly [West Virginia] in the Sixties*, reprinted by the Randolph County [W.Va.] Historical Society in 1969.

31. The author verified the Rosser speech by reading the news report in the next day's Raleigh paper.

32. Jackson's staff in the Maryland Campaign also included: Maj. George H Bier, C.S. Navy, chief of ordnance; Col. S. Crutchfield, chief of artillery; Col. William L. Jackson, vice aide de camp; Capt. R. E. Welbourne, chief staff officer. The staff might have included: Lt. Col. William S. H. Baylor, inspector general; Surgeon H. Black; Charles James Faulkner, assistant adjutant general; Lt. S. S. Harris, assistant inspector general; E. F. Ritton, assistant adjutant general. *List of Staff Officers, Confederate States Army, 1861-1865* (Washington, 1891).

33. *Battles and Leaders* 2, p. 622.

34. Bradley T. Johnson in *Battles and Leaders* 2, pp. 615-16.

35. John Bowers, *Stonewall Jackson: Portrait of a Soldier* (New York, 1989), pp. 185-88.

36. Douglas' marginal notation in copy of William A. Owen, *In Camp and Battle with the Battalion Washington Artillery of New Orleans* (Boston, 1885), p. 119. Douglas' personal library, Antietam National Battlefield.

37. Douglas' marginal notation in G. F. R. Henderson, *Stonewall Jackson and the American Civil War* (London, 1998), p. 538. Douglas personal library.

38. *Battles and Leaders* 3, p. 322.

39. Douglas to Helen McComb "Miss Tippie" Boteler, November 16, 1861. Henry Kyd Douglas Collection, Perkins Library, Duke University; Douglas, *I Rode with Stonewall* (Chapel Hill, N.C., 1940), pp. 265, 376-77.

40. Numerous sources cite or describe this area, including: Ezra A. Carmen draft undated memoir. Box 1, Ezra Ayers Carmen Papers, Manuscripts Division, Library of Congress; J. Thomas Scharf, *History of Western Maryland* 1 (Philadelphia, 1882), p. 229; Douglas draft undated memoir, chapters 15-17, Paper 15. Antietam National Battlefield Library; Diary of Jedediah Hotchkiss. Jedediah Hotchkiss Papers, Manuscripts Division, Library of Congress; and *The Atlas to Accompany the Official Records of the Union and Confederate Armies* (Washington, 1891-95), Plates XCIV and LXXXIII. The Truit farm was leased to the Best family.

41. William G. Willman, Frederick County (Md.) Historical Society, to the author, January 24, 1988, and April 27, 989; Thomas J. Moore to Hill, June 3, 1885. Hill Papers, Virginia State Archives. The "clover field" area, on the later Battle of Monocacy ground, is still under cultivation, nearly in pristine condition, and can be seen to the east alongside Maryland Highway 355.

42. Chilton wrote seven "originals": for Jackson, Longstreet, McLaws, Stuart, Walker, Taylor and his files. His and Jackson's "modified" copies to Hill omitted paragraphs I and II.

43. This copy became the "Lost Order."

44. Douglas was a procrastinator, and once said, "Procrastination is the thief of time. And I ofttimes think that quotation must have been expressly intended for me." Douglas G. Bast, Western Maryland expert on Douglas, in a February 7, 1983, lecture at the Washington County Free Library, Hagerstown, Maryland. See note 56 for a discussion of Bast's source.

45.Douglas to Helen McComb "Tippie" Boteler, September 27, 1862. Douglas Collection, Perkins Library.

46. *List of Staff Officers;* also, Moses Gibson to Hunter McGuire, March 1, 1897. Hotchkiss Papers, Reel 32. Gibson joined Jackson's staff on detail on August 8, 1862, and served with that corps until the 1865 surrender, serving as chief clerk in the medical and inspector general offices. The transfer must have been sudden. Pendleton, the senior staff aide, did not mention it—perhaps was unaware—in his newsy letter to wife Nancy, October 20, 1862, in which he mentioned Douglas frequently regarding their shared tent arrangements. A. S. Pendleton to Nancy Pendleton, October 20, 1862, William N. Pendleton Papers, Southern Historical Collection, University of North Carolina.

47. Douglas to Boteler, [ca. Christmas 1862]. Douglas Collection, Perkins Library.

48. The Comte de Paris, *History of the Civil War in America* 2 Henry Coppee, ed. (Philadelphia, 1907). Chilton reverted to the inferior rank of lieutenant colonel and served another year in the field.

49. Jedediah Hotchkiss to W. F. Mason McCarty, October 1, 1896. Hotchkiss Papers, Reel 32, Library of Congress.

50. Hunter Holmes McGuire to Jedediah Hotchkiss, January 22, 1897. Jedediah Hotchkiss Papers, Alderman Library, University of Virginia.

51. Jedediah Hotchkiss to G. F. R. Henderson, January 27, 1897. Hotchkiss Papers, Library of Congress.

52. Jubal A. Early quoted in Hotchkiss to McCarty.

53. *I Rode with Stonewall*, 151; *Battles and Leaders* 2, pp. 622, 624.

54. *I Rode with Stonewall*, p. 159.

55. Walter H. Taylor, *General Lee: His Campaigns in Virginia, 1861-1865.* (Reprint: Dayton, O., 1975), p. 125.

56. True, the final word may never be known, but Douglas G. Bast of Boonsboro, the man considered to be Western Maryland's expert on Douglas, may hold the only "smoking gun." He possesses numerous Douglas diaries under lock and key, allows no one to read them, and in 1991 refused to discuss their contents with the author.

Besides these diaries, Douglas manuscripts are hard to locate. Not all manuscript guides are reliable (i.e., manuscripts are not at the Universities of North Carolina and Virginia). Duke University holds some, the Antietam National Battlefield holds his personal library, and about 20 post-war letters mostly on routine business are scattered.

57. William Allan, "Review of General Longstreet," *Southern Historical Society Papers* 14, 1886, p. 106

58. William Allan, *The Army of Northern Virginia in 1862* (Boston, 1892), p. 343.

59. Hal Bridges, *Lee's Maverick General* (New York, 1961), p. 98.

60. Bruce Catton, *Reflections on the Civil War* (New York, 1981), p. 130.

61. Bruce Catton, *This Hallowed Ground* (New York, 1955), p. 199.

62. Chilton did not conjecture.

63. *Confederate Military History* 4 (Atlanta, 1899), pp. 107-109.

64. John Esten Cooke, *Stonewall Jackson: A Military Biography* (New York: 1876), p. 316.

65. Burke Davis, They Called Him Stonewall (New York, 1954), p. 321.

66. Stephen W. Sears, *Landscape Turned Red,* p. 127.

67. *I Rode with Stonewall*, 151; *Battles and Leaders* 2, pp. 622, 624.

68. Clifford Dowdey, *The Land They Fought For: The Story of the South as the Confederacy, 1832-1865* (Garden City, N.J., 1955).

69. Shelby Foote, *The Civil War; A Narrative: Fort Sumter to Perryville* (New York, 1958), p. 668.

70. John McKnight Bloss (27th Indiana, a finder of the Lost Order), January 6, 1892.

71. Douglas Southall Freeman, *R. E. Lee: A Biography* 2 (New York, 1934), p. 363.

72. G. F. R. Henderson, *Stonewall Jackson and the American Civil War* (London, 1898), pp. 504-505.

73. Robert Selph Henry, *The Story of the Confederacy* (Indianapolis, 1931), pp. 185-86.

74. Robert E. Lee to D. H. Hill, February 21, 1868. Daniel Harvey Hill Collection.

75. Allan Nevins, *The War for the Union* (New York, 1960), p. 219.

76. Frederick Maurice, ed. *An Aide-de-Camp of Lee: Charles Marshall* (Boston, 1927), p. 158.

77. George B. McClellan to D. H. Hill, July 1, 1969. Hill Papers, Virginia State Archives.

78. James V. Murfin, *Gleam of Bayonets: The Battle of Antietam and the Maryland Campaign of 1862* (New York, 1965), pp. 336-37.

79. Francis Winthrop Palfrey, *Campaigns of the Civil War: The Antietam and Fredericksburg* (New York: 1882), pp. 21-22.

80. The Comte de Paris, p. 318.

81. Edward A. Pollard, *The Lost Cause: A New Southern History of the War of the Confederates* (New York: 1866), p. 314.

82. Stephen W. Sears, *Landscape Turned Red*, p. 349.

83. Kenneth P. Williams, *Lincoln Finds a General: A Military Study of the Civil War* 1 (Bloomington, Ind., 1949), p. 375.

"Men of the Twenty-third, when I tell you to charge, you must charge. . . ."

"MY GOD! BE CAREFUL!"
Morning Battle at Fox's Gap, September 14, 1862

D. Scott Hartwig

One of the unusual features of the offensive that Union Maj. Gen. George B. McClellan devised to capitalize upon his army's discovery of Special Orders no. 191 was that it did not take into the account the real possibility that the Confederates might defend the mountain passes through South Mountain. Nothing more than a reconnaissance of gaps was planned for the morning of September 14. On the 13th Brig. Gen. Alfred Pleasonton's Union cavalry had pressed Maj. Gen. J. E. B. Stuart's Confederate horsemen along the National Road from Catoctin Mountain, across the Middletown Valley, to the base of South Mountain. Here, the Federals were confronted with Southern infantry, deployed to defend Turner's Pass, the gap through which the National Road crosses the mountain. Pleasonton sent back a request for infantry support to Maj. Gen. Ambrose E. Burnside, commanding the Right Wing (I and IX Corps) of the Army of the Potomac. Burnside forwarded the request to IX Corps commander, Maj. Gen. Jesse L. Reno, who in turn ordered Brig. Gen. Jacob D. Cox, commanding the Kanawha Division of Ohio troops, the most forward infantry element of the army, to furnish Pleasonton with the necessary force. The details of the operation were left to Cox and Pleasonton. The cavalry general came to Cox's tent that evening and requested the support of only one brigade, to report at 6 a.m. As Cox recalled, Pleasonton believed the infantry which he had encountered in Turner's Pass was nothing more than a rear-guard and he deemed a single infantry brigade sufficient force to enable his cavalry to get through. Cox distinctly remembered years later that "no battle was expected at Turner's Gap." on September 14.[1]

Pleasonton requested that the brigade of his Old Army friend, Col. George Crook, support the reconnaissance. "I wished to please him [Pleasonton]," Cox recalled, "and not thinking it would make any difference to my brigade commanders, intimated that I would do so." But when Col. Eliakim P. Scammon, Cox's First Brigade commander, was told about the arrangement, he objected. Crook's brigade had led the march on the 13th. As was the custom, it was Scammon's turn to lead the march on the 14th. By right, Scammon believed *his* brigade should support Pleasonton. Cox attempted to explain that it was only out of courtesy to Pleasonton that he had proposed the change. Scammon was unmoved. "The point of professional honor touched him," wrote Cox. Scammon was a West Pointer, class of 1837, and had been commissioned in the Corps of Topographical Engineers. His career had been promising, but in 1856, while building military roads in the New Mexico territory, he was dismissed from the service for "conduct to the prejudice of good order and military discipline." This black mark on his record no doubt still burned fiercely and partly explains his persistence on a minor point. Cox consented to Scammon's demand and he sought out Pleasonton to explain why. "Crook (who Pleasonton was visiting at the time) took the decision in good stride," recalled Cox, but "Pleasonton was a little chafed, and even intimated that he claimed some right to name the officer and command to be detailed." Pleasonton's bluster did not intimidate or move Cox. Scammon would march at 6:00 a.m.[2]

Colonel Eliakim P. Scammon, commander of the First Brigade, Kanawha Division. He originally commanded the 23rd Ohio Volunteer Infantry.

Miller's *Photographic History of the Civil War*

Sunday, September 14 dawned bright in Middletown Valley with the promise of a pleasant late summer day. It was the sabbath but war was at work and there would be no respite. Promptly at 6:00 a.m. Scammon had his brigade under arms and filing onto the National Road. The controversy with Pleasonton over who would accompany the reconnaissance, "had put Scammon and his whole brigade upon their mettle, and was a case which a generous emulation did no harm." Scammon's westerners were an independent, tough group of soldiers. Early in the campaign there had been a confrontation with corps commander Jesse Reno when some soldiers of Col. Rutherford B. Hayes' 23rd Ohio had taken straw from a nearby stack to feed some artillery and cavalry horses.

Post-war image of Brig. Gen.. Jacob D. Cox, commander of the Kanawha Division

Loyal West Virginia from 1861 to 1865

Reno came upon the men engaged in foraging forbidden by orders and accosted the men while blurting out, "you damned black sons of bitches." He and Hayes had some words on the subject—which according to Hayes were cordial—but as the story spread through camp it was told that Reno was seen to put his hand on his pistol while Hayes men, unimpressed by Reno's rank, picked up their weapons to defend their colonel if the need arose. The part of the story about the soldiers going for their weapons probably was apocryphal, but it illustrated the aggressive spirit of the men.[3]

Since their upcoming mission was only a reconnaissance, the men left their knapsacks in camp to lighten their load. Scammon counted three regiments numbering approximately 1,455 officers and men. Two troops of West Virginia Independent Cavalry and Captain James R. McMullin's 1st Battery, Ohio Light Artillery (six 10-lb. Parrot Rifles]) accompanied the infantry. So too did Cox. With commendable curiosity he breakfasted early in order to ride along with Scammon so he could see how Pleasonton intended to use his brigade.

The beauty of the morning was shaken by the crash of artillery up ahead. Pleasonton had unlimbered two batteries, Capt. Horatio G. Gibson's C & G, 3rd U.S. (six 3-inch rifles) and Lt. Samuel N. Benjamin's E, 2nd U.S. (four 20-lb. Parrots), which Burnside had temporarily loaned the cavalry, upon a high clear hill situated south of the National Pike and one-half mile north of the point where the Old Sharpsburg Road leaves the turnpike. There were no specific targets except to fire into Turner's Gap. Pleasonton simply wanted to see if he would draw a response. He did. Lane's Georgia Battery, which was positioned upon open ground on the summit of Hill 1280. (For ease of understanding,the hill positions at South Mountain will be referred to by their elevation.) The two Federal batteries concentrated their fire upon the Georgians. Twice the Southern guns were silenced and finally Lane changed his position to escape the heavier Union fire. Between lulls in the artillery exchange the rumble of artillery drifting up from Harper's Ferry could plainly be heard.[4]

As Cox and Scammon preceded the Union brigade across Catoctin Creek, Cox was astonished to see standing by the roadside Colonel Augustus Moor, the Second Brigade commander, who had been captured in Frederick by Hampton's cavalry two day's earlier. Cox asked him how he had come to be wandering alone along the National Road. Moor explained he had been paroled the evening before and was returning to Federal lines on foot. Cox recalled their brief conversation: "'But where are you going?' said he. I answered that Scammon was going to support Pleasonton in a reconnaissance into the gap. Moor made an involuntary start, saying, 'My God! be careful!' then checking himself, added, 'But I am paroled!' and turned away."[5]

Moor had said enough for Cox. Trouble lay ahead. He galloped after Scammon and told him what Moor had said, and added that he was returning to camp to bring up the Crook's Brigade as support. As Cox rode back he paused to speak with each regimental commander in Scammon's Brigade, warning them "to be prepared for anything, big or little—it might be a skirmish, it might be a battle." Spurring on at a gallop, Cox rode into the camp of Crook's Brigade and ordered its commander to assemble his command and march at once. While drums or bugles sounded assembly, Cox wrote a note to Reno explaining that he believed the enemy were in force on the mountain, and that he was taking both brigades along on Pleasonton's reconnaissance as a precaution. After sending this message off Cox rode forward to see Pleasonton, whom he found near the batteries shelling Turner's Gap. Cox learned that Scammon and Pleasonton already had conferred about the prospect that the enemy was occupying Turner's Gap in some strength. Both men agreed that Turner's Gap might be outflanked

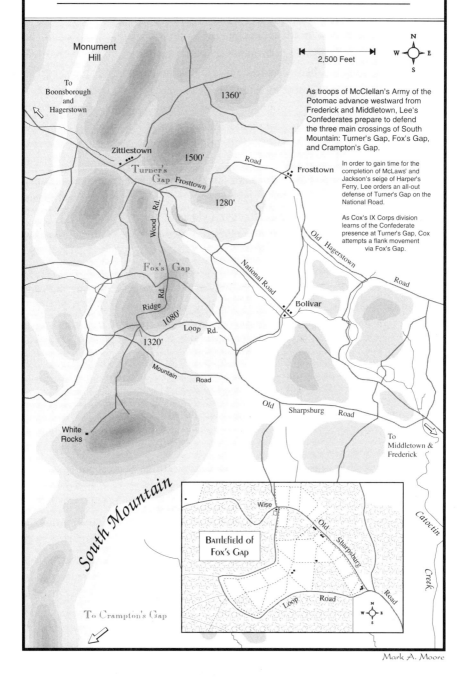

Prelude to Antietam, September 1862
SOUTH MOUNTAIN: Vicinity of Fox's Gap, Maryland

Monument Hill

2,500 Feet

N
W — E
S

To Boonsborough and Hagerstown

1360'

Zittlestown

1500'

Turner's Gap

Road

Frosttown

Frosttown

1280'

Wood Rd.

Fox's Gap

Ridge Rd.

1080'

Loop Rd.

1320'

Mountain Road

White Rocks

Old Hagerstown Road

National Road

Bolivar

Old Sharpsburg Road

To Middletown & Frederick

As troops of McClellan's Army of the Potomac advance westward from Frederick and Middletown, Lee's Confederates prepare to defend the three main crossings of South Mountain: Turner's Gap, Fox's Gap, and Crampton's Gap.

In order to gain time for the completion of McLaws' and Jackson's siege of Harper's Ferry, Lee orders an all-out defense of Turner's Gap on the National Road.

As Cox's IX Corps division learns of the Confederate presence at Turner's Gap, Cox attempts a flank movement via Fox's Gap.

South Mountain

To Crampton's Gap

Wise

Battlefield of Fox's Gap

Old Sharpsburg

Loop Road

Road

N
W — E
S

Catoctin Creek

Mark A. Moore

by marching up the Old Sharpsburg Road to Fox's Gap. While Scammon's infantry executed the turning maneuver, Pleasonton would divert the enemy with his cavalry by demonstrating in front of Turner's Pass. Cox agreed to the plan, but made it clear that if his division became engaged, he, and not Pleasonton, would direct operations. Cox later wrote that Pleasanton "cordially assented."[6]

If it came to a fight the topography of South Mountain offered significant advantages to the defender. The mountain crests rose from 1000 to 1500 feet. "These summits are like scattered and irregular hills upon the high rounded surface of the mountain top," wrote Cox. Fox's and Turner's gaps were 200 to 300 feet lower than the surrounding mountain crests. A heavy forest covered much of the mountain. In some areas a thick, almost impenetrable growth of mountain laurel grew upon the forest floor. There were some small farms, however, with meadows and cultivated fields that had been hewn out of this difficult land, principally along the southeastern slopes of the mountain. The early farmers had found their soil filled with granite boulders which they collected as the land was cleared and built sturdy walls to mark field and property boundaries.[7]

Access over the mountain before the construction of the National Road had been by either the Sharpsburg or Hagerstown Roads. The armies of 1862 were not the first the Sharpsburg Road had seen. In 1757 British General Edward Braddock had used it to cross his army over South Mountain during the campaign that ended in disaster at the Battle of the Monogahela near Fort Pitt. This road originates at the point where the National Road crosses Catoctin Creek. In 1862 it was narrow and rough, and the climb up South Mountain was (and still is) a hard and steep grade. It crosses the mountain at Fox's Gap, about one mile south of Turner's.

Besides these roads there were numerous farm and logging roads and paths that bisected the main roads and, in some instances, offered access over the mountain. For defender or attacker, there were three roads of particular importance in the Fox's Gap area. The first was a farm road (which, for the purposes of this essay, will be called the "Loop Road") that left the Sharpsburg Road as it began to ascend the mountain. The Loop Road ran obliquely southwest up the slope of the mountain for nearly one mile until it turned west and climbed steeply to the summit of Hill 1100, where it joined a road running south from the Mountain House (a stone house at the summit of the Fox's Gap). This road, called the Ridge Road, left the Old Sharpsburg Road at the summit of Fox's Gap, immediately east of the mountain farm of Daniel Wise, and roughly ran along the summit of Hill 1080, until it met the Loop Road. Near the intersection of these two roads, several wagon roads and trails led down the west side of the mountain to the valley south of Boonsboro. The third road, called Wood Road, left the National Road east of the Mountain House, and ran south for nearly one mile until it emerged at the Sharpsburg Road at Wise's farm.[8]

For the attacker this road network partially compensated for the natural terrain advantages the defender enjoyed. By using the numerous approaches available both Turner's and Fox's Gaps might be flanked. To cover all the approaches adequately, the Confederates were forced to stretch their thin forces over a wide front.

Crook's Brigade, accompanied by Capt. Seth J. Simmonds Kentucky Light Artillery (two 20-lb. Parrots and four 10-lb. Parrots), had turned out promptly after Cox's call-up and at about 7:30 a.m. reached the Sharpsburg Road turnoff. Scammon's Brigade was in front by nearly one-half hour's march. It was nearly two miles to the summit of Fox's Gap. The troops marched slowly and took frequent rests due to the roughness of the road and its steep grade, and to keep the ranks closed up. Meanwhile, the artillery continued to shell the Turner's Gap area. Cox increased the Union firepower by unlimbering McMullin's battery and Simmonds 20-lb. Parrotts near Pleasonton's batteries, so that 18 rifled guns were concentrated together. As Scammon's regiments were slowly ascending the Sharpsburg Road a courier from Reno caught up with Cox to tell him that the corps commander approved his actions and would support him with the entire corps.[9]

When Scammon's brigade had marched one-quarter mile beyond Mentzer's saw mill, the alert gunners of Capt. J. W. Bondurant's Jeff Davis Battery (two 3-inch rifles and two 12-lb. howitzers), which had just unlimbered near Fox's Gap, observed the moving column and opened with case shot from their 3-inch

guns. The shells screeched over the startled Ohioans. Scammon promptly deployed Captain Gilmore's troop of cavalry as skirmishers and sent them forward. They encountered Confederate skirmish-

Lieutenant Colonel Rutherford B. Hayes, commander of the 23rd Ohio Volunteer Infantry.

Rutherford B. Hayes Library

ers, probably of Rosser's 5th Virginia cavalry, who quickly withdrew uphill to the woods crowning the level plateau on the crest of Hill 1080.[10]

The artillery greeting and enemy skirmishers convinced Scammon that the direct approach to Fox's Gap up the Sharpsburg Road was defended. He learned through his guide, local resident John Miller, of the existence of the Loop Road and the prospects it offered of gaining the flank of the Confederate position. Scammon summoned Lt. Col. Rutherford B. Hayes, the commander of his leading regiment, the 23d Ohio Infantry. Hayes was destined to be president one day—so too was a commissary sergeant in the 23d named William McKinley—but for now, Scammon had a difficult mission for the young lieutenant colonel. He ordered Hayes to take his large regiment of 765 officers and men up the Loop Road, gain the flank of the rebel battery, and capture it. "If I find six guns and strong support?" asked Hayes. "Take them anyhow," Scammon replied.[11]

John Miller accompanied Hayes as his regiment filed onto the Loop Road, which Hayes described as no more than a "mountain path." A detachment of Capt. Gilmore's West Virginia cavalry, under the command of Sergeant A. B. Farmer, accompanied the infantry. Hayes deployed Company A of his regiment as skirmishers, and forged uphill through a dense forest.[12]

Once Hayes had started, Scammon deployed companies A and F, of Col. Carr B. White's 12th Ohio Infantry as skirmishers to relieve Gilmore's dismounted cavalry. These two companies apparently followed the Loop Road. The remaining eight companies of White's regiment either followed their skirmish companies some minutes later or pushed through the woods east of and parallel to the Loop Road. Colonel Hugh Ewing's 30th Ohio Infantry, about 400 officers and men, drew a task just as difficult as Hayes' mission. Ewing's orders were to turn the enemy's left, drive them from Fox's Gap, and hold the summit until reinforced. He deployed a powerful body of skirmishers under Lt. Col. Theodore Jones, and followed with the balance of the regiment deployed in column.[13] Scammon's tactics were sound given the unknown dispositions and strength of the enemy in front. Ewing would fix the enemy in front while Hayes and White turned his flank. It was nearly 9 a.m.[14]

D. H. Hill rose early on the 14th and arrived at the summit of Turner's Gap before sunrise. Unwelcome news awaited him. It was a note from Stuart explaining that he had ridden to Crampton's Pass, about ten miles northeast. Years later, Hill charitably wrote that Stuart "was too gallant a soldier to leave his post when a battle was imminent, and doubtless believed that there was but a small Federal force on the National Road." It is unlikely that Hill spoke so kindly of the

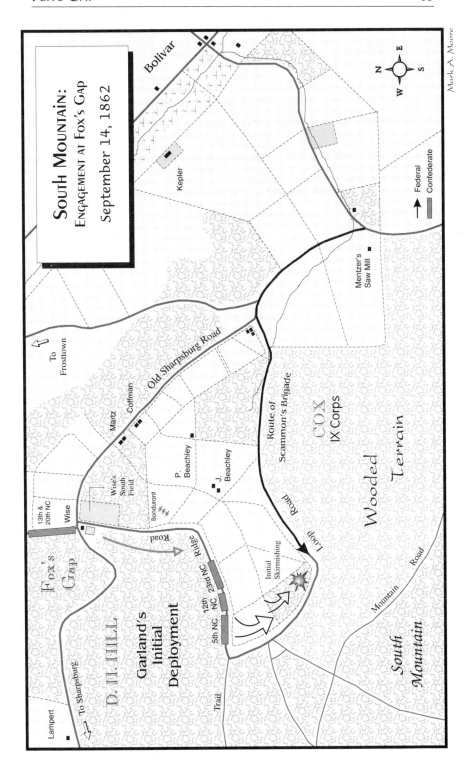

SOUTH MOUNTAIN:
ENGAGEMENT AT FOX'S GAP
September 14, 1862

Federal
Confederate

Bolivar

Kepler

To
Frosttown

Old Sharpsburg Road

Coffman

Martz

P.
Beachley

J.
Beachley

Wise's
South Field

Bondurant

13th &
20th NC

Wise

Fox's
Gap

D. H. HILL

Garland's
Initial
Deployment

To Sharpsburg

Lampert

23rd NC

12th
NC

5th NC

Ridge

Road

Trail

Initial
Skirmishing

Route of
Scammon's Brigade

COX
IX Corps

Wooded
Terrain

Loop

Road

Mentzer's
Saw Mill

South
Mountain

Mountain

Road

Mark A. Moore

cavalryman that morning. Not only was Stuart gone, but there were no cavalry or pickets left behind for scouting out the enemy. In an important oversight, Stuart had failed to inform Hill that he had left Col. Thomas Rosser's 5th Virginia Cavalry at Fox's Gap. Brigadier General Samuel Garland's Brigade and Bondurant's Battery, at least, were on the summit. Hill found them resting by the roadside near the Mountain House when he arrived on the mountain. As far as Hill knew, Garland, Col. A. H. Colquitt and their supporting batteries were the only Confederate forces on South Mountain.[15]

A swift scan of the ground from the summit of Turner's Gap and probably some discussion with one of Colquitt's outpost officers convinced Hill that more than just two brigades were needed on the mountain. Orders were dispatched to bring up Brig. Gen. George B. Anderson's North Carolina brigade of 1,200 men. Brigadier General Roswell Ripley's brigade and Brig. Gen. Robert Rodes' brigade were left at Boonsboro to watch the roads and protect Hill's divisional trains. Whatever force the enemy had in the Middletown Valley and whether they intended to move upon South Mountain that morning were unknown. Until he learned some answers to these questions Hill hesitated to draw any more troops from Boonsboro.[16]

After sending for Anderson, Hill rode forward with Colquitt to have a closer look at the approaches to Turner's Pass and to inspect the Georgian's disposition of his brigade. Colquitt had picked his ground well and his regiments and skirmishers were strongly posted. Hill made no changes to his dispositions other than to instruct him to connect his right with Garland, whom Hill planned to send to defend Fox's Gap. Without cavalry to picket his front, Colquitt could tell Hill little about the strength or dispositions of the enemy in the Middletown Valley, but he offered the opinion that they had withdrawn during the night. Hill was unconvinced. Accompanied by Major J. W. Ratchford, his assistant adjutant general, he rode off to have a look at the ground at Fox's Gap.[17]

The two men probably followed the Wood Road south from the Mountain House. They had traveled approximately three-quarters of a mile when they heard voices of command and the rumbling of wheels coming from the direction of the Sharpsburg Road and Fox's Gap. Unaware of the presence of Rosser's cavalry, Hill believed it was the enemy moving to turn his right. Without investigating further, the two officers turned back for Turner's Pass. At the Mountain House he found Garland, alerted by the artillery fire, with his brigade under arms and ready to march. In an army rich in talented leaders, Samuel Garland was one of its bright rising stars. The 31-year old general had received his professional training at the Virginia Military Institute. In the winter of 1861-1862 he had lost

Brig. Gen.. Samuel Garland

Library of Congress

his wife and the tragedy nearly broke his spirit. He rallied, however, and led his brigade with skill and bravery through the Peninsula Campaign. "I never knew a truer, better, brave man," wrote Hill of the young Virginian. A new woman had recently entered Garland's life and rumors were circulating that they were to be married. But for the present, Hill had a challenging and difficult mission for the brigadier.[18]

Hill's orders to Garland were to sweep south through the woods to Fox's Gap and to hold the Sharpsburg Road "at all hazards." To underscore the importance of the assignment Hill pointed out that the very safety of the army depended upon holding the Federals in check. If they were able to force their way to the western side of the mountain before Lee and Longstreet came up, a disaster might result. Garland had no questions and started his brigade and Bondurant's Battery promptly along the Wood Road. Hill recalled that Garland "went off in high spirits."[19]

Garland's brigade of North Carolinians counted five regiments numbering approximately 1,100 officers and men. Bondurant added two 3-inch rifles and two 12-lb. howitzers for artillery support. Had Hill known the ground and the road and trail system more fully, he would have realized how inadequate this force was for the duty entrusted to them. All of Garland's regiments had suffered severe casualties on the Peninsula and were thin in numbers. During the respite enjoyed by Hill's Division following the Peninsula Campaign, the brigade had drawn new uniforms and replaced lost and damaged equipment. Manpower losses, however, had only been partially reconstituted by the addition of some conscripts. There had been little opportunity to train these recruits. Sergeant E. M. Dugand of the 5th North Carolina observed that the conscripts in his regiment could not even "load a gun." Nevertheless, Garland was a skilled soldier, and he was sustained for the most part by competent regimental leadership. His commanders could be expected to make effective use of the terrain and to get every bit of fight out of the slim number of veteran riflemen they could put on the firing line.[20]

As Garland's column emerged from the woods north of Fox's Gap, they came upon Tom Rosser with the 5th Virginia Cavalry and a section of Major John Pelham's horse battery. Rosser had been picketing the gap since early that morning and could offer some information about the terrain. After a brief conference Garland made his dispositions. To properly cover the approaches to Fox's Gap he found it necessary to deploy the brigade across a broad frontage. The 13th and 20th North Carolina deployed north of the Sharpsburg Road (with their right flank touching that road) and with open ground to their front. The left of these two regiments did not extend far enough to connect with Colquitt's right, leaving a gap 400 yards wide between the two brigades.[21]

Garland took the rest of his brigade south of Fox's Gap past the farm of Daniel Wise, whose house and garden were located at the southwest corner of the intersection of the Sharpsburg and Ridge Roads. East of Wise's farmhouse, across the Ridge Road, Wise maintained a large level pasture of about two acres, known afterwards as "Wise's Field." The south and east borders of the field were enclosed by a woods that wrapped around the field and followed the course of the Sharpsburg Road down the slope of the mountain. The woods stopped at the edge of a field which enclosed the J. Coffman farmyard. South of the woods were fields under cultivation. The perimeter of this open ground was roughly defined by the Ridge, Loop and Old Sharpsburg roads. The fields were in pasture, wheat stubble, or corn, intersected by numerous stone walls that defined field and property boundaries. Garland led the 5th, 12th and 23rd North Carolina along the Ridge Road to the summit of Hill 1080 where he overlooked this open ground. The summit was a level plateau that extended approximately 40 yards east from the Ridge Road before the ground dropped off and declined sharply toward the woods enclosing the Loop Road. The western side of the Ridge Road was enclosed by a thick forest that followed the course of the road as it curved to meet the Loop Road. The two roads joined one another on the wooded summit of Hill 1320.

Garland placed his strongest regiment, Col. Duncan K. McRae's 5th North Carolina Infantry with more than 400 effectives on the right of the brigade, in position near, but north of the important intersection of the Ridge and Loop roads. To McRae's right and front the ground climbed steadily to the summit of Hill 1320, where Rosser's 5th Virginia Cavalry and Pelham's two guns were stationed. Captain Snowden Snow's 12th North Carolina, a mere 92 muskets, formed on the Ridge Road to McRae's left. Colonel Daniel H. Christie's 23rd North Carolina also deployed in the Ridge Road, to the left of the 12th. Christie's men enjoyed the protection of a stone fence bordering the road. The space between the left of the 23rd North Carolina and the woods around Wise's Field Garland filled with Bondurant's Battery, which he ordered unlimbered in an open field enclosed by stone walls, south of Wise's Field. The three infantry regiments stacked arms and broke ranks, lounging in the Ridge Road. From right to left, the brigade's frontage covered approximately 1,300 yards. According to the tactics of the day it should have covered no more than 350 yards. There were intervals between every regiment. The largest gap—between the left of the 23d and right of the 20th—extended a full 250 yards, although this was partially filled by Bondurant's guns. Garland was dangerously extended but until the enemy displayed their force he could not concentrate.[22]

After completing his dispositions, Garland rode forward with McRae to reconnoiter the open ground east of the Ridge Road. They were on the alert since Bondurant had spotted an enemy column marching up the Sharpsburg Road and fired several shells at it. But the Federals had sought cover and were not to be seen. All appeared tranquil until the sharp-eyed Alabamians of Bondurant's battery spotted "a few men slowly and stealthily approaching us near the north east corner of the clearing." They were skirmishers of the 30th Ohio. Garland and McRae had also seen enemy soldiers, moving along the Loop Road. It was probably Company A of the 23d Ohio. Garland concluded the enemy activity he observed might mean the Federals were attempting to move a force across his front to seize a position on the slope of Hill 1320. He instructed McRae to push a force of 50 skirmishers into the woods to the 5th's right oblique front to investigate.[23]

It was nearly 9:00 a.m. when McRae's skirmish line cautiously moved out with muskets at the ready across the fields and pastures to explore the woods that concealed the Loop Road. The 5th's skirmish line had not covered more than fifty steps when musketry fire rang out. At the edge of the woods the North Carolinians bumped into Company A of the 23d Ohio. Instantly both sides opened fire. Several Federals fell in the first volley and a prisoner was seized. Garland promptly moved to reinforce the skirmish line by ordering McRae to advance his entire regiment to its support. The 5th pushed through a dense woods so thick that McRae reported "it was impossible to advance in line of battle." The woods eventually gave way to a clearing where they could see a heavy line of Federals advancing through the woods on the opposite side.[24]

The Federals were Hayes' 23d Ohio. Before encountering McRae's skirmish line Hayes had observed Confederates in the area and had thrown out Company F to his left and Company I to the right as flankers. It was this formidable skirmish line, along with Company A, that precipitated the engagement with the North

Carolinians. Upon observing the 5th North Carolina advance down the slope of Hill 1080 Hayes hastily ordered his regiment into line, a trying task because the emergency forced the regiment to form by facing by the rear rank with "some companies inverted and some out of place." The officers and sergeants also struggled with the dense mountain laurel in trying to get the men into a semblance of a line. Hayes did not pause to correct his awkward formation, but pushed forward aggressively over broken, difficult ground to meet the approaching enemy. As the Ohioans struggled through the forest to the edge of the clearing, McRae's North Carolinians greeted them with a volley that killed and wounded several men. "I feared confusion," wrote Hayes, so he "exhorted, swore, and threatened" his men. The 23d stood their ground and returned fire.[25]

Greasy white smoke wreathed the opposing battle lines as they blazed away at one another. The advantage was with McRae, whose regiment was well formed to deliver its fire. At some points, however, the Ohioans delivered as good as they got. Robert E. Cornwall of Company A wrote that he and his comrades "killed 8 that I see before the Regt got up to us." Still, Hayes knew his men could not stand the terrific fire for long. One member of the regiment recalled that "[b]ullets pattered about us like raindrops on the leaves. . .Then we heard the voice of Colonel Hayes saying: 'Men of the Twenty-third, when I tell you to charge, you must charge...Charge Bayonets.'" With a yell the 23rd surged forward from the woods. The North Carolinians delivered "a cloud of bullets" into the advancing Union line but did not check it. The untried and shaky conscripts of McRae's regiment were unnerved and many broke for the rear. McRae raced after them and by "strenuous exertion of officers and veterans," the recruits were rallied. The balance of the regiment had fallen back from the forest clearing to the first belt of woods, where they continued the battle.[26]

Hayes halted his regiment briefly to reform its broken line, and pushed forward again. The rapid musketry firing that had slackened when the 5th gave ground quickly intensified as the reformed North Carolinians brought the advancing 23d under a murderous fire. "I soon began to fear we could not stand it," wrote Hayes, and he ordered a second advance. This charge drove the North Carolinians clear out of the woods, through a cornfield, and up the slope of Hill 1080. As the Ohioans emerged from the timber they came under an accurate and destructive fire from a regiment of Confederate infantry positioned behind a hedgerow and stone wall on the plateau of Hill 1080. The Federals took cover behind a stone wall which ran between the cornfield and edge of the timber. "Most of our loss occurred at this point," reported Maj. James M. Comly of the 23rd. Hayes again attempted to employ the aggressive tactics that had succeeded thus far. He ordered a charge, but this one failed to get started. As he shouted the command to charge a bullet shattered Hayes left arm, the shock of the wound forcing him to lie down. He recalled afterwards:

> I laid down and was pretty comfortable. I was perhaps twenty feet behind the line of my men, and could form a pretty accurate notion of the way the fight was going. The enemy's fire was occasionally very heavy; balls passed near my face and hit the ground all around me. I could see wounded men staggering or carried to the rear; but I felt sure our men were holding their own. I listened anxiously to hear the approach of reinforcements; wondered [why] they did not come.[27]

In addition to the murderous fire that raked the front of the 23rd, the regiment began taking fire from their left flank. This was undoubtedly delivered by dismounted troopers of Rosser's 5th Virginia, who had advanced to relieve the pressure on Garland's right. Someone on the left of the 23rd shouted a warning which was heard by Hayes. He stood up and called to Capt. James L. Drake, commanding Company H, the left-flank company, to wheel back and face this new threat. The effort sapped Hayes' strength and he lay down again. A young wounded North Carolinian lay nearby and the two men had "a considerable talk," that Hayes recalled was "right jolly and friendly" amidst the storm of battle.[28]

Captain Drake pulled his company back perhaps twenty yards to face Rosser's threat. In the noise and confusion the remainder of the regiment observed the movement and promptly fell back on a line with Drake, leaving their wounded colonel lying between the hostile lines. Major Comly stopped by Hayes and inquired if he had wanted the whole regiment to fall back. Hayes replied no, but said "if the line was now in good position to let it remain and to face the left companies as I intended."[29]

Sharp firing continued for perhaps fifteen to twenty minutes, then by seemingly mutual consent it died out and an unsteady lull settled over the field. Fearing he might have been abandoned by his regiment, Hayes called out, "Hallo, Twenty-third men, are you going to leave your colonel here for the enemy?" Six men instantly responded and bounded forward to the rescue only to be driven back by heavy fire. This renewed the combat and both sides soon blazed away at one another. Finally, Lieut. Benjamin W. Jackson of Company I dashed forward through the heavy fire and managed to get Hayes back to the cover of the woods. A dressing was applied to his wound, then he walked on his own about one mile to the home of Widow Coogle, from where he was transported to Middletown.[30]

The Confederates who had checked the advance of Hayes were Col. Daniel H. Christie's 23d North Carolina, who along with the 12th North Carolina had been ordered forward by Garland to the support of the 5th North Carolina. After his initial orders to McRae to send forward a detachment of skirmishers, Garland rode to his left to see how matters were developing upon that part of his front. But the storm broke upon his right and spread to his center. The left remained quiet and Garland started for the right at the gallop. As he rode past Bondurant's battery, which was under fire from skirmishers of the 30th Ohio, he ordered the Alabamians to limber-up and fall back by the right piece. When he reached his right he promptly ordered the 23d and 12th regiments to advance. The 23d advanced about forty yards from the Ridge Road into an open field behind a hedgerow and old stone fence, from which position they fired with deadly effect upon the 23d Ohio and later upon the 12th Ohio. The 12th North Carolina, burdened with a young and inexperienced commander, did not perform as stoutly. They moved upon the 23d Ohio, probably while that regiment was still engaged in the woods with the 5th North Carolina, and fired one wild volley, whereupon Capt. Snow became un-nerved shouting, "fire and fall back." More than half the regiment departed the field with their captain, but 30 to 40 members stumbled upon the 13th North Carolina and fought with that regiment the remainder of the day.[31]

McRae's regiment came tumbling back in retreat soon after the collapse of the 12th North Carolina. McRae reported to Garland that he believed the Federals had massed a large force in the woods with the intention of turning the brigade's right. He suggested that Bondurant shell the woods to dislodge or uncover whatever force the Federals might have concealed. Garland replied that he had withdrawn Bondurant, but agreed with McRae that the threat to the brigade's right appeared ominous. A staff officer was dispatched to bring the 13th and 20th regiments south of the Sharpsburg Road. Garland remained a few moments longer with McRae, then rode off to meet and place the two regiments.[32]

Garland met the 20th North Carolina, followed by the 13th, in the vicinity of the intersection of the Ridge and Old Sharpsburg Roads. By this time skirmishers of Ewing's 30th Ohio were pressing their way up the slope of the mountain, threatening the left of the brigade position south of the Sharpsburg Road. To parry this force Garland led both regiments south of the woods bordering Wise's Field. He placed the 20th North Carolina, under Colonel Alfred Iverson—a man who would later lead this same brigade to disaster at Gettysburg—on the left of the 23d North Carolina. Due to the absence of cover, however, Iverson was unable to advance in order to connect with the left of the 23d, and formed instead on the Ridge Road, to the left and rear of Colonel Christie's regiment. Iverson described his position as "a level plateau about 100 yards wide in thick chestnut undergrowth, open fields in front sloping down steep hills, the bottom of which we could not see; in our rear a precipitous rocky, wooded descent." He advanced skirmishers to the brow of the Hill 1080 plateau to cover his front and prevent surprise. The soldiers of the 13th North Carolina, under an excellent officer, Lt. Col. Thomas Ruffin Jr., were "directed to take position in an open field upon the brow of a high hill." Presumably, this position was to the left and front of Iverson, possibly in the same field previously occupied by Bondurant. Bondurant, meanwhile, unlimbered in the area of Farmer Wise's garden, where their guns could sweep Wise's Field in front and the open ground south of the Sharpsburg Road. The re-deployment improved Garland's situation but his flanks remained vulnerable and his regiments were not in close contact with one another.[33]

During Garland's re-deployment to the right, Scammon fed his last regiment into the fight. With Hayes sharply engaged with the Confederate right and while Ewing was moving upon their left, Scammon determined to test the Confederate center with Col. Carr B. White's 12th Ohio. The 12th had arrived at the edge of the woods, on the right of the 23d, and facing the open pasture that extended to the plateau of Hill 1080. The 12th was ordered to advance over this open ground to drive off what appeared to be a Confederate regiment, which in reality probably was the 20th North Carolina's skirmish line, which could be observed in position on the brow of the plateau 300 yards distant. To reduce casualties while advancing over open ground White deployed his entire regiment in skirmish order. At a signal, the 12th delivered a volley, burst out of the woods and dashed forward. The 23d North Carolina shifted some of their fire to this new threat, but they did not check the advance. Neither did Iverson's skirmishers. They beat a retreat to the Ridge Road leaving 15 to 20 dead and wounded behind. As White's men reached the plateau of Hill 1080 they instantly came under fire from Iverson's regiment on the Ridge Road, from the left of the 23d North Carolina, and from sharpshooters posted in trees in the woods behind the Ridge Road. White pulled his men under the edge of the plateau, where they were in defilade. The 12th had advanced beyond the 23d Ohio on the left, which still remained in the woods of Hill 1320, and the 30th Ohio, which had encountered stubborn resistance in attempting to establish itself on Hill 1080. Until they came up on his flanks, White and his men were content to hug mother earth.[34]

While White's 12th regiment had established itself under the brow of the Hill 1080 plateau, Col. Hugh Ewing's 30th Ohio, with its front covered by a "cloud of skirmishers," had advanced steadily up the open slopes of Hill 1080, south of the Sharpsburg Road. Their advance soon brought them into view of Lane's Battery, which had re-located to a patch of cleared ground on the summit of Hill 1280, over one mile distant at Turner's Gap. Lane immediately opened an enfilading fire upon them. Then, one of the Union batteries in the valley below mistook Ewing's men for Confederates and began shelling them. Lane's enfilading fire was bad enough, but the "friendly fire" from the rear threw confusion into the ranks and brought the advance to a halt. But Ewing managed to restore order and pushed his command forward until they reached the plateau of Hill 1080, south of the woods bordering Wise's Field. This placed Ewing on the flank of Bondurant's guns, which he made dispositions to attack by changing front to the left. His skirmishers began firing at the unsupported artillerymen, causing Garland to order the battery to limber-up and withdraw, but not before they killed and wounded several of Ewing's men with a parting blast of canister. No sooner had Bondurant retreated than Ewing learned that a strong enemy force had displayed itself on the regiment's right flank. It was the 13th and 20th North Carolina moving up from their initial positions north of the Sharpsburg Road. Ewing pushed his heavy skirmish line forward to a rail fence and changed front to the rear with the remainder of his regiment. They were soon confronted by the 13th North Carolina in the open ground in front, triggering a fierce exchange of musketry.[35]

The 13th North Carolina soon took fire not only from Ewing's skirmishers but also from Federals concealed in the woods on Hill 1320. The Federals in the woods could not be seen so Ruffin directed his regiment's fire against Ewing's skirmishers, who could be clearly seen behind a rail fence on the 13th's left. "Our men were cool and fired with precision and effect," reported Ruffin. The Federal skirmish line melted away, but the fire from the woods in front continued. Garland, concerned about his vulnerable left flank, had remained with the 13th throughout their battle with the 30th Ohio. It was his style of leadership to be near the point of danger. But Ruffin thought he was unnecessarily exposing himself. "General, why do you stay here? You are in great danger," Ruffin warned. "I may as well be here as yourself," Garland replied. Ruffin responded that as a regimental commander it was his duty to be with the regiment, but Garland's duty was to superintend the brigade from a safe position. Before Garland could reply, Ruffin was struck in the hip. He advised Garland of his wound and the general turned to a member of his staff and gave an order in a low voice. An instant later, Ruffin heard a groan and turned to see his commander on the ground, writhing in pain from a mortal wound. Garland was gathered in a blanket and carried from the field.[36]

The fall of Garland and the ineffectiveness of the 13th North Carolina's fire caused the wounded Ruffin—who remained with his regiment—to pull his command back 50 yards from the brow of the hill, probably to the Ridge Road, and on the left of the 20th North Carolina. Bondurant by now had repositioned his guns and they sent what Ewing reported was "a hail of grape" into his ranks. The Ohioan had also learned of Confederate reinforcements approaching the battlefield from the direction of Turner's Gap. Not deeming it prudent to draw more upon his command than it could handle, Ewing pulled his men back where they found shelter from Bondurant's guns and Ruffin's musketry.[37]

Garland's wounding left Col. McRae in command. "I felt all the embarrassment the situation was calculated to inspire," he later commented in his report. It was evident to him that the Federals were present in greater strength than his small brigade could handle alone. He called for Capt. D. P. Halsey, Garland's assistant adjutant general., and sent him galloping to Hill with a request for immediate reinforcements.[38]

Although McRae's regiments had checked the initial Federal effort to seize the high ground south of Fox's Gap, they had been unable to prevent the 12th and 30th Ohio from establishing themselves at the edge of the plateau of Hill 1080. Both regiments, however, were pinned down and unable to make further progress. Scammon thought close artillery support might give his infantry the edge they needed to dislodge Garland's North Carolinians from their covered positions. He sent a request to Cox for a section of guns, which the division commander in turn forwarded to Capt. McMullin. According to James E. D. Ward, of the 12th Ohio, McMullin "at first demurred, complaining that Old Granny (as Scammon was called) did not know what he was about." But the battery commander was assured that the 12th Ohio would support his guns. This was good enough for McMullin, who remarked he would "trust his 'soul' in the keeping of that regiment," and he ordered Lt. George L. Crome to take his section forward.

The climb up the mountain proved extremely difficult for the battery's horses and Crome had to resort to manual force to get his section into position. Infantrymen from the 12th Ohio pitched in with Crome's gunners and the two 10-lb. Parrots were hauled forward and placed in the open pasture in front of the 12th, on the plateau of Hill 1080. The 20th North Carolina, protected by a stone wall and dense woods, were forty yards distant. Crome's gunners rammed double charges of canister down their tubes and sent the deadly charges crashing into the thicket in front. White's infantry did what they could to support the frightfully exposed artillerymen with small arms fire. Crome and his men served their pieces bravely but they never stood a chance. Iverson ordered Capt. James B. Atwell to deploy his company as skirmishers and use the cover of a stone wall, which ran from the regiment's left down the mountain, to gain a position from which they could silence the Union guns. "In a moment the sharp crack of his rifles told the work was being done," wrote Iverson. Lt. R. B. Wilson of the 12th Ohio recalled that "the men about our guns were picked off rapidly." Volunteers were requested from the ranks of the infantry and Crome himself served as a gunner for one of his fallen men. The gallant guns crews and their infantry volunteers managed to discharge four rounds of double-canister into their front before Atwell's riflemen dropped Crome and silenced his guns for good. Lt. Wilson recalled that Crome had just loaded the piece he was serving "and had leveled it, and was giving the command to fire to a corporal of Co C of our regiment who held the lanyard when he fell dead behind his piece as the last shot was fired." Actually, Crome was not killed instantly. Although struck in the heart he lived for two hours before expiring. The violent death of the young, courageous officer haunted Lt. Wilson's memory. Thirty-seven years later he wrote, "[i]t was a tragic scene that I shall never forget."[39]

While Crome bravely fought their hopeless and costly fight, Cox reinforced Scammon's foothold on the plateau of Hill 1080. The 23d Ohio's soldiers were ordered to lie down and crawl forward to take position on the left of the 12th Ohio. Their advance brought them to within thirty yards of the 23d North Carolina, "but we were concealed by the hill," wrote John M. Clugston of the 12th. Samuel W. Compton, also of the 12th Ohio, recalled they were so near the Confederates that he "could hear them giving orders almost as plainly as our own." During the fighting between Scammon and Garland, Crook's brigade had arrived and formed in support of Scammon. Cox ordered Lt. Col. Augustus H. Coleman's 11th Ohio, 430 strong, to move and protect the left flank of the 23d Ohio, and to parry the threat Rosser's cavalry posed. In taking position the regiment endured a fire upon its flank from the 5th and 23d North Carolina. They also had to grope through mountain laurel described as "almost impenetrable." Cox sent Lt. Col. Melvin Clark's 36th Ohio, a huge regiment of 800 effectives, forward to fill a gap that had developed between the 12th and 30th Ohio. Lieutenant Colonel Gottfried Becker's 28th Ohio, which numbered 775 officers and men, took position on the right and rear of the 30th Ohio to strengthen the right of the division. When Cox had completed his deployment there were four Ohio regiments, the 23d, 12th, 36th, and 30th, from left to right, somewhat over 3,000 men, poised under the edge of the plateau of Hill 1080 and ready to assault Garland's line. It was probably close to 11:30 a.m. While the Ohio infantrymen waited for the signal to charge, Col. Crook recalled that the soldiers amused themselves by hoisting their caps upon their ramrods which the keen-eyed Confederate marksman quickly perforated.[40]

To Duncan McRae's relief, his urgent call for reinforcements received a prompt response from D. H. Hill. The division commander had ordered Brig. Gen. George B. Anderson's North Carolina brigade of 1,174 officers and men up from Boonsboro when Garland's and Cox's battle had broken out. Hill deployed the brigade on the Frosttown Road, immediately north of the National Road. When Capt. Halsey galloped up with McRae's appeal for reinforcements, Hill instructed Anderson to detach the 2nd and 4th North Carolina under the senior colonel, C. C. Tew of the 2nd, and have them report to McRae. "We are faced to the right," recalled Lt. John C. Gorman of the 2nd, "and away we go up the side of the mountain [along the Ridge Road] at a double quick." The regiments passed "lots of wounded limping down the mountain, trickling blood at every step." One stretcher that passed the column bore the body of Garland, whose life was rapidly ebbing away.[41]

Colonel Tew rode ahead of his men and to report to McRae that his two regiments, numbering approximately 450 fighting men, were close behind. McRae, seeking to relieve himself from the onerous burden of command, questioned Tew about the date of his colonel's commission which, it turned out, pre-dated McRae's. He offered Tew command, but Tew had the good sense to decline, and offered to place his regiments wherever McRae suggested. McRae's achilles heel was his dangling left flank, so he asked him to post his regiments on the left of the 13th North Carolina. With Bondurant's guns providing support McRae hoped this would render the left reasonably secure.[42]

Tew brought his regiments into line on Ruffin's left, and they immediately engaged skirmishers of the 30th Ohio at a range of 100 to 200 yards. The colonel observed that his force was inadequate to cover the ground necessary to adequately defend the position, for a large unprotected space remained on his left. He sent a staff officer to Gen. Anderson to request reinforcements to help fill it. Meanwhile, Tew's skirmishers practiced their deadly trade with their Federal counterparts from Ohio. After nearly thirty minutes of anxious waiting Tew received orders from Anderson to "flank to the left" an unspecified distance, but apparently still south of the Sharpsburg Road. Tew obeyed, although possibly perplexed by his orders, thus breaking the connection with Ruffin's 13th North Carolina. McRae immediately sent Capt. Charles Wood of the brigade staff speeding off to notify Hill of Anderson's curious notion of support, and "to explain to him my situation, and to request re-enforcements." With misplaced confidence that Hill would push forward reinforcements, McRae directed Ruffin to move his regiment to the left to maintain connection with Tew's right flank. Ruffin took post in the Ridge Road in front of Wise's Farm, protected by the high stone walls that flanked the road at that point. His new posting left a gap of 250 to 300 yards between the 13th's right flank and the 20th's left flank. McRae planned to fill this gap by shifting the 5th North Carolina over from the right flank. He scurried to his right to do so (McRae had no horse) but discovered that under an earlier order the 5th had advanced from the Ridge Road into the open field on the right of the 23rd North Carolina where, he believed, "it was dangerous to withdraw it." There were no other troops that could be spared and McRae could only cling to the slender hope that he would be reinforced before the enemy discovered the yawning gaps in his line.[43]

But Cox's division was like a coiled snake, ready to strike at the moment McRae was most vulnerable. The muskets of the waiting Federal soldiers bristled with fixed bayonets. At the signal to advance, the 23d Ohio crawled on their hands and knees to the crest of the plateau, then an officer shouted, "Up and at them." The regiment leaped to its feet and with a "long extended yell" rushed upon the 23d North Carolina directly in their front. At the same moment, on the 23d Ohio's right, the infantrymen of the 12th Ohio reacted by jumping to their feet. Instantly the men were commanded to lie down. "Never did men lie quicker even when shot," recalled Samuel W. Compton. A volley crashed from the line of the 20th North Carolina, forty yards away. Compton recalled that "the few that stood were either killed or wounded." But the majority of the soldiers escaped injury and rose and, with bayonets glinting in the sun and yells bursting from their throats, surged forward toward Iverson's North Carolinians. On the 12th Ohio's right, the 36th and 30th Ohio likewise advanced, but without the shock and fury that characterized the charge of the 12th and 23d.[44]

As the 23rd Ohio dashed forward to close with Col. Christie's 23d North Carolina, "a deadly fire was poured into our ranks," wrote one Ohioan. At point-blank range the Federals halted and "gave them [the 23rd NC] a far more destructive volley, and then charged up on them with our bayonets." The Ohioans surged up to the left of the 23rd North Carolina and a desperate melee ensued in which Sgt. Maj. Eugene L. Reynolds of the 23rd Ohio died by a bayonet thrust. Then the Ohioans discovered a gap in the wall and poured through with bayonets slashing and muskets clubbed. Colonel Christie ordered a retreat which swiftly degenerated into a rout, being hotly pursued by the Ohioans. Those not fleet enough to escape were killed or wounded, including both surgeons of the North Carolina regiment. Not being recognized as noncombatants in the close quarter combat, the two physicians were shot down. E.

M. Dugand, of the 5th North Carolina, was witness to the ferocity of the combat. He observed two men of the 23d North Carolina run down by Ohioians and killed by the bayonet.[45]

"We completely routed the enemy," recorded John Clugston of the 23d Ohio. The force of the charge by Clugston's regiment shattered the left of the 23d North Carolina. The right of that regiment, in company with the 5th North Carolina, streamed to the right and rear in retreat. Captain Thomas M. Garrett, in command of the 5th North Carolina, attempted to rally his regiment by halting his color bearer on the Ridge Road, but a bullet from the 23d Ohio dropped the standard bearer and the stampeding retreat continued, carrying Garrett along with it. The North Carolinians plunged "in great disorder down the steep and bewildering mountain side," Clugston remembered. The 5th regiment's losses numbered five killed, 10 wounded and 33 captured, some of whom were wounded. The 23d North Carolina counted 13 killed (all enlisted men except for the two surgeons) four wounded and 46 captured. The 23d Ohio paid heavily for its victory. Between the earlier combat with both the 5th and 23d North Carolina, and its final charge, the regiment had lost 32 killed, 95 wounded and three missing. Only two other Union regiments' losses at South Mountain would surpass these figures.[46]

While the 23d Ohio overwhelmed the right of Garland's Brigade, the 12th and 36th Ohio smashed its center, routing the 20th North Carolina. Following the one volley Iverson's regiment was able to get off, the 12th Ohio rose to their feet and with a "wild cry" rushed the Carolinians. Before the Southerners could reload, "our line was over the fence and among them with the bayonet," recalled Lt. R. B. Wilson. Solomon R. Smith of the 12th Ohio recalled the close-quarter fight "was a carnival of death; hell itself turned loose." Bayonets flashed and fell and musket charges exploded at point blank range. While the 12th Ohio met the 20th North Carolina head on, the 36th Ohio stormed unchecked into the woods on the 20th's left to envelop their line. "There was nothing to do but to get away or surrender," wrote Iverson. Most chose the former and "fled like deer" down the western slope with the exultant Federals in close pursuit.[47]

"We let into their backs and did great execution," wrote the 12th Ohio's Samuel Compton. One bullet struck down Jimmie Gibson of the 20th North Carolina, a former student of D. H. Hill. He called out to his close chum, Texan Dan Coleman—whose courage and great physical strength had landed him in the ambulance corps—"Great God, Dan, don't leave me." Coleman dashed through the Federal fire to within ten yards of the enemy, scooped up Gibson and ran off unscathed. Colonel Iverson joined the rush to escape the bayonets of the Ohioans. He recalled making "terrific leaps down that mountain." Some distance to his

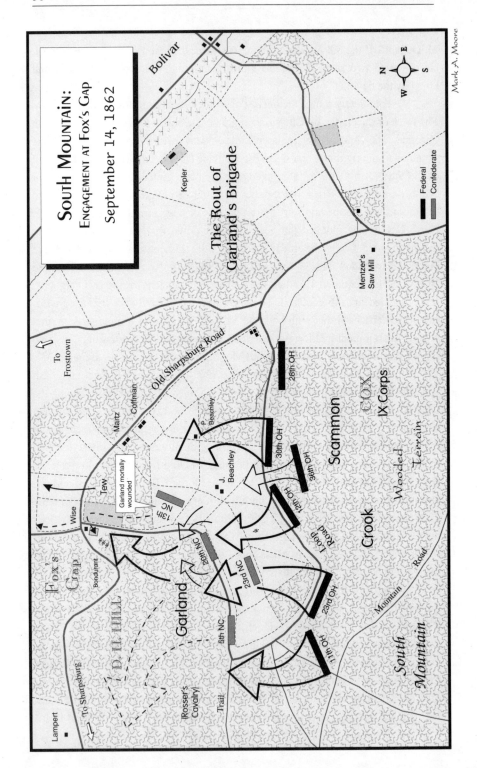

SOUTH MOUNTAIN:
ENGAGEMENT AT FOX'S GAP
September 14, 1862

The Rout of
Garland's Brigade

Federal
Confederate

Mark A. Moore

front, he observed Col. McRae running down the mountain. With refreshing honesty Iverson noted, "I must have been the fastest runner for I caught up with him and together we went to the foot of the mountain." Fred Foard, also of the 20th North Carolina, heard McRae shout at the chaplain of one of Garland's regiments "who was bounding over the tops of laurel bushes like a kangaroo— 'Parson—Parson—God Damn it, come back here; you have been praying all your life to get to heaven and now that you have a short cut you are running away from it.'" Several of Iverson's men who chose to fight died by the bayonet. Lieutenant Wilson saved one "bright looking young soldier" of Iverson's command from this horrible death when he seized the gun of a man from his company "who was very greatly excited [and] was about to run his bayonet" through the body of this unfortunate lad.[48]

The violent charge of the 12th and 36th Ohio left seven dead, nine wounded, and 42 missing or captured in the 20th North Carolina. "My regiment was scattered in every direction and it took the remainder of the day to get them together," recalled Iverson. Some elements of the 12th North Carolina who had not left the field with their captain earlier in the battle had fallen in with Iverson and suffered severe casualties. Colonel White's 12th Ohio pursued the fleeing North Carolinians through the dense forest for nearly one-quarter mile, until, as Lt. Wilson recalled, "the pursued and pursuers became scattered in the dense undergrowth." White called a halt to reform his regiment. Bondurant's battery attempted to succor its broken infantry support by blasting the 12th Ohio's position with canister and shell. But the damage had been done. The center and right of Garland's brigade had been overwhelmed and driven from the field. Their defeat left the position of Rosser's cavalry untenable and he withdrew his troopers and artillery north of the Sharpsburg Road. As the troopers pulled out the 11th Ohio scrambled forward to take possession of Hill 1320 and secure Cox's left flank on this dominating ground. McRae, Christie, Iverson and Garrett were able to rally elements of their regiments near the western base of the mountain, but their part of Garland's Brigade was finished as a fighting force for the remainder of the day.[49]

By this point, only Colonel Thomas Ruffin's 13th North Carolina and Bondurant's battery remained an intact fighting force south of the Sharpsburg Road. The plucky North Carolinian had engaged the advance of the 30th Ohio in his front and held them in check when his right flank came under a heavy fire. The flanking fire surprised Ruffin, for he was under the mistaken impression that the rest of the brigade still extended "in one continuous line" to his right. He sent his adjutant to look into the situation who returned to report that "the enemy had obtained the [Ridge] road on our right, and were coming down upon us from that direction." Ruffin ordered his regiment to move to the left, hoping to come in contact with Anderson's Brigade, but that officer, who had brought his remaining regiments, the 14th and 30th North Carolina, south of the National Road, had pulled the 2nd and 4th North Carolina farther north along the Ridge Road until they were 300 to 400 yards distant from the hard-pressed 13th. Men from the 30th Ohio had penetrated into this gap so Ruffin sought an avenue of retreat by moving to the rear. Instead of finding safety, they encountered the 12th Ohio.[50]

After lying under Bondurant's artillery fire for several minutes, the 12th Ohio was ordered by Scammon to charge the battery, which was situated about 600 yards to the 12th's right and front, near Wise's cabin. Colonel White moved his men through a dense laurel thicket under a severe fire from the Alabamians guns. They emerged in rear of Wise's cabin, near his rock wall enclosed garden, just as Ruffin's regiment attempted to retreat to the rear. Bondurant's battery chose this opportune moment to get out while it still could, and it thundered away to a position in Wise's pasture north of the Sharpsburg Road. A severe fight now swirled about Wise's farm and garden. Ruffin saw bluecoats all around him and nearly despaired that his regiment could escape. Captain Leonard H. Hunt of Company C suggested to the colonel that they charge the Federals in front and withdraw in the confusion. Ruffin employed Hunt's bold suggestion and led his regiment forward against what probably was elements of the 30th or 36th Ohio. It is likely he did not encounter the full weight of either of these large regiments, for the Federals gave way before the aggressive counterattack. Ruffin now skillfully changed front to the right and engaged the 12th Ohio and elements of the 36th Ohio. "A terrific fight ensued," recalled the 12th's Lieutenant Wilson. Wilson observed the color bearer of the 13th North Carolina jump up upon the wall of Wise's garden. Admiring his courage, the Federals shouted for him to surrender. He refused and "in an instant a dozen balls pierced his body and he fell dead." The flag fell into the garden and was seized by Private Hoagland of Wilson's company. Ruffin, nevertheless, managed to temporarily hold the 12th Ohio in check. In the meantime, however, elements of the 30th Ohio infiltrated his rear. Ruffin promptly faced his command about and charged, dispersing the enemy and opening an escape route to the north. He led his command across the Sharpsburg Road and continued north until he encountered G. B. Anderson's brigade. There he found D. H. Hill with the North Carolinians. "I shall never forget the feelings of relief which I experienced when I first caught sight of you," wrote Ruffin to Hill later. "You rode up to me, and, shaking my hand, said that you had given us up for lost and did not see how it was possible for us to have escaped." Hill instructed Ruffin to attach his regiment to Anderson's Brigade. Ruffin had escaped, but not without severe loss. Out of 212 effectives, there were 13 killed, 19 wounded and 24 captured (14 of whom also were wounded).[51]

When Ruffin withdrew north of the Sharpsburg Road, Cox's Kanawha Division had cleared the last Confederate defenders from south of this road and secured their grasp upon the commanding high ground of hills 1080 and 1320. The Sharpsburg Road was threatened and Hill's right flank was turned. It was almost noon. A lull in the infantry fighting settled over the field. Cox and Garland's struggle had consumed nearly three hours. Scattered across the pastures, cornfields, thickets, behind stone walls, and littering Farmer Wise's garden, lay crumpled, bleeding bodies in blue and gray. Elsewhere, the wounded begged for assistance, hobbled away, or were carried off the field. Cox's division had smashed Garland brigade, but the North Carolinians' stubborn defense had exacted a significant toll upon the Ohioians. Scammon lost 262 officers and men, including 62 dead. Crook contributed 62 more casualties in his two regiments engaged. "It was time to rest," wrote Cox. The boundless energy brought on by the excitement of combat had worn off and exhaustion had taken its place. The tiring climb up the mountain, followed by three hours of fighting, had taken a physical toll on the Ohioans. Ammunition in Scammon's brigade was undoubtedly low. The division needed to catch its breath and take stock of the situation. It had done well. A Confederate infantry brigade had been swept from the field with heavy casualties. Colonel Carr White reported that the ground around Wise's Farm was "literally covered with the enemy's dead and wounded." White also boasted two captured battle-flags, one national flag, and a large bag of prisoners. Although White exaggerated Garland's losses, they had been severe enough: Garland and 43 others dead, 168 wounded, and 168 missing or captured, approximately 37 percent of the brigade's strength.[52]

Besides the defeat of Garland, Cox's division had gained the advantage of position. The captured ground commanded the Sharpsburg Road and threatened both Hill's flank and rear. Cox was quick to post his regiments to take advantage of the ground and to assure, if he was counterattacked, that he could hold on to what he had gained. "Our own losses had not been trifling," wrote Cox, "and it seemed wise to contract our lines a little, so that we might have some reserve and hold the crest we had won till the rest of the Ninth Corps should arrive." The Ohioans had cleared the Wise Farm and intersection of the Ridge and Sharpsburg Roads but, Cox noted, "the hollow at the gap about Wise's was no place to stay."

Bondurant's guns, repositioned in the pasture north of the Sharpsburg Road, commenced shelling the gap, as did Lane's rifled pieces, from north of the National Pike, and Major John Pelham's section of horse artillery pounded it from high ground west of Fox's Gap.[53]

While he secured the ground his division had won, Cox questioned his prisoners to learn who he had engaged and the number of troops the enemy had upon the mountain. Either his prisoners stretched the truth for Cox's benefit or were simply ignorant (not unlikely), for they told the Ohioan that Hill's division and Stuart's cavalry were on the mountain, and that Longstreet was in close support. Clearly it was more than Cox's two brigades could handle. As if to confirm the prisoners' information, Hill put up a bold front with his artillery, banging away furiously at Cox's position. Cox knew that the 9th Corps was marching to reinforce him. Until their leading elements arrived, he determined to "hold fast to our strong position astride the mountain top commanding the Sharpsburg Road."[54]

Cox later came under criticism for not pushing his division on to the Mountain House and seizing Turner's Pass. D. H. Hill advanced this notion in his 1886 article for *Century Magazine*, when he wrote that after Cox defeated Garland, "there was nothing to oppose him [Cox]. My other three brigades had not come up; Colquitt could not be taken from the pike except in the last extremity." So, according to Hill, he ran two guns down from the Mountain House and collected a line a "dismounted staff-officers, couriers, teamsters, and cooks" to give the appearance of infantry supports. "I do not remember ever to have experienced a greater feeling of loneliness," he wrote. It made for stirring reading but it was pure fiction. G. B. Anderson's brigade, the 13th North Carolina, and Bondurant's battery, a force of approximately 1,200 to 1,300 men and four guns stood between Cox and Turner's Gap, not a line of clerks and cooks. It is unlikely that there were any clerks or cooks on the mountain at all since the non-combatants had been left at Boonsboro.[55]

Ezra A. Carman, himself a participant in the Maryland Campaign as colonel of the 13th New Jersey and later a historian of balanced judgment, wrote of he Kanawha Division's commander:

> Had Cox pressed his advantage there is little room to doubt that he could
> have seized and held Fox's Gap and the old Sharpsburg road; but he knew
> nothing of the enemy's strength, did not know what he might encounter in the
> woods and dense thickets lying beyond the ridge road; naturally supposed
> that his enemy was in force to hold the position against his small division.

Cox already had demonstrated his aggressive spirit by taking on Garland in a meeting engagement on unfamiliar ground. But he was not reckless. His men had been engaged in combat for three hours and he faced, according to his prisoners, a Confederate division of five brigades plus cavalry. In light of these facts, Cox's decision to halt and solidify the advantage he had gained can hardly be criticized. It was the prudent decision of a good soldier.[56]

Notes

1. Special Orders no. 191 were the operational orders of the Army of Northern Virginia in its movement designed to capture the Union garrison at Harper's Ferry. As such, they detailed the movements of nearly every command of the army. They were discovered by two Union non-commissioned officers near Frederick, Maryland, shortly before noon on September 13. Jacob D. Cox, *Military Reminiscences of the Civil War*, (New York, 1900), pp. 277-278. Hereinafter cited as *Reminiscences*. Jacob D. Cox, "Forcing Fox's Gap and Turner's Gap," in Robert U. Johnson and Clarence C. Buel, eds., *Battles and Leaders of the Civil War*, 4 vols. (New York, 1884-1888), v. 2, p. 585. U.S. War Department, *War of the Rebellion: The Official Records of the Union and Confederate Armies*, 128 vols. (Washington, D.C., 1880-1901), series I, vol. 19, pt. 1, p. 209. Hereinafter cited as *OR*. All references are to series I unless otherwise noted.

2. Cox, *Reminiscences*, p. 278.

3. Ibid. Rutherford B. Hayes, *Diary and Letters of Rutherford B. Hayes*, edited by Charles R. Williams (Columbus, OH, 1922-1926), v. 2, p. 347.

4. Martin Sheets diary, Civil War Times Illustrated Collection (CWTI), United States Army Military History Institute (USAMHI), Carlisle Barracks, PA. *OR* 19, pt. 1, pp. 461, 210, 435-436. Hugh Ewing Diary, Ohio State Archives.

5. Cox, *Reminiscences*, p. 280. See also, Cox, "Forcing Fox's Gap," p. 586. To the 20th Century reader, Moor's refusal to provide more information when he clearly knew it is astonishing. But this was the 19th Century, where a man's word counted for something—at least with some men.

6. Cox, *Reminiscences*, pp. 280-281. Cox, "Forcing Fox's Gap," p. 586.

7. Cox, *Reminiscences*, p. 275. Ezra A. Carman, "History of the Antietam Campaign," pp. 432-434, Ezra A. Carman Papers, Manuscript Division, Library of Congress.

8. Hill 1100 is actually a spur of a peak known as Lamb's Knoll, which is more than 1,700 feet at its summit.

9. Cox, *Reminiscences*, p. 281. Carman, "Antietam Campaign," p. 429. *OR* 19, pt. 1, pp. 458, 463-464. In his report Cox stated that only two sections of McMullin's battery unlimbered near the turnpike. McMullin's report implies that his entire battery went into

position. The disposition of Simmond's remaining guns is unknown until later in the morning when a section was sent up to support the infantry at Fox's Gap.

10. Carman, "History," p. 429. Cox, *Reminiscences*, p. 281. James Abraham, Letters and Memoirs, USAMHI.

11. Hayes, *Diary and Letters*, v. 2, p. 355.

12. Ibid. James Abraham memoir, USAMHI.

13. R.B. Wilson to Carman, July 22, 1899, Carmen Papers, Library of Congress. *OR* 19, pt. 1, pp. 464, 469. U.S. Army Generals' Reports of Civil War Service, Vol. IV, Roll 3, Record Group 94, National Archives (NA). The 12th Ohio numbered approximately 300 effectives.

14. Hayes, *Diary and Letters*, v. 2, p. 355. *OR* 19, pt. 1, p. 461.

15. *OR* 19, pt. 1, p. 1019. Daniel H. Hill, "The Battle of South Mountain, or Boonsboro," *B & L*, 2, p. 561.

16. *OR* 19, pt. 1, pp. 1019-1020.

17. George D. Grattan, "The Battle of Boonsboro Gap or South Mountain," *Southern Historical Society Papers*, v. 39, pp. 36-37. Hereinafter cited as *SHSP*. *OR* 19, pt. 1, pp. 1019-1020, 1052. Carman, "Antietam Campaign.' *Supplement to the Official Records*, (Wendell, NC, 1995), pt. I, v. 3, p. 581. Hill, "Battle of South Mountain," v. 2, pp. 561-562. Hill was mistaken that he had to bring Colquitt back from the base of the mountain and reposition him. See Grattan.

18. Hill, "Battle of South Mountain," v. 2, p. 562. Ezra Warner, *Generals in Gray*, (Baton Rouge, 1959), pp. 98-99.

19. Hill, "Battle of South Mountain," v. 2, p. 562.

20. *OR* 19, pt. 1, p. 1041. *B & L*, v. 2, p. 316. Garland's Brigade had suffered 844 casualties during the Seven Days' fighting. E. M. Dugand to John A. Gould, no date. Carman Papers, New York City Library. A number of Federal soldiers noted that Garland's men were well uniformed. For one account, see R. B. Wilson to Carman, July 22, 1899, Carman Papers, LC.

21. Carman, "Antietam Campaign," p. 434. *OR* 19, pt. 1, pp. 1040, 1045. Hill, "Battle of South Mountain," v. 2, p. 563.

22. E. M. Dugand to Carman, April, 1892, Carman Papers, New York Public Library (NYPL). Dugand wrote Carman that the regiment was composed of "400 conscripts." Walter Clark, *Histories of the Several Regiments and Battalions From North Carolina in the Great War 1861-1865*, (Reprint; Wendell, NC, 1982), v. 1, pp. 219, 627. *OR* 19, pt. 1, p. 1040. Hill, "Battle of South Mountain," v. 2, p. 563. Carman, "Antietam Campaign," pp. 434-435. John Purifoy to Carman, July 15, 1899 and August 7, 1900, Carman Papers, Library of Congress.

23. John Purifoy to Carman, August 7, 1900, Carman Papers, LC. *OR* 19, pt. 1, p. 1040.

24. *OR* 19, pt. 1, p. 1040. E. M. Dugand to Gould, Carman Papers, NYPL. Carman, "Antietam Campaign," 436.

25. Hayes, *Diary and Letters*, v.2, p. 355. Carman, "Antietam Campaign," p. 436.

26. Robt. Cornwall letter, October 3, 1862, USAMHI. Charles R. Williams, *Life of Rutherford Birchard Hayes*, (Houghton Mifflin, 1914), p. 199. *OR* 19, pt. 1, p. 1040. Dugand to Gould, Carman Papers, NYPL.

27. Hayes, *Diary and Letters*, v. 2, p. 356. *OR* 19, pt. 1, pp. 467, 1040.

28. Ibid., pp. 356- 357.

29. Ibid., p. 356.

30. Ibid., p. 356. Carman, "Antietam Campaign," p. 437.

31. *OR* 19, pt. 1, pp. 1040-1041. John Purifoy to Carman, July 15, 1899. Carman Papers, LC. Walter Clark, *North Carolina Regiments*, v. 1, p. 627.

32. *OR* 19, pt. 1, p. 1041.

33. *OR* 19, pt. 1, pp. 1041, 1045, 465. Purifoy to Carman, August 7, 1900, Carman Papers, LC. Iverson's deployment of skirmishers is extrapolated from, R. B. Wilson to Carman, July 22, 1899, Carman Papers, LC. It was probably this skirmish force that Col. Carr B. White identified as a Confederate "regiment" in his report. See *OR* 19, pt. 1, p. 464. Although some accounts place the 13th North Carolina in Wise's Field initially, it is apparent from both Ruffin's report and Ewing's report, that the first position of the 13th south of the Sharpsburg Road, was in the open ground south of the woods bordering Wise's Field.

34. *OR* 19, pt. 1, pp. 462, 464. Carman, "Antietam Campaign," p. 438. R.B. Wilson to Carman, July 22, 1899, Carman Papers, LC.

35. *OR* 19, pt. 1, pp. 461, 469. U.S. Army General's Report of Civil War Service, Vol. 4, Roll 3, RG 94, NA. Hugh Ewing Diary, September 14, 1862, Ohio Historical Society. Ohio Antietam Battlefield Commission, *Antietam, Report of the Ohio Antietam Battlefield Commission*, (Springfield, 1904), p. 77.

36. *OR* 19, pt. 1, pp. 1046, 469. Hill, "Battle of South Mountain," v. 2, pp. 563-564.

37. *OR* 19, pt. 1, pp. 1046, 469. Adjt. Genls. Report of C.W. Service, Vol. IV, Roll 3, RG 94, NA.

38. *OR* 19, pt. 1, p. 1041.

39. *OR* 19, pt. 1, pp. 459, 462, 464. J.E.D. Ward, *The Twelfth Ohio Volunteer Infantry*, (Ripley, OH, 1864), p. 59. Wilson to Carman, July 22, 1899, Carman papers, LC. D. H. Hill, *Bethel to Sharpsburg*, (Raleigh, 1926), v. 2, p. 370. Alfred Iverson to D. H. Hill, August 23, 1885, Daniel H. Hill Papers, Southern Historical Collection, University of North Carolina at Chapel Hill.

40. John M. Clugston diary, Sept. 14, 1862, Rutherford B. Hayes Library. *Youngstown Mohoning Register*, October 9, 1862. Samuel W. Compton Papers, Samuel Perkins Library, Duke University. Cox, *Reminiscences*, p. 283. *OR* 19, pt. 1, pp. 459, 472. Horton & Teverbaugh, *A History of the Eleventh Regiment* (Dayton, 1866), p. 72. Three companies of the 36th Ohio, probably about 200 men were detached to guard some roads on the left of the division and were not present during the morning fighting. See, Lester L. Kempfer, *The Salem Light Guard, Company G, 36th Regiment Ohio Volunteer Infantry* (No city, No date), p. 87. George Crook Reminiscence, Crook-Kennon papers, USAMHI. Timing of actions is nearly impossible to determine at South Mountain. Cox

wrote that the fight with Garland was over by noon, hence, it is reasonable to estimate
that his dispositions were completed by about 11:30 a.m.

41. *OR* 19, pt. 1, pp. 1041, 1048-1049. John C. Gorman, "Memoirs of a Rebel,"
edited by George Gorman, *Military Images*, no. 3, Nov.- Dec., 1981, pp. 4-5.

42. *OR* 19, pt. 1, p. 1041.

43. *OR* 19, pt. 1, pp. 1049,1046,1041. Gorman, "Memoirs of a Rebel," pp. 4-5.
Clark, *North Carolina Regiments*, v.2, pp. 220-221.

44. Cox, "Forcing Fox's Gap," v. 2, p. 587. Cox, *Reminscences*, 283. John M.
Clugston diary, Rutherford B. Hayes Library. *Youngstown Mohoning Register*, Oct. 9,
1862. Samuel W. Compton Papers, Perkins Lib., Duke University. *OR* 19, pt. 1, p.
1042.

45. Clark, *North Carolina Regiments*, v. 2, p. 221. Dugand to Gould, Carman
Papers, NYPL.

46. John Clugston Diary, Rutherford B. Hayes Library. *OR* 19, pt. 1, p. 1042.
Losses are compiled from Weymouth T. Jordan, Jr., *Roster of North Carolina Regiments*, (Raleigh, 1975), v. 5. *OR* 19, pt. 1, 187.

47. Samuel B. Compton papers, Perkins Library, Duke University. R. B. Wilson to
Carman, July 22, 1899, Carman Papers, LC. Sol. R. Smith, "South Mountain," *National
Tribune*, Jan. 17, 1895. *OR* 19, pt. 1, p. 465. Iverson to D. H. Hill, Aug. 23, 1885, D. H.
Hill Papers.

48. Samuel B. Compton papers, Perkins Library, Duke University. R. B. Wilson to
Carman, July 22, 1899, Carman Papers, LC. *OR* 19, pt. 1, p. 465. Iverson to D. H. Hill,
Aug. 23, 1885, D. H. Hill Papers.

49. Jordan, *Roster of North Carolina Regiments*, v. 5. Out of 92 effectives in the
12th North Carolina, they lost 58, including 23 missing or captured. Benjamin Collins
Reminiscences (12th NC), Southern Historical Collection, University of North Carolina
at Chapel Hill. R. B. Wilson to Carman, July 22, 1899, Carman Papers, LC. *OR* 19, pt.
1, p. 465. Hill, "Battle of South Mountain," v. 2, pp. 566, 587.

50. *OR* 19, pt. 1, p. 1046. Hill, "Battle of South Mountain," v. 2, p. 564.

51. *OR* 19, pt. 1, pp. 465, 1046. Hill, "Battle of South Mountain," v. 2, p. 564.
Ruffin's account in *B & L* differs in some details from his report. D. H. Hill, *Bethel to
Sharpsburg*, v.2, p. 371. R. B. Wilson to Carman, July 22, 1899, Carman Papers, LC. J.
E. D. Ward, *History of the Twelfth Ohio Volunteer Infantry*, p. 59.

52. *OR* 19, pt. 1, pp. 465, 287. Carman Papers, "Antietam Campaign," LC. Carman gives Garland's losses at 49 killed, 164 wounded and 176 captured or missing.
However, a study of the North Carolina rosters by the author reveals the losses stated in
the text. Cox, *Reminiscences*, p. 282.

53. Cox, *Reminiscences*, p. 285. Cox, "Battle of South Mountain," v.2, p. 587.54.
Cox, "Forcing Fox's Gap," v. 2, p. 587. Cox, *Reminiscences*, p. 285. *OR* 19, pt. 1, p.
459.

55. Hill, "Battle of South Mountain," 2, pp. 566-567. *OR* 19, pt. 1, pp. 1019-1020.

56. Carman, "Antietam Campaign," p. 445.

"The brigade is cut to pieces, but I shall remain with them to the last."

A BRIGADE COMMANDER'S FIRST FIGHT

The Letters of Colonel Walter Phelps, Jr. during the Maryland Campaign

edited by Tom Clemens

Nothing in Walter Phelps Jr.'s 30 years of life prepared him for the situation he faced on September 14, 1862 on the slopes of South Mountain in western Maryland. Phelps, a lumber merchant from Glens Falls, New York, was a successful businessman, husband and father. He had been a militia officer for several years, and in May 1861 he volunteered to serve the Union, helping to organize a regiment of local men. Fourteen months after leaving home at the head of this regiment, Col. Phelps had become a seasoned campaigner. He had served credibly in the Union Army for over a year, participating in campaigns in central Virginia, but on this clear fall day in 1862 he was facing his first *major* battle.[1]

His regiment, the 22nd New York Volunteer Infantry, was mustered into United States service in June 1861. Three quarter's of a year later, as part of Maj. Gen. Irvin McDowell's I Corps, Phelps had participated in several fruitless marches and small skirmishes, but no large battles. He fell ill in the summer of 1862 and on July 31 was granted 30 days leave.[2] His brigade, currently commanded by Brig. Gen. John Hatch, previously had earned the nickname "Iron Brigade" while it was commanded by Brig. Gen. Christopher C. Auger, due to their good discipline and marching ability. (There were several units that used the term "Iron Brigade" in 1862. It is not until 1863 that a single "Iron Brigade" emerges in he Army of the Potomac.[3]) During Col. Phelps' absence the brigade underwent several dramatic changes. General Hatch moved up to command Brig. Gen. Rufus King's division, of what was soon designated I Corps, Army of the

Potomac, which was commanded by Maj. Gen. Joseph Hooker. Colonel Timothy Sullivan of the 24th New York Infantry succeeded to command of the brigade. Under his command, the brigade was badly mauled at Second Manassas, losing 772 men.[4]

While the battered elements of the 22nd New York were suffering severe losses in their first major fight, Col. Phelps was trying to return to the regiment and share their fate on the battlefield. His letters to his wife, Eliza, reflect his earnest endeavors to join his command.

Washington Aug. 29 1862
Friday 12 M
Dear E[liza],

I reached here yesterday with Herman Van Dusen. . .I reported to Gen. Wadsworth as soon as I reached here & was informed that I could not join my regiment for a day or two as the rebels had possession of the roads & it was impossible to get there. There are a great many officers situated as I am, unable to get out to their regiments. The rebels are in the rear of Pope & have been this side of Manassas. Our brigade has had some work to do. You do not know my anxiety to be with my regiment now. There are rumors of all kinds afoot in the city. Of course many without foundation, but I believe Pope has been out-generaled. His enemies cite his first order about there being no such thing as a retreat. Gen. Wadsworth told me last night Pope was surrounded & was short of provisions. I am in the hopes that it may not be as bad as represented, but I am confident of one thing & that is that Gen. Wadsworth will not allow me to attempt to join my regiment on account of the guerilla in Pope's rear. I will write you again before I leave. Let me hear from you soon.

Y[ou]rs Aff[ectionate]ly
W Phelps, Jr[5]

As part of General McDowell's III Corps of Maj. Gen. John Pope's Army of Virginia, the 22nd New York Infantry suffered grievously in the loss of officers, losing six killed, 13 wounded and four missing. Lieutenant Colonel Gorton Thomas, who took command of the 22nd New York while Phelps was on leave, was mortally wounded, and the regiment also sustained casualties of 157 enlisted men. Although these figures were unknown to Phelps at the time, his anxiety continued as reports of the battle drifted into Washington.[6]

Colonel Walter Phelps, Jr.
Mass. Commandery, MOLLUS; USAMHI

Washington Aug. 31, 1861
Sunday 10 ½ A.M.
Dear E,

I wrote you on Friday morning. In the afternoon I went to see Gen. Wadsworth in reference to rejoining my regiment. He informed me that I could not do so at present or until something decisive was know in reference to the position of our army & the circumstances of their situation. I met Secretary Stanton at the general's and had some conversation with him. He informed that Popes Army has been fighting all day but did not know with what success (recollect this was on Friday). Yesterday hearing it reported that heavy cannonading was distinct from the battlefield, Herman and myself went down to the river bank and remained there nearly two hours. The firing was distinct & rapid. At 5 ½ PM it became terrific, Washington was in a high state of excitement & many absurd rumor gained confidence.

Up to Friday night at 7 o'clock the 22nd had lost no men at least in killed, although exposed for two days exposed to heavy artillery fire. Lt. Colonel Fowler of the 14th Brooklyn came in last night wounded. He was shot in the leg, the ball passing entirely through the fleshy part but injuring no bone. He was wounded Friday night about 7 PM and left the field. Up to that time I have no information of my regiment. Col. Fowler says they have behaved nobly & that the entire brigade has won the admiration of the commanding officers. They are termed the iron brigade for their coolness, intrepidity and stolidity under fire.

I return tomorrow by the wagon that brought the Col. I am exceeding anxious to learn the details of yesterday's battle. To day we are having rain possibly the result of the heavy firing of yesterday. I shall write you again the first opportunity after joining the regiment. I hope my brave fellows may not suffer much, but if they escaped yesterday it will be miraculous. Gen. Casey ordered me yesterday to drill some of the new regiments until I could leave town but as I now know where the regiment is & have a wagon to carry me to the field he cannot deny me permission to leave. The wagon is being mended to day & I hope to leave bright & early tomorrow.

Affly
W Phelps Jr[7]

The poignancy of Phelps' next letter is quite moving as he surveys the destruction in his regiment. He notes the loss of many friends and comrades and hopes to restore his regiment before it is committed to combat again. Unfortunately, much of the Army of the Potomac was not allowed to recuperate, but was immediately ordered to pursue Confederate General Robert E. Lee's Army of Northern Virginia as they proceeded into Maryland.

Head Qrs. 1st Brigade
Upton Hill Va
Thursday Sept. 4, 1862

Dear E,

The old brigade is again encamped on the ground so long occupied by them last winter. I reached the regiment last night and staid [sic] in the log house where I had passed so many happy hours with you and friends whom I shall never see again. It is sad. I am now in command of the brigade and have my head quarters in the house occupied last winter by Gen. Auger. My office is in the room where the piano was and where we passed so many pleasant evenings. Col. Frisby was killed last Saturday.[8] Lt. Col. Thomas died yesterday morning about 9 o'clock at Brown's Hotel. Poor fellow, he died a hero. I followed his remains from his room to the wagon in front of the hotel. When I contrast the present scenes about me with the past I can hardly imagine the reality, it seems like a dream. I do not realize that I shall never see again Capts. McCoy, Clendon & Cadwell and numbers of other who have fallen. Poor Atherly, too[,] I miss him exceedingly.[9] War news to me is a stern reality, it is stripped of all pomp and tinsel and of all happy circumstances that once surrounded it. All agree that the 22d Reg. acted splendidly in the battles of last week. I do not know what orders the brigade may have for the present, but think they will be allowed to recruit, it has been terribly cut up. Gen. Hatch I like very much. He told me yesterday as matters had terminated, he was thankful I was not with my regiment, he thinks I would have fallen. It appears he telegraphed me to come on but I never received the telegram.[10] I joined my regiment the first moment I could, it can hardly be called a regiment now. Every officer & man in the brigade thinks it has been sacrificed. How long are these things to be? James Wythe, poor fellow was killed on Friday night.[11] I have but 4 line officers doing duty with the regiment & but 240 men. The other regiments in the brigade are about the same. Charley Bellamy is well, so is Dr. Holden. Henry Cronkhite is wounded but will get on well. Capt. Cameron is doing well & will probably save his arm. Lt Cushing is well. Dr. Cromwell's son (Lake George) is killed. Everything is yet confused and I cannot get accurate accounts. Mr. Bates was taken prisoner, but returned to camp last night.[12]

A great many of my men were taken prisoners but have been paroled. Write me often directing as before. Kiss Annie for me. Remember me to all

Affly Yrs
Walter Phelps Jr

Soon after his return to the regiment Phelps was suddenly thrust into temporary command of the brigade, while his old brigade commander, Brig. Gen. John P. Hatch, assumed command of what had been King's Division, I Corps, Army of the Potomac.

Head Quarters 1st Brigade
Upton Hill Va Sept. 6, 1862
Dear E,

I have just received orders to have the brigade ready to move at a moment's notice. I think we shall move towards Washington. I shall take Qr. Master Schenck for one of my aids [sic]. Capt. Strong is acting as my Adjutant General. I will write again tomorrow or the next day if possible. The loss in killed, wounded and missing in the brigade is about 800. The 22nd lost about 220.[13]

On the seventh of September Phelps received a letter from Eliza that added to his discomfort. Evidently unnamed persons in Glens Falls were accusing Phelps of cowardice for failing to be with his regiment at the disaster of Second Manassas. Phelps was quite stung by this criticism and wrote a lengthy letter justifying all of his actions, and describing his attempts to join his regiment.

Phelps' father-in-law had notified him of "a petition. . .being circulated to have me dismissed from the service." Incensed, Phelps dashed off a letter on September 13 offering a challenge to his critics. He then described how such a petition would have to be presented to the Secretary of War and if verified, he then would be dismissed from the service. Phelps threw down the glove, directing his wife Eliza to "[s]ay to your Father I wish him to propose this plan to the getters up of the paper & that I will pay expenses to Washington for that purpose if they succeed. If they do not succeed, they must pay their own. I enclose you an order on James Beull for $100. Let no one see it but your Father. If you have no occasion to use it destroy it."[14]

What is striking about this letter is that while Phelps is concerned about his honor and reputation, the Maryland Campaign is progressing rapidly towards a series of climactic battles. A few hours after Phelps wrote his letter to Eliza the famous "Lost Order" was presented to Maj. Gen. George B. McClellan. The next day, September 14, Gen. McClellan ordered his army to move against the Confederate forces holding the passes through South Mountain. With a fight looming in the immediate future, Phelps keenly felt the need to demonstrate his courage in battle.

Colonel Sullivan of the 24th New York Infantry returned to the brigade on September 7 and relieved Phelps of brigade command. However, Phelps' comments to Eliza on September 13 that "it is possible I may have an opportunity to distinguish myself as a brigade commander," proved prophetic. On the morning of September 14 in the streets of Frederick, Phelps was given brigade command again by Gen. Hatch..[15]

Thus, as he faced his first major battle, Phelps had his own brigade, not one in which he only was in temporary command. Unfortunately, his new command had been thinned out by casualties, disease and hard marching. The regiments in Phelps' brigade, the 22nd, 24th and 30th New York and the 14th Brooklyn, were augmented by the addition of the 2nd U. S. Sharpshooters, bringing the total strength of the brigade to about 500 officers and men. Phelps led them into battle at South Mountain that afternoon, earning the plaudits of generals Hatch and Doubleday.[16] It is easy to sense the pride Phelps took in describing his actions in battle to Eliza two days after the fight.

Head Qrs. 1st Brigade
Sept. 16
Camp near Potomac
7 miles beyond Middletown MD

Dear E,

I have been in command of the brigade several days. Sunday Sept. 14 I led the brigade against five rebel regiments, drove them from their position and held it until reinforced by Gen. Doubleday & Gen. Ricketts.[17] Gen. Hatch approved highly of my movements. We had a terrible engagement, it was a general one. I formed my brigade in line of battle & steadily advanced up the mountain, driving the enemy before me, until they reach a line heavy fence. Here they made a desperate stand, but I then drove them from their position. The brigade has covered itself with glory. My brigade remained on the battlefield during the night, the 22d behaved splendidly. They killed two rebel officers, one a Col Strang[e] of the 19th Va. The rebel dead lay in heaps in front of my brigade line, the 22d lost 12 men killed and 26 wounded.[18] I took occasion yesterday to compliment the brigade upon their splendid fighting, the 14th did finely, in fact all the regiments behaved as well as I could have wished. I got one ball through my coat, with that exception escaped. I have now in my command 5 regiments & one battery of artillery of 6 pieces. We have (the Army) gained a great victory & the army has taken some 3,000 prisoners. At least 5,000 of the rebels killed & wounded. Yesterday the rebels opened upon us with their batteries & I was obliged to move the brigade out of range. Lieut. Cushing & Lieut. McCoy behaved nobly. Lieut. Burgey was wounded early in the engagement but his conduct was all I could have desired. Gen. Hatch was wounded and Gen. Reno was killed. I begin to realize that we are at war. I cannot now give the names of killed & wounded. Major McKee was not able to get to the regiment in time for the action, he was like me in that respect, my courage was questioned, his cannot be.[19] Keep writing. The Qr. Master is well, he has been acting as one of my aids [sic] and behaved nobly. I am greatly indebted to him. Write often. We get no mails yet, love to all

Yr Aff H[usban]d
W Phelps Jr

Proud as he might have been of the accomplishments of his brigade and undoubtedly relieved in a personal sense, bigger challenges faced Phelps the next day. At dawn on the 17th of September Phelps' Iron Brigade, only 450 strong, was assigned to support Gibbon's western brigade as it assaulted the now-famous Cornfield. In the maelstrom of fire many men fell and many had their courage tested beyond question. Again, the relief in Phelps' description of the action to his wife shows his concern about the questioning of his courage.

[on Confederate Stationery]
no other paper to write on
Head Quarters 1st Brigade
In the field near Boonsboro
Thursday Sept. 18, 1862

Dear E,

My escapes so far have been wonderful. I was under a most terrific fire yesterday with the brigade for 3 ½ hours. I have endeavored to do my duty. It remains with the officers & men of the brigade to say whether I have or not. Lieut. Cushing is killed I cannot give the names of the others as we cannot get onto the field. I have sent men for Cushing's body, say to his friends that he died nobly the bravest of the brave & fell at the head of his men.[20] The brigade is cut to pieces, but I shall remain with them to the last. I have passed through everything for the past few days. I cannot now describe anything, the sights of the battle field are awful to behold, but familiarity with them makes me feel differently. A shell struck between the Qr. Master's horse & my own yesterday on the field, but did no damage. The 2d USS[harp]S[hooters] alone lost 50 or 60 men in killed and wounded. I have not got the reports of the other regiments. Our flags are cut in shreds with the enemy balls. I captured a rebel flag yesterday, or rather one of my regiments captured it. The ball is opening again & I must cease. We lay [on] our arms last night but were not attacked. I had two orderlies shot at my side. Qr. master safe.[21]

W Phelps Jr

A few days later Phelps amplified his recollections of Antietam in a letter to Eliza. A note of self confidence is evident here as he relates his conduct in the battle:

. . .Gen. Doubleday (of Ft. Sumpter [sic] notoriety) now in command of the Division, sent for me last night & complimented me on the manner of my leading the brigade in the actions of Sunday the 14th and Wednesday 17th. I have also received the congratulations of General Patrick and other officers.[22] I am pleased to know that so far, I have received the approbations of the officers and men of the brigade. I was under very heavy fire Sunday had men fall all about me, but [I was] excepted miraculously, but the fire of Sunday bore no comparison to the one of Wednesday. I do not know how I escaped. I assure you that at night I offered the most fervent prayer of the thanksgiving for my wonderful preservation through the dangers of the battle fields. Fortunately I am very cool under fire & the fact of my quietly lighting my pipe when the shot & shell were flying about cutting down my men seemed to enspirit the men and gave them confidence. I have not had my clothes off for 10 days, oh for the luxuries of a bath. My cough troubles me very much and my lungs are becoming very sore, but I shall not complain when there is such pressing necessity for every officer and man to be in the field. Besides, my courage would be questioned by the Glens Fall people. I don't think any officer or man would question it.

What has become of the petition to the Governor for my dismissal from service that Ellis was circulating?[23] I presume you will the particulars of the battle from Qr. Master Schenck, he was one of my aids & behaved most gallantly. I was obliged to send him often with orders through the most galling fire, but he never quailed or hesitated. He is a brave fellow. Keep any papers that contain any accounts of the brigade or division & send them to me. Send this to Mother or write her. Love to all. Kiss Annie for me

Yrs. Affly
W Phelps Jr

Phelps again earned the praise of General Doubleday for his conduct at Antietam.[24] Members of the brigade performed well also, as reflected in Phelps' reports and letters, but not everyone seemed to have pleased the colonel. In February 1863 he drew up charges and specifications against Col. William M. Searing, (then Lt. Col.) of the 30th New York. According to Phelps, Searing was charged with four offenses, the most serious being cowardice. He accused Searing of abandoning the regiment as it marched to battle on September 16. He also charged that Searing refused a direct order, delivered by one of Phelps' aides, to take command of his regiment. According to Phelps, Searing said "he had already lost one horse and did not want to lose another, nor risk his life to lead only fifty men to battle." There is no record that the charges were ever brought to court martial, and Searing was honorably discharged with his regiment in June 1863.[25]

This incident not only illustrated Phelps' dedication to duty, but also his intolerance of officers unwilling to abide by the same code. Not only had Phelps successfully led his brigade in two sharp engagements, but he had won praise from superiors for his conduct. Evidently he satisfied his critics in Glens Falls as well. His letter of the September 18 asked about what happened to the petition to remove him from office. Everything seemed to have settled down, however, and Phelps' accusers made no more efforts to have him removed from command. He had passed the test of combat and proved his competence and courage.

Colonel Phelps retained command of his brigade through the rest of his term of service. His conduct in the battles of Fredericksburg and Chancellorsville was solid, and his letters to his wife mentioned several compliments paid him by senior officers. When his three New York regiments with two-year enlistments mustered-out in June 1863, nearly every commissioned officer present signed a petition encouraging Phelps' promotion to brigadier general. In addition, his personal papers contain numerous letters of recommendation from generals Doubleday Wadsworth, Hatch, King, Gabriel Paul, John Reynolds, Erasmus Keyes and Solomon Meredith, endorsing his nomination for brigadier general.[26]

Instead of getting a promotion, however, Phelps went home with his regiment. Whether his promise to his mother and his wife to come home was the reason, or his avowed fondness for Gen. McClellan at a time when the "Young Napoleon's" star had fallen, or the simple fact that Phelps' beloved brigade had disbanded, his military career had come to an end. Phelps returned to a warm welcome in Glens Falls which included the presentation of a gold medal from his staff. He went into the iron business after the war, but his health problems seem to have continued, and he died suddenly while on a business trip to Vermont in 1878.[27]

Phelps had accomplished much during his war service. He commanded a brigade from September 1862 until June 1863. His performance was commended in four major battles and numerous skirmishes. Despite the initial doubts of some naysayers in his hometown, he had proven himself, not only to his superiors and his men, but to his critics, and no commander can ask for greater praise than that.

Notes

1. Walter Phelps, Jr. Papers, U.S. Military History Institute, Carlisle, PA.
2. Letter from Ass't. Surgeon Meredith Clymer, USV, July 31, 1862. Compiled Service Records, Colonel Walter Phelps Jr. -RG 94, National Archives, Washington, DC.
3. Mark M. Boatner, *Civil War Dictionary*, (New York, 1959), p. 428. William F. Fox, *Regimental Losses in the American Civil War 1861-1865*, (Albany, 1898), p. 117.

The New York Iron Brigade will be the subject of an article by the author in a forthcoming issue of *Civil War Times Illustrated*.

4. *The War of the Rebellion: Official Records of the Union and Confederate Armies in the War of the Rebellion*, 128 vols. (Washington, DC, 1890-1901) series I, Volume 12 pt. 2, p. 254. Hereinafter cited as *OR*. All references to are to series I unless otherwise noted. Frederick Phisterer, *New York in War of Rebellion*, (New York, 1912), p. 167.

5. Herman Van Dusen was a civilian friend of Phelps who was also from Warren County, New York. He frequently appears in Phelps' letters to his wife. James S.Wadsworth, also from New York, was a brigadier general at this time in the war, and was the military governor of the District of Columbia. Major General John Pope was the commander of the Union Army of Virginia, which engaged the Army of Northern Virginia at the Battle of Second Manassas. Phelps Papers, USAMHI; Ezra J. Warner, *Generals in Blue*, (Baton Rouge, 1964), p. 532., Boatner, *Civil War Dictionary*, pp. 658-9.

6. Edwin Stanton was Secretary of War at this time, and was evidently conferring with Wadsworth concerning the fate of Maj. Gen. John Pope's Army of Virginia as well as the dangers confronting the nation's capital. Maj. Gen. Silas Casey was a veteran of the Peninsula Campaign who was commanding a provisional brigade in the defenses of Washington. His revision of the basic drill manual had just been adopted by the U.S. government; evidently, he had confidence in Phelps' ability to drill new troops. In 1862 Casey, a West Point graduate, had forty years of army service. Lieutenant Colonel Edward B. Fowler of the 14th Brooklyn, officially the 84th New York Infantry, survived his wounds and was eventually breveted to major general in 1865. *OR*, 12 pt. 2, p. 254; Phisterer, *New York in the War*, p. 167

7. Warner, *Generals in Blue*, p. 74-5. Roger D. Hunt & Jack R. Brown, *Brevet Brigadier Generals in Blue*, (Gaithersburg, MD, 1990), p. 213.

8 Major General Christopher C. Auger graduated from West Point in 1843 and had commanded Phelps' brigade in the spring of 1862 until mid-summer, when he assumed command of a division under Maj. Gen. Banks. He was seriously wounded at the battle of Cedar Mountain, but recovered and later commanded the XXII Corps. Boatner, *Civil War Dictionary*, p. 34 -5. Col. Edward Frisbee commanded the 30th New York Volunteer Infantry. Hailing from Trenton, Oneida County, New York, he was a few weeks past his 53rd birthday, when he was killed on August 29, 1862. Rufus W. Clark, *Heroes of Albany, Memorial of Patriot-Martyrs of the City and County of Albany*, (Albany, 1866), p. 118.

9. Robert E. McCoy, age 30, enlisted at Ft. Edward NY in May 1861 as captain of Company B. He was killed on August 29, 1862. *Report of the Adjutant General, State of New York, 22nd Infantry* (Albany, 1865), p. 381 Hereinafter referred to as *NYAGR*.

Miles P. S. Cadwell, age 26, enrolled in the 22nd at Port Henry, and was the Captain of Company K. He too was killed on August 29, 1862. *NYAGR*, p. 328. George Clendon, age 34, was from England originally but enrolled in Glens Falls during the organization of the regiment. Although severely wounded, Clendon did not die at Manassas. He recovered and rejoined the regiment as Major before being discharged for disability in March of 1863. *NYAGR*, p. 333. Joseph Atherly, Surgeon of the 22nd New York Infantry, was a close friend of Phelps. He was 39 years old and died of disease while Phelps was on leave, on August 12, 1862. *NYAGR*, p. 313.

10. Brigadier General John Hatch was in command of brigade to which the 22nd New York was assigned. He graduated from West Point in 1845 and had commanded cavalry units until assigned to this brigade. Warner, *Generals in Blue,* p. 216-7.

11. James Wythe, age 30, enlisted as a private at Sandy Hill, NY and served in Company H. He was killed on August 29, 1862. Evidently, he and Phelps were well acquainted. *NYAGR*, p. 430.

12. Duncan Cameron mustered in as First Lieutenant of Company G in June 1861. He was promoted to captain on March 1, 1862. He survived his arm wound and returned to Albany. *NYAGR*, P. 329. Charles T. Bellamy, age 21 when he joined Company E of the 22nd in May 1861 was quickly promoted to commissary sergeant and then second lieutenant on March 26, 1862. He was from Glens Falls and Phelps refers to him as "Charlie," suggesting familiarity. *NYAGR*, p. 317. Henry O. Cronkhite, age 22, enlisted in July 1861. He also was from Glens Falls. He served as a private in Company E, and again Phelps refers to him as though he knows him well. *NYAGR*, p. 338. Austin W. Holden served as Captain of Company F from May 1861 until August 18, 1862 when he mustered out. Six days later he mustered-in as Assistant Surgeon and served as such until the regiment mustered out in June 1863. He was 42 years old when the war began. *NYAGR*, p. 363. Phelps' writing is very unclear here, but he probably refers to another Glens Falls friend, Lt. Charles Cushing. Enlisting at age 21 in 1861, Cushing rose from private in Company E to Second Lieutenant by January 8, 1862. He survived the holocaust of Second Manassas only to be killed the next month at Antietam. *NYAGR*, p. 339. Bates is the regimental Chaplain. He may have elected to stay with the wounded of his regiment, or to help inter the dead. Either practice was typical of chaplains during the war. He was from Troy, NY and 53 when he enlisted in 1861. Dr. Cromwell's son is probably Edward Cromwell. He enlisted at Albany in October of 1861 at age 21. He was mortally wounded on August 29, 1862 and died on August 31. Phisterer, *New York in the War*, pp. 1982-1993.

13. Capt. Thomas J. Strong enrolled at Sandy Hill, NY in May of 1861 as Captain of Company H, 22nd New York. In 1863 he became Major and then Lt. Colonel of the 22nd, and subsequently served as Lt. Col. in the 16th New York Heavy Artillery. Phisterer, *New York in the War*, p. 1992; James W. Schenck Jr., the Regimental Quartermaster, was also Phelps' brother-in-law. He was 25 years old in September of 1861 when he enlisted at Arlington VA. *NYAGR*, p. 403. The losses of the brigade at Second Manassas were 726 officers and men, killed wounded or missing. Phisterer, *New York in the War*, p. 167. *OR* 12, pt. 2, p. 254 lists 772 total casualties. Either way, Phelps' estimate is close. Both sources agree that the losses in the 22nd were 180 total casualties.

14. Letter to E[liza], September 13, 1862, Phelps Papers, USAMHI.

15 *OR* 19, pt. 1, p. 231. Gen. King was removed from command permanently on this day, which put Hatch in command of the division. Phelps was the senior colonel present in Hatch's brigade, and thus assumed command. David S. Sparks, ed., *Inside Lincoln's Army*, (New York, 1964), p.143.

16. *OR* 19, pt. 1, pp. 220-3, & p. 232. Strengths of the brigade and the 22nd are hard to determine. Phelps' comment in the Sept. 4 letter says he has about 240 men and all the other regiments are about the same. That would put the brigade, with the four New York regiments, somewhere between 900-1,000 men, a figure hard to reconcile with the tablets at Antietam National Battlefield, which state the brigade fought on Sept. 17 with 450 men. Phelps also claims that the 30th New York had only 50 men on the 17th. The addition of the 2nd USSS must have been done to bolster the numbers, perhaps because there was severe straggling on the march from Washington. The number 550 was determined by adding the nearly 100 casualties from the battle of South Mountain to the 450 stated on the War Department tablets at Antietam. *OR* 19, pt. 1, p. 184, and Antietam National Battlefield tablets on Cornfield Avenue, Sharpsburg, MD.17. Brigadier General Abner Doubleday commanded a brigade in the same division with Phelps. His brigade was sent to reinforce Phelps, although by that time Doubleday had assumed command of the division from the wounded Gen. Hatch. Later in the evening Phelps' brigade was reinforced by a brigade from Brig. Gen. James B. Ricketts' division of I Corps. *OR* 19, pt. 1, pp. 221 & 258.

18. The figures in the *Official Records* and Phisterer show 10 enlisted men killed, one officer and 19 enlisted men wounded. Since Phelps wrote the *OR* report it is hard to account for this discrepancy. *OR* 19, pt. 1, P. 184, *Phisterer*, Vol. I, p. 173.

Colonel John Bowie Strange commanded the 19th Virginia Infantry. He was in the first class to be graduated from the Virginia Military Institute, founded the Albemarle Military Institute and was president of Norfolk Academy. He was killed at South Mountain on September 14, 1862. Robert Krick, *Lee's Colonels*, (Dayton, 1992), p. 362.

19. Daniel Burgy, 28 years old, was from Ft. Edward when he enlisted as Second Lieutenant in Company I of the 22nd NY. Effective September 3, 1862, he was transferred and promoted captain of Company E. Lt. Cushing also was in Company E, the "Glens Falls" company, and Phelps refers to it frequently. Lt. James W. McCoy probably was the younger brother of Robert McCoy, who was killed at Second Manassas. Both are from Ft. Edward. Major John McKee Jr., who began his enlistment at age 35 as Captain of Company B, was promoted to major in September 1861 and would attain the rank of lt. col. shortly after Antietam. Phisterer, *New York in the War,* pp. 1989-91; *NYAGR*, pp. 326, 339, 381, 383. Major General Jesse Reno commanded the Ninth Army Corps. He was killed at South Mountain while leading his men at Fox's Gap. *OR* 19, pt. 1, p. 423.

20. Charles Cushing was 21 years old when he enlisted as a private in May 1861. He was from Glens Falls and had worked his way up through the ranks to lieutenant in February 1862. (Emphasis in original.) *NYAGR*, p. 339.

21. C.A. Stevens, *Berdan's United States Sharpshooters in the Army of the Potomac 1861-1865,* (Dayton, 1984) pp. 202-3; Lt. Humphreys, 2nd USSS Letters, Antietam

Collection, Dartmouth College; Stephen W. Sears, *Landscape Turned Red,* (New York, 1983), pp. 194-5. These three sources disagree as to the particular regiment's colors which were captured. Stevens does not elaborate on it, Sears says it was the 1st Louisiana Infantry from Starke's brigade, Humphreys says it was a "lone star flag from a Georgia regiment under Lawton." Doubleday's report, *OR* 19, pt. 1, p. 224, says the 2nd USSS captured two flags, but does not specify whose flags. Certainly Phelps was justifiably proud of the accomplishment. The 2nd USSS casualties are listed as 66 total casualties in *OR*, 19, pt. 1, p. 189. Again, Phelps' estimate is very accurate. On page 234 of the same source Phelps says the losses of the brigade were 186, which he calls 43% of the brigade, while the losses of South Mountain are described as 25 percent. These figures contrast with the chart of losses on page 189, which list 154 total casualties for September 17.

22. Brigadier General Marsena Patrick was a West Point graduate and long-time professional soldier who commanded another brigade in the division. He soon would become Provost Marshal of the Army of the Potomac. Boatner, *Civil War Dictionary*, pp. 622-3.

23. The person who probably accused Phelps of cowardice was Zabeina Ellis. He was 44 years old when he enlisted as a private in the 22nd New York, on September 30, 1862, less than two weeks after the battle of Antietam. Whether this enlistment was an atonement for his criticism, or some other motive, cannot be determined. In later letters Phelps wrote Eliza that he is determined to be fair to Ellis, despite the false rumors Ellis helped spread. *NYAGR*, p. 345; Phelps Papers, USAMHI.

24 *OR* 19, pt. 1, p. 226.

25. Phelps Papers, USAMHI. A search of the Court Martial Records in the National Archives, Washington DC, show no records of Searing ever being tried on these charges, or any other.

26. Phelps Papers, USMHI.

27. "Portrait of Late Colonel Presented." Phelps scrapbook, Phelps Papers, USAMHI.

"These brave men were mowed down like the corn surrounding them."

CLASH IN THE CORNFIELD

The 1st Texas Volunteer Infantry in the Maryland Campaign

George E. Otott

Dawn had barely driven away the nighttime shadows when the shells crashed through the treetops, hurling branches and splinters among the tired and hungry soldiers below. Within minutes, staff officers dashed through the camp with orders to fall into line. The 226 officers and men of the 1st Texas Volunteer Infantry angrily scrambled from campfires to rifle stacks, strapped on cartridge boxes and cursed their luck. The whizzing projectiles and broken tree limbs, more bothersome than lethal, had interrupted their first regular meal in nearly three days.

Less than two hours after falling into line, the Battle of Sharpsburg ended for the 1st Texas. During that time, Brig. Gen. John Bell Hood's Division, which included the 1st Texas, turned back the first Federal breakthrough of Gen. Robert E. Lee's lines. But the fighting shattered Hood's division and decimated the 1st Texas. Though the war lasted another two and a half years, no other regiment, North or South, lost as large a percentage of its manpower in a single battle.

Most of the men in the 1st Texas answered the Confederacy's first call for troops in April 1861. They were from east Texas counties and formed companies under the command of local leaders. Eight of the companies traveled independently to New Orleans where they mustered into Confederate service and sought transfer to the seat of war in Virginia. They arrived in Richmond by July 1861 and were organized as the 1st Texas Infantry Battalion under the command of former U. S. Senator and political bully, Col. Louis T. Wigfall of Texas. They were the first troops from the Lone Star State to reach a major theater of operations.[1] As the summer wore on, other Texas companies arrived and the battalion was upgraded to the 1st Texas Regiment.[2]

In November 1861, the army brigaded the 1st Texas with the 4th and 5th Texas regiments, the only other Lone Star units to serve in the Virginia theater. Cemented by blood and hard experience, it was an association that lasted until the war's end. Also assigned to the brigade at that time was the rugged and dependable 18th Georgia. Wigfall was promoted to general and given command of the new brigade, which soon became known as the Texas Brigade. Lt. Col. Alexis T. Rainey was promoted to colonel to command the 1st Texas.

During the war's first winter, the Texas Brigade guarded batteries on the Potomac River near Washington. In March 1862, while the Confederate army was *en route* from Northern Virginia to the Peninsula to counter the Union offensive there, a 31-year-old former cavalry lieutenant, Brig. Gen. John Bell Hood, was assigned to command the Texas Brigade after Gen. Wigfall was elected to the Confederate Congress. Hood became the Texans' most famous commander and his name has been linked with the Texas Brigade ever since. On May 7, 1862, the Texas Brigade received its baptism of fire on the Peninsula in a small battle at Eltham's Landing. The 1st Texas suffered most of the brigade's casualties and proved to be an aggressive fighting unit. Both Hood and the Texas Brigade attracted attention and showed promise of even better fighting ahead. Three weeks later, eight understrength, battle-hardened South Carolina companies of Hampton's Legion joined the brigade.

During the brutal summer of 1862, when Lee's army was forged in combat from Richmond to the Potomac, the Texas Brigade was conspicuous. At the Battle of Gaines' Mill on June 27, the 4th Texas spearheaded an assault by Hood's Brigade that shattered a strong Federal position after a long day of bloody failures by other Confederate units. This decisive action of the Seven Days battles turned back Maj. Gen. George B. McClellan's offensive up the Peninsula and gave Lee his first victory. On August 30, at the battle of Second Manassas, the 5th Texas blazed to the forefront of Lt. Gen. James Longstreet's counterattack. Longstreet's attack smashed the Union army of Maj. Gen. John Pope, and the subsequent retreat of the Federal army virtually cleared northern Virginia of enemy soldiers. But while the 4th and 5th Texas won laurels at Gaines' Mill and Second Manassas, the 1st Texas, although present, missed most of the heavy fighting. They soon had another chance. After failing to catch and crush the beaten Federals after Second Manassas, Lee planned to continue on Northern soil his successful combination of bold movement and aggressive fighting, hoping to further damage the enemy army. By crossing the Potomac River Lee also hoped to liberate Marylanders sympathetic to the South and to gain additional time for the Confederacy to gather subsistence and forage from northern Virginia.

The Texas Brigade's success during the Seven Days gained Hood command of a division in a newly formed infantry corps under Longstreet.[3] Small by Army of Northern Virginia standards, Hood's Division consisted of the Texas Brigade and a brigade of Mississippi, Alabama and North Carolina regiments under a 26-year-old teacher and Citadel graduate, Brig. Gen. Evander McIver Law. Upon Hood's promotion, command of the Texas Brigade passed to its senior officer, 38-year old Colonel William T. Wofford of the 18th Georgia. Before the war, Wofford had been a lawyer, legislator and newspaper editor, and had served in the Mexican War.[4]

Despite Hood's success at Second Manassas, he was placed under arrest by Longstreet after the battle for refusing to obey an order from Maj. Gen. Nathan "Shanks" Evans to relinquish a few captured ambulances. Longstreet ordered Hood to Culpeper to stand trial. Lee's invasion plans preempted military protocol, however, and Hood marched north with his division, but remained in the rear under arrest.

"I never saw such a pretty country. . ."

On September 4, 1862, Lee's army began fording the Potomac River near Leesburg, Virginia. The Texans crossed on September 6. Barely waist deep and a quarter of a mile wide, the river for several hundred yards was filled with grimy, tattered Southerners who laughed and sang to the accompaniment of regimental bands. "In we bulged," remembered Pvt. John Stevens of the 5th Texas, "our bands playing, and the boys yellin', as jolly as any who had gone before or any who came after us."[5] The Texans were in high spirits and confident of victory.

When the 1st Texas marched onto Maryland soil, it was led by 30-year-old Lt. Col. Philip A. Work. A Kentuckian by birth, Work was raised in Texas and attended that state's Secession Convention in 1861.[6] After Texas seceded, he recruited the Woodville Rifles in Tyler County and was elected captain. The Woodville Rifles became one of the original 1st Texas companies and was designated Company F. Work led his company until May, 1862 when he was promoted to the rank of lieutenant colonel upon Rainey's elevation to colonel. On June 27, Work assumed command of the regiment when Rainey was wounded in the Battle of Gaines' Mill.[7]

Lieutenant Colonel Philip A. Work,
commander of the 1st Texas during the Maryland Campaign

Confederate Research Center, Hillsboro, Texas

Second in command of the 1st Texas was 30-year old Maj. Matt Dale. Born in Tennessee and a resident of Palestine, Texas, Dale represented his district prior to hostilities for one term in the Texas Legislature.[8] At the outbreak of war, Dale enlisted in the Reagan Guards of Anderson County and was elected to the position of second lieutenant. Dale served as a company officer until he was promoted to major in May, 1862.[9]

One 1st Texan who was happy to be in Maryland was 22-year old Pvt. Samuel T. Blessing of Company L. A Marylander by birth, Blessing found himself within a dozen miles of his mother's home when the regiment crossed the Potomac. Once on his native soil, he could not resist the urge to take "French leave" to surprise his home folks. The surprise was on Blessing, however, when his mother's Unionist neighbors informed the authorities that a Rebel was in the area. Blessing managed to escape from a squad of Federals sent to capture him and caught up with the regiment a few days later.[10]

Although they were ragged and many were barefoot, the 1st Texans enjoyed the fair September weather and the bountiful Maryland countryside as Lee moved his army northward to Frederick.[11] The marches were leisurely and the column rested for two days along the banks of the Monocacy River. Private Watters Berryman of Company I was impressed with Maryland, a state virtually untouched by war. "I never saw such pretty country or an old one in my life," he wrote, ". . .splendid crops have been raised in this part of Maryland and everything is good to eat."[12] Along the way many of the local citizens gathered to watch the rebel army that had so recently thrashed the Union host under General Pope. Corporal O. T. Hanks of Company K thought some of the locals appeared awe-struck as the Texans marched by.[13]

The 1st Texas passed through Frederick on September 10, 1862. While marching through the city, Corp. Hanks heard a woman shout: "Here comes the Bonnie Blue Flag now, come and see it."[14] The "Bonnie Blue" was actually the state flag of Texas, known as the Lone Star flag. One of two regimental battle flags carried by the 1st Texas, the Lone Star flag had two horizontal bars, white over red, to the right of a blue vertical bar with a large white star. The colorful banner had been sewn by Mrs. Louis T. Wigfall and was presented to the 1st Texas in 1861 by Lula Wigfall, daughter of the general, at a ceremony outside of Richmond.[15] By September 1862, the battle honors "Eltham's Landing," "Seven Pines," "Gaines Farm," and "Malvern Hill" had been painted on the flag.

The men of the 1st Texas were proud of their Lone Star flag. It was carried in a silk oilcloth case and never unfurled except for reviews, dress parades and battle. The other Texans in the brigade were also proud of the flag. One member of the 4th Texas later recalled, "[w]hen we saw it waving in the Virginia breeze, it was a sweet reminder of home, a thousand miles away."[16] Along with the Lone Star banner, the 1st Texas also carried a Confederate battle flag of the Army of Northern Virginia pattern: a square red flag with a blue St. Andrew's cross containing 13 white stars.

The 1st Texas flags were much more than just army insignia functioning as guiding and rallying points for the regiment in battle. The Confederate battle flag symbolized the Texans' participation in a new nation rebelling against an unjust Union. The Lone Star flag represented the communities and the state from which the 1st Texas companies sprang. It symbolized the emotional ties of the Texans to their families, friends and neighbors hundreds of miles away. In addition, both battle flags symbolized the soldiers' bonds to each other and to the regiment, which was a military community also comprised in large measure of family members, friends and neighbors. For all of these reasons, the flags had to be vigorously defended, as if defense of the flags symbolized defense of home, family and nation.[17]

At Frederick, General Lee boldly divided his army. He ordered "Stonewall" Jackson with three divisions to cooperate with three of Longstreet's divisions in an attempt to capture the Federal garrison at Harpers Ferry, Virginia, located west of the Blue Ridge Mountains. When Lee's army crossed the Potomac east of the mountains Lee had assumed the Federal garrison at Harpers Ferry would retreat into Maryland, thus opening a line of communication for Lee's army through the Shenandoah Valley. When the Federals did not abandon Harpers Ferry, Lee decided to capture its 12,000-man garrison.

While the bulk of his army converged on Harpers Ferry in three separate columns, Lee ordered his remaining force, consisting of Maj. Gen. Daniel H. Hill's Division of Jackson's Corps and Hood's and Maj. Gen. David R. Jones' Division of Longstreet's Corps, to push on to Boonsboro by way of Turner's Gap in South Mountain. Maj. Gen. J.E.B. Stuart's cavalry would remain east of South Mountain to keep an eye on the Union army, commanded by General McClellan and cautiously approaching Frederick from the south and east.. At Boonsboro, Lee would await the return of the Harpers Ferry columns before proceeding with his original plans. Lee issued detailed written orders to his generals explaining how the army would be divided and the role of the principal generals in the campaign.

From Frederick, the Texans marched northwest on the macadamized Washington Turnpike and passed through Turner's Gap on September 12. Based on an erroneous report of a Federal force marching on Hagerstown, Lee once again divided his army and ordered Hood's and Jones' divisions to that place, leaving Hill's Division at Boonsboro to guard Turner's Gap. The Texans marched into Hagerstown on the 13th. They were only ten miles below the Pennsylvania line and anticipated another rest while waiting for Jackson's force to capture Harpers Ferry.

In the meantime, McClellan advanced to Frederick somewhat quicker than Lee expected and the leading Federal units clashed with Stuart's cavalry east of South Mountain on September 13. Bad luck intervened that same day when McClellan came into possession of a lost copy of Lee's plans for dividing the Southern army. Lee was surprised and worried by McClellan's proximity to South Mountain. If McClellan crossed the mountain before the Federal garrison at Harpers Ferry surrendered, the large Union army would be in a position to attack the rear of the Confederate column operating on Maryland Heights, across the Potomac River from Harpers Ferry. To prevent this, on the night of the 13th Lee ordered Hood and Jones to start their divisions back to Turner's Gap the next morning. It was good that he did. As a result of finding Lee's orders, McClellan directed his army to depart Frederick early on the 14th and to force a crossing of South Mountain at Turner's Gap.

For the 1st Texas, the easy marches were over. It was a grueling 14 miles to South Mountain over a dusty road and under a hot sun. For nine hours they pressed on. By the time the brigade neared the foot of South Mountain, the Confederates on the summit were in trouble. D. H. Hill had earlier moved his division from Boonsboro to Turner's Gap and was up there alone, facing the bulk of McClellan's army. Enemy shells overshot the ridge and exploded on the western slope.[18] On the road ahead of the Texans, troops of Jones' Division snaked up the mountain to the relief of Hill's beleaguered men.

As the Texans began to ascend the mountain they passed Gen. Lee. Annoyed because of Hood's arrest, they repeatedly yelled: "Give us Hood!" Lee raised his hat and replied, "You shall have him, gentlemen!" The Texans cheered and Hood was restored to command. When Hood galloped to the front of the division, "his head uncovered and his face proud and joyful," the cheers of the Texans deepened into a roar.[19]

Hood hurried his two brigades to the summit of the mountain, where they formed a line of battle along the crest north of the Washington Turnpike. Large numbers of Federals were massed on the eastern face of the mountain. Hood was soon ordered to move to the south where some of Hill's and Jones' Confederates were in danger of being pushed off the ridge. Hood led his brigades along a small path through woods choked with underbrush. Shouts and cheers of the Federals were heard to their left where the enemy was driving Brig. Gen. Thomas F. Drayton's Brigade of Jones' Division over the summit and toward Hood's column.

As daylight faded, Hood finally halted his men, formed them into line facing the crest, and ordered bayonets fixed. Just up the slope the Federals, flushed with success, bore down on them through the trees. Hood yelled "Charge!" and the Texans and Law's brigade stepped off with a rebel yell. The enemy recoiled before the onrushing Confederates and retreated over the mountain, but nightfall put an end to the fighting before the Texans could close with them.[20] The Texans' brief role in the battle was strenuous but mostly painless: one 1st Texan was wounded and only a handful of others in the Texas Brigade were wounded or missing.[21]

During the night, Lee learned that the left wing of McClellan's army had pushed Stuart's cavalry out of Crampton's Gap, six miles south of Turner's Gap. He also learned that Jackson expected Harpers Ferry to surrender the next day. Concluding that holding the South Mountain passes was impractical against McClellan's large army, Lee ordered Longstreet to withdraw the three Confederate divisions from the mountain and take the Boonsboro Turnpike to Sharpsburg, eight miles to the southwest. A small town of 1,300 people, Sharpsburg was located at the intersection of several important roads. The Boonsboro Turnpike, which the Confederates from South Mountain and the pursuing Federal army would take, entered Sharpsburg from the east. The Harpers Ferry Road, which Jackson would take to join Lee, entered from the south. Leading away from the town to the southwest was a road to Boteler's Ford, three miles away and the only practical Potomac crossing in the region.[22] Finally, the Hagerstown Turnpike headed north to Hagerstown and then into Pennsylvania. The local road net would allow Lee to concentrate his scattered divisions at Sharpsburg and to confront McClellan's army, rather than give up Maryland without a fight. If necessary, Lee could use Boteler's Ford as an escape route.

The Texas Brigade started toward Sharpsburg early on the 15th and, being the rearguard, deployed in line of battle several times to keep the Federals from pursuing too closely.[23] Fortunately for Lee, McClellan was true to form and did not aggressively pursue.

"We were nearly barefooted and worn out with marching."

The Texans crossed Antietam Creek over the Middle Bridge at about noon on the 15th. They turned into the fields south of the Boonsboro Road and formed a line of battle between the creek and the town.[24] There they joined D. R. Jones' Division along the low hills facing the creek. D. H. Hill's Division was deployed in line north of the road. Across the Antietam, enemy columns filled the fields and roads, creating the illusion of an almost endless field of blue.[25] Later in the afternoon, long columns of Federals were seen moving northward toward the Upper Bridge and Lee's left flank, where McClellan, at his own slow pace, would ultimately start the battle.

While Lee and McClellan deployed their forces around Sharpsburg during the forenoon of September 15, the Federal garrison at Harpers Ferry surrendered to Jackson. Starting that night, and into the 16th, Jackson sent five of the six divisions with him toward Sharpsburg, where Lee hoped they would arrive before McClellan attacked. Maj. Gen. A. P. Hill's Division would remain in Harpers Ferry for as long as it would take to receive the surrender of Union troops and guns.

Until Jackson's forces arrived, Lee had to contend with the Federal army with only the three divisions under Longstreet and D. H. Hill. Lee responded to McClellan's massing of troops near the Upper Bridge on the afternoon of the 15th by ordering Longstreet to redeploy Hood's Division to the left of D. H. Hill's line north of the Boonsboro Road. Leaving his artillery behind, Hood led his infantry on the Boonsboro Road to Sharpsburg, where they turned north onto the Hagerstown Turnpike. As the Texans trudged along, vigilant Federal gunners across Antietam Creek spotted them and opened fire with long-range batteries, wounding several of the men.[26] About a mile out of town, Hood halted his division near a small white church, known locally as the Dunker Church. Law's Brigade stopped in the trees along the turnpike just north of the church and the Texas Brigade halted along the turnpike south of the church.[27] The men rested on their arms in adjacent pastures and woods.

The weary Texans rested near the Dunker Church for the remainder of the 15th of September. Captain George Todd of Company A recalled that "we were nearly barefooted and worn out with marching and skirmishing when we went into camp. . . ."[28] Todd was a 23-year old native Virginian whose family moved to Texas when he was a small boy. He went back to Virginia to attend college and at the outbreak of war was a lawyer in Jefferson, Texas. Though Todd's men were relieved for the time from marching and fighting, they were hungry. Because of McClellan's sudden advance against South Mountain, Hood's Division had been separated from the army commissary wagons since early on the 14th. The Texans were without a regular issue of rations since leaving Hagerstown, subsisting mostly on corn and green apples.[29] They foraged what they could from the fields and houses within easy reach of their camp near the Dunker Church. Many of them picked roasting ears from a large cornfield several hundred yards to the north. The stalks were head high and ready for harvest.

If any of the Texans resting near the Dunker Church had bothered to take note of their surroundings, they would have noticed a gently rolling farmland framed on three sides by woods. The open farmland was dominated by high ground in a pasture across the turnpike from the Dunker Church. Starting behind the church, a woodlot, known after the battle as the West Woods, stretched northward along the turnpike some 300 yards before cutting back to make room for two roadside clover fields. West of the clover fields, the woods continued to the north for another 600 yards and ended opposite the David R. Miller farm that straddled the turnpike. The high ground in the pasture across from the Dunker Church dipped northward across the Smoketown Road into a topographic low, a broad swale that narrowed into a ravine in the West Woods. From the swale, the ground then rose again to form a northeast-trending plateau that crossed the turnpike about 400 yards north of the Dunker Church. The plateau dominated the northwest corner of the pasture and continued into a large cornfield on the David Miller farm some 750 yards from the church. It was the same field from which some of the Texans gathered their most recent meal, and would be known to history as "the Cornfield." Beyond the Cornfield and nearly a mile from the church was a patch of trees later known as the North Woods. The pastures and the Cornfield were bounded on the east by another patch of timber, later known as the East Woods, that ran parallel to the turnpike and some 500 yards from it. The Hagerstown Turnpike and the Smoketown Road were bounded on both sides by heavy post and plank fences.

The 1st Texas remained near the Dunker Church the night of the 15th and for most of the 16th, a crucial day for Lee. McClellan did not attack, deciding instead to precisely place his infantry for a general assault at dawn on the 17th starting against the Confederate left flank. This decision resulted in a squandered opportunity for McClellan by allowing Lee an entire day to bring up most of Jackson's force from Harpers Ferry. Enough Federals were on the field during the 16th to have allowed a more aggressive commander to severely punish Lee's force at Sharpsburg. But while McClellan sat and planned, Lee reinforced and regrouped.

The Texans most likely were unaware of the larger events as the 16th passed. They were perhaps more concerned that their rations had still not arrived. Enemy batteries east of Antietam Creek lobbed shells at them sporadically throughout the day, but there were no casualties.

Late in the afternoon, two of Jackson's divisions arrived on the field from Harpers Ferry. The first, Brig. Gen. John R. Jones' Division, was ordered to extend the Confederate lines westward from Hood's left. Jones formed his division in two north-facing lines: Jones' own brigade and Col. Andrew J. Grigsby's Stonewall Brigade in the clover field west of the turnpike and Brigadier Generals William E. Starke's and William B. Taliaferro's brigades in the West Woods behind the first line.[30] Jones sent three batteries from his division artillery to Nicodemus Hill, northwest of the West Woods and about 500 yards from the turnpike, where they joined a battery from Jeb Stuart's Horse Artillery. Just before dark, Ewell's Division, commanded by Brig. Gen. Alexander R. Lawton, marched up the turnpike. Two of Lawton's four brigades, under Brig. Gen. Jubal Early and Brig. Gen. Harry T. Hays, moved into positions supporting the left flank of Jones' Division. The brigades commanded by Col. Marcellus Douglass and Col. James A. Walker halted in the woods behind the Dunker Church.[31] Four batteries of Col. Stephen D. Lee's artillery battalion of Longstreet's Corps had arrived the previous night and spent most of the day in a sheltered position behind the ridge just east of the church.[32]

While Jackson's men marched from Harpers Ferry on the 16th, the Federals moved closer to the Confederate left flank in preparation for the attack to be launched at dawn the next day. In mid-afternoon, Maj. Gen. Joseph Hooker's I Corps crossed the Antietam over the Upper Bridge and at a nearby ford. Massed in heavy columns and with Maj. Gen. George Meade's division of Pennsylvania Reserves in the lead, the Federals advanced westward in a north-bending arc, slowly heading for the high ground near the Hagerstown Turnpike. D. H. Hill saw the blue column in his front and ordered one of his batteries to fire at the inviting target.[33] Undeterred, the Federal column pressed on, snaking around the low hills and woods to minimize their exposure to Hill's guns, before turning south onto the Smoketown Road that led toward the East Woods.[34] When Union cavalrymen screening Meade's advance approached Samuel Poffenberger's farm lane, Confederate skirmishers from Law's Brigade opened fire on them. Immediately, the Bucktails of the 13th Pennsylvania Reserves, also known as the Pennsylvania Bucktails, from Brig. Gen. Truman Seymour's brigade rushed forward into skirmish positions and started to bang away at Law's men.[35]

Hood decided to redeploy his division to confront the Federals, who were approaching from the northeast. From its original position along the turnpike, Law's Brigade advanced in line of battle across the pasture to the East Woods.[36] The Texas Brigade, deployed along the turnpike south of the church, faced by the left flank and marched behind Law and into the pasture beyond the Smoketown

Road. There Wofford reformed his brigade in the usual order from left to right: Hampton's Legion, commanded by Col. Martin W. Gary; 18th Georgia, commanded by Lt. Col. Solon Z. Ruff; the 1st Texas, Lt. Col. Work commanding; 4th Texas, commanded by Lt. Col. Benjamin F. Carter; and 5th Texas, temporarily commanded by Capt. Ike Turner. A hundred skirmishers from the 4th Texas filtered into the East Woods to support Law's skirmishers contesting the enemy's advance in the fields beyond.[37] Hood requested artillery support from Colonel Lee, who sent over two guns from Capt. Andrew Burnett Rhett's Battery posted near the Dunker Church. Rhett galloped up the turnpike to the top of the plateau, turned in front of the Cornfield, and wheeled into position near the left of the Texas Brigade.[38]

The Texans stood in the pasture and waited anxiously as the Federal column drew near. Beyond the East Woods, Seymour's Pennsylvania regiments maneuvered from column into line and moved up to support the skirmishing Bucktails, who were pushing Law's pickets into the East Woods. It was about dusk.[39] The popping of musketry intensified as Law's men, under cover of the trees and reinforced by the contingent from the 4th Texas, disputed the Federals' advance. Rhett's guns opened fire on the them, hurling canister shells across the front of the Texas Brigade. To counter Rhett's salvos, Gen. Seymour deployed Capt. James H. Cooper's Battery B, Pennsylvania Light Artillery on high ground just east of the North Woods.[40]

While Seymour's brigade pressed Law's skirmishers, Gen. Meade took Lt. Col. Robert Anderson's and Col. Albert Magilton's Pennsylvania brigades, marching in column behind Seymour's brigade, and led them westward across the fields toward the North Woods. The Texans saw them in the distance, their "lines of battle in echelon with banners waving, drums beating, and bugles blowing . . . . more like they were on grand review than going into battle."[41] Confederate gunners on Nicodemus Hill also spotted them and opened a noisy fire on the Pennsylvanians.[42] Meade led his two brigades into the North Woods from where he could see Rhett's Battery firing across the pasture into the East Woods. The Rebel gunners were framed by the infantry of Jones' Division and the Texas Brigade. As Anderson and Magilton formed their battle lines in the North Woods and threw out skirmishers, Meade ordered up Capt. Dunbar C. Ransom's Battery C, Pennsylvania Light Artillery. It was growing dark when Ransom wheeled his pieces into position in front of the North Woods and opened fire on Rhett's guns, with some of the shells landing close to the 1st Texas. The shelling was too hot for Rhett, who withdrew his section to its original position near the Dunker Church, where he resumed firing from a safer distance.[43] Just before Rhett pulled out, three guns from Capt. William T. Poague's Rockbridge Artillery of Jones's Division galloped up the turnpike to the top of the plateau, wheeled into position on the left of the road and fired over the Cornfield at Ransom's battery and the Pennsylvania Reserves in the North Woods. Ransom and Poague pounded away at each other until dark.[44]

While the artillery duels heated up, Law's skirmishers streamed out of the East Woods. The aggressive Hood ordered his division forward. The Texas Brigade advanced to the edge of the Cornfield, except for the 5th Texas, which fronted the East Woods.[45] The 1st Texas and the other regiments along the edge of the Cornfield faced away from the axis of Seymour's advance and did not engage the Federal infantry. They were masked from the fire of Cooper's and Ransom's artillery by the Cornfield and the topography. On the right of the brigade, the 5th Texas pushed into the East Woods, where they relieved the 4th Texas skirmishers who were falling back to their own regiment with the Federal skirmish line on their heels. As soon as the 4th Texans were out of the way, the 5th opened a spirited fire that turned back the Federals in their front.[46] On the right of the 5th Texas, Law's regiments moved into the East Woods and in a sharp fight drove the Bucktails through the woods and into their reserves beyond.[47] At least one battery of S. D. Lee's artillery battalion near the Dunker Church joined the fray.[48] But before the fighting developed into a battle involving Seymour's entire brigade, darkness fell and the skirmish quieted to sporadic picket clashes and long-range artillery fire. All the while, more Federals moved to the front. Hooker's other two divisions, commanded by Brig. Gen. James B. Ricketts and Brig. Gen. Abner Doubleday, crowded into the fields beyond the North and East Woods. Farther to the northeast, the two divisions of Maj. Gen. Joseph K. Mansfield's XII Corps, which had crossed the Antietam during the late afternoon, went into camps near the Martin Line farm.

In the darkness, the Texans watched the Federal artillery shells arch over their lines, looking like "balls of fire in the heavens."[49] Colonel Work, who could see the "lighted fuses [of the shells] as plainly as a glowworm's light," apparently sent a picket line into the Cornfield to warn of any renewed enemy advances.[50] The Federals had their own pickets out and several violent encounters occurred as jittery soldiers rustled among the cornstalks in the dark. A few of the 1st Texans were either careless or confused and were captured by the Federal pickets, who turned them over to the 12th Massachusetts Infantry of Gen. Rickett's division. The prisoners, including Capt. Howard Ballenger of Company M, remained under guard by the Bay State men throughout the night. Captain Ballenger seized the opportunity to impress his captors with tall Texas tales of the size of the

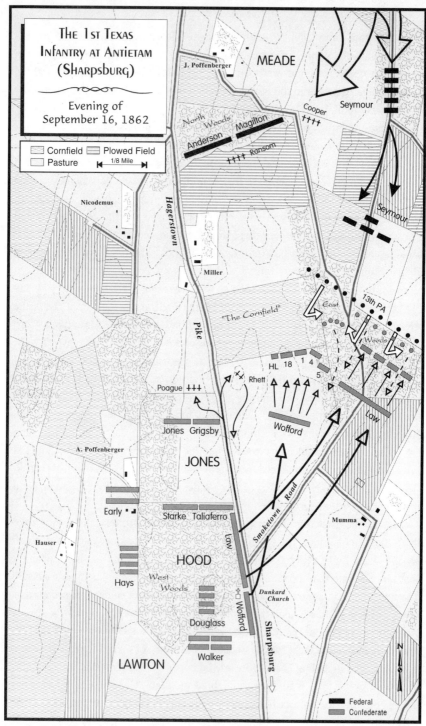

The 1st Texas
Infantry at Antietam
(Sharpsburg)

Evening of
September 16, 1862

Cornfield   Plowed Field
Pasture   1/8 Mile

Mark A. Moore

Confederate forces in the vicinity, and was the first to tell them that Harpers Ferry had fallen to Jackson.[51]

Sometime during the afternoon or evening, Hood's wagons finally arrived with rations. After the fighting died down, Hood sought out Gen. Lee and asked if his division could be replaced by other troops so that his men could cook and eat. Lee sent Hood to see Jackson, who commanded the only reserves in the area. Jackson agreed to relieve Hood with two brigades from Lawton's Division if Hood promised to come to their support the moment he was called. Hood agreed. Sometime between ten and eleven o'clock Wofford and Law quietly pulled their brigades out of line while Douglass' and Walker's brigades moved out of the West Woods and took their places.[52]

Hood withdrew his division into the West Woods behind the Dunker Church where the hungry Texans expected to find rations waiting for them. They were no doubt disappointed to learn that their meal was not yet ready to be issued. Some of the men couldn't wait and cooked more roasting ears gathered from the Cornfield they had just vacated.[53] The rest of the men rolled up in their blankets to get as much sleep as empty stomachs would allow. During the night, under dark clouds and a light rain, desultory skirmish firing between the pickets periodically flared into sharp exchanges.[54] For the 1st Texas, there was no skirmish duty to relieve the stress of impending combat, and those unable to sleep had to quietly endure the waiting.

The skirmish in the East Woods did little more than establish where the opposing battle lines would lie when fighting renewed in the morning. And there must have been few soldiers on the field who doubted that it would be renewed with vigor. By midnight of the 16th, six of Lee's nine divisions were on the field. Of the Army of Northern Virginia's three remaining divisions, two left Harpers Ferry at midnight and Maj. Gen. A. P. Hill's Division was expected to leave there in the morning. Lee's plan was to hold Sharpsburg against McClellan's expected attack and to wait for an opportunity to counterattack.

McClellan, too, had made his preparations and intended to attack the Confederate left in the morning. Hooker's I Corps, consisting of the three divisions massed in and around the North and East Woods, was to open the attack early on the 17th. Mansfield's XII Corps, massed near the Martin Line farm, was to support Hooker. McClellan planned for his other army corps to attack the Confederate center and right as the battle progressed.

"They were knocked out of the ranks by dozens."

Just before dawn on September 17, 1862 the long-awaited rations, mostly flour, were distributed to the Texans. The hungry men crowded around campfires to prepare their meal. Most of them moistened the flour into dough which they wrapped around ramrods and cooked over the flames.[55] They had to hurry. As the darkness lifted and it became light enough to see, pickets along the front started firing and the armies began to stir.

Hooker ordered Doubleday, whose division had camped on the Joseph Poffenberger farm, to push three brigades down the Hagerstown Turnpike, past Anderson's and Magilton's brigades in the North Woods, and to attack the Confederates beyond the Cornfield. After Doubleday's troops passed, Meade was to move Anderson's and Magilton's brigades forward to support the attack. Hooker ordered Ricketts' division to attack through the Cornfield and the East Woods, where Seymour's brigade of Meade's division was up early and ready to resume the fight it started the evening before. The Federal objective was the high ground around the Dunker Church, which Hooker considered the key to the battlefield. Hooker had 8,600 men to throw against the Confederates. Although the XII Corps was nearby, there were no orders from McClellan for them to join Hooker in the initial attack.

To oppose Hooker, Jackson had three divisions of infantry consisting of ten brigades, a total of 7,700 men. On the left of the Confederate line, Early's Brigade of Lawton's Division moved to the west to support the Confederate artillery on Nicodemus Hill. Jones' four brigades were still deployed in two north-facing lines west of the turnpike. Douglass' and Walker's brigades of Lawton's Division were in a battle that stretched eastward from the turnpike into the pasture where it bent southeasterly to the Samuel Mumma farm. Four batteries of S. D. Lee's artillery, deployed since 3 a.m. on the high ground near the Dunker Church, supported Lawton. Massed in the West Woods as a reserve were Hood's two brigades and Hays' Brigade of Lawton's Division. During the evening of the 16th, Brig. Gen. Roswell Ripley's Brigade of D. H. Hill's Division moved into position near the Mumma Farm to support S. D. Lee's guns. Hill, in command of Lee's center, had placed his other four brigades along a sunken farm lane to the south. As long as McClellan did not attack in the center of General Lee's line, some or all of Hill's brigades were available to support Jackson.

The battle began as soon as it was light enough to see. Seymour's Pennsylvanians moved into the East Woods where they stirred up the Confederate pickets of Walker's Brigade. As distant targets became discernible, S. D. Lee's veteran gunners opened fire on any Federals in sight, firing over the heads of Lawton's men.[56] At about the same time, the Confederate guns on Nicodemus Hill opened on Doubleday's infantry and artillery in the fields surrounding the J. Poffenberger farm. Doubleday's batteries immediately returned fire and the big Union guns across the Antietam added their thunderous volleys.[57] With yet an hour until sunrise, the battle already was swelling ominously.

In the West Woods, the efforts of the Texans to cook and eat their rations proved futile. Before their dough could be cooked into bread, Federal cannonballs swept through the trees overhead and landed among the men. Almost immediately, orders to fall in and prepare for action rang out amid the growing din of battle. The Texans abandoned their campfires and within minutes the still hungry men were under arms and standing in line. The storm of shells crashing through the trees continued unabated. To avoid the shells, the brigade was moved around the hill located behind the Dunker Church and the men were ordered to lie down.[58] Breakfast had to wait as the Texans laid low and anxiously listened to the battle sounds grow louder and stronger.

Doubleday and Ricketts started their divisions forward sometime between 5:30 and 6:00 under a heavy fire from the Confederate batteries.[59] As the Union infantry advanced, Batteries C and F of the 1st Pennsylvania Light Artillery, commanded by captains James Thompson and Ezra W. Matthews, deployed in the pasture north of the Cornfield to support the attack.[60] In the East Woods, Seymour's brigade pushed Walker's skirmishers out of the trees, but when the Pennsylvanians emerged from the woods themselves they met a blistering fire from Walker's main line. Walker's crashing volleys signaled the beginning of the infantry fight at Sharpsburg that day. Hell on earth was about to break loose in the normally peaceful fields and woods of western Maryland.

Fortunately for the Confederates, the Federals attacked in piecemeal episodes. Walker's men had already repulsed Seymour's attack when Col. Abram Duryea's Brigade of Rickett's division entered the Cornfield and bore down on Douglass' Georgia Brigade. The Georgians shredded the New Yorkers and Pennsylvanians when they stepped out of the head-high corn. Duryea fought back gamely until some of Walker's Confederates opened fire on his line. Within minutes, Duryea's regiments were wrecked and driven back through the corn.

Hartsuff's Federal brigade of Rickett's division advanced through the remnants of Duryea's brigade and into the Cornfield and East Woods. Within minutes Hartsuff was shot and Col. Richard Coulter took over the brigade. Like Duryea's before, Coulter's regiments emerged from the corn into a withering fire from the Confederate line. But the Confederates also took a beating. Colonel Douglass requested help from Harry Hays' tough Louisiana Brigade, which earlier in the morning had moved to a support position in rear of Douglass' line. Colonel Lee's gunners helped contain the enemy advance with well directed artillery fire as Hays' "Tigers" swept across the pasture in line of battle and opened fire on Coulter's Yankees. With help from the right flank regiments of Douglass' brigade, and from two artillery pieces from Colonel Lee's battalion that had earlier pushed across the Smoketown Road, the Louisianans drove the Federals back into the corn.[61] Coulter rallied his men, turned on his pursuers and, with the help of the Federal batteries, forced the Confederates back into the pasture, killing Douglass in the process. But Coulter's men fell fast and his counterattack stalled at the edge of the Cornfield just as Ricketts' last brigade, commanded by Col. Peter Lyle, passed through Seymour's shot-up regiments in the East Woods and entered the gruesome pasture beyond.[62]

Meanwhile, Brig. Gen. John Gibbon's "Black Hat" brigade, in a column of regiments with the 6th Wisconsin in the lead, led Doubleday's division through the North Woods and toward the Miller farm. Following Gibbon were the brigades of Col. Walter Phelps and Brig. Gen. Marsena R. Patrick, as well as Capt. Joseph B. Campbell's Battery B, 4th U.S. Artillery.[63] After clearing Rebel skirmishers from among the Miller buildings, Gibbon's black hatters swept past the farm and into the Cornfield. The 6th Wisconsin straddled the turnpike with three of its ten companies extending into the clover field on the right. Gibbon's 2nd Wisconsin lined up on the left of the 6th while his 7th Wisconsin and 19th Indiana closed up behind the first line. Phelps' brigade of New Yorkers followed Gibbon into the corn. When Gibbon's brigade reached the top of the plateau about halfway into the Cornfield, Jones' and Grigsby's Virginia brigades in the cloverfield together with Rebel skirmishers in the northern reaches of the West Woods opened a heavy fire into the 6th Wisconsin, slowing their advance. The Confederate infantry were supported by Poague's Battery in the cloverfield.[64]

To counter the fire, Gibbon ordered up Lt. James Stewart's section of Campbell's battery, which wheeled into position in the field just south of the Miller barn and started shelling the Confederates. Gibbon then diverted the 7th Wisconsin and 19th Indiana into the West Woods to protect the flank of his forward line. Doubleday was on the scene and ordered Patrick's brigade, which had crowded into the Cornfield behind Phelps, into the West Woods as well. On the way, Patrick detached the 80th New York to support Stewart's section and the 23rd New York to keep an eye on the Confederate guns on Nicodemus Hill. Patrick's two remaining regiments, the 21st and 35th New York, followed Gibbon's 7th Wisconsin and 19th Indiana into West Woods.[65]

The battle raged in full fury as northerners and southerners pummeled each other mercilessly along Jackson's entire front. In the eastern half of the Cornfield and in the East Woods, Rickett's division was stalled against Lawton's brigades. Along the turnpike and in the West Woods, however, Doubleday's Federals pressed forward. The 7th Wisconsin and 19th Indiana, supported by Patrick, cleared the Confederates out of the northern reaches of the West Woods.[66] Free of flanking fire, the 6th and 2nd Wisconsin, with Phelps' brigade only 25 paces behind, resumed their advance through the corn. Stewart's two pieces near the Miller barn poured a heavy fire into Jones' and Grigsby's brigades in the clover-field, adding to the deadly fire of Doubleday's infantry. The Virginians resisted as best they could, but soon broke and retreated into the West Woods. Gibbon and Phelps pushed through the cornstalks and toward the pasture. Lawton's Confederates held their fire until the Federals reached a rail fence bordering the southern edge of the corn, then unleashed a furious volley into the Yankee line. Major Rufus Dawes of the 6th Wisconsin later recalled: "Men, I can not say fell; they were knocked out of the ranks by dozens."[67] Undaunted, the Wisconsin men scrambled over the fence and returned fire as some of Phelps' New Yorkers closed up through the corn and filled the gaps in their line.

Douglass' Georgians could not hold and fell back until Starke's Louisiana Brigade and Taliaferro's Virginia/Alabama Brigade charged out of the West Woods diagonally across the southeastern clover field and up to the post and rail fence along the turnpike. They blasted Gibbon's line and forced the 6th Wisconsin and Phelp's men back to the edge of the Cornfield.[68] But the Confederate counterattack was doomed. Gibbon and Phelps poured a murderous fire into the Southerners' line while Stewart's guns ripped the flank of Starke's Brigade. The Confederates melted back into the West Woods, leaving a line of dead and wounded along the turnpike fence. Jones' Division was wrecked, Jones himself was wounded and Starke was dead.

While Doubleday and Ricketts pounded Jackson's divisions, Generals Anderson and Magilton of Meade's division led their Pennsylvania brigades in close columns out of the North Woods and across the open fields to low ground between the Miller orchard and the Cornfield. By that time, Capt. Dunbar R. Ransom's Battery C, 5th U.S. Artillery and Capt. John Reynold's Battery L, 1st New York Artillery, had taken positions in the fields north of the Cornfield, adding their ordnance to Matthews' and Thompson's guns.[69]

With ample artillery support, the soldiers of Gibbon and Phelps pressed forward with a cheer.[70] On their left, Coulter's Federals, though badly used up, were still firing. Farther to the left Lyle's regiments crowded out of the East

Woods. This time the Federals were irresistible. Lawton's beaten line dissolved. Many of the Confederates turned and ran into the West Woods, some being shot as they climbed the turnpike fences. Others retired sullenly, turning to shoot at the Northerners, who were pressing directly toward the Dunker Church. With Jackson's two divisions smashed, the left flank of Lee's line was seriously threatened. It was only 7 a.m.

"The dogs of war were loose, and havoc was their cry."

The Texans waited quietly in the woods while the noisy battle rattled their nerves. After the war, Cpl. W. D. Pritchard of Company I described the tension that perhaps most men felt while waiting under fire:

> . . .this is the time that tries the souls of men. Standing inactive, conscious of unseen danger, with bullets whistling over and around them, the increasing rattle of musketry in front, with now and then the ominous shriek of a shell as it tears through the ranks, taking out perhaps a file of men. . . .The strain upon the men is terrible. It takes more than brute courage to make him stand. There must be some higher, nobler feeling to prompt him or he will run in this moment of his great trial.[71]

A few minutes before 7 a.m., a staff officer from Lawton's crumbling division delivered an urgent plea for Hood's promised assistance. Hood instantly ordered his two brigades forward.[72] The temperature was in the high 60s with a relative humidity of about 70 percent and light winds out of the west—a pleasant morning in spite of the fact that the Texans were about to face the most intense violence humans could then produce.[73] The 1st Texas would in the next forty minutes earn a front-rank spot for bloodletting in the Civil War.

Hood's 2,300-man division was deployed in a double line of battle in the West Woods behind the Dunker Church, with the 900 men of the Texas Brigade behind Law's 1400-man brigade.[74] When the order was given to advance, Law's Brigade faced to the right and formed a column of fours. The head of the column then turned left and the brigade snaked through the woods, filed past the Dunker Church, and entered the Smoketown Road through a gap in the turnpike fences. Behind them, the Texas Brigade stepped off through the trees in line of battle.[75] When Law reached the turnpike himself, he saw "but few of our troops on the field, and these seemed to be in much confusion, but still opposing the advance of the enemy's dense masses with determination."[76] The Federals he saw belonged to Gibbon's, Phelps', Coulter's and Lyle's brigades. Out of sight and perhaps unknown to Law, the 19th Indiana, 7th Wisconsin and Patrick's New Yorkers were in the northern reaches of the West Woods. Also unseen were Meade's Pennsylvania brigades massed in the low ground between the Cornfield and the Miller orchard. Law's regiments marched a short way up the Smoketown Road before turning left into the pasture. There Law began to deploy his regiments into line of battle: from left to right the 2nd Mississippi, 11th Mississippi and 6th North Carolina. The 4th Alabama remained in column in the Smoketown Road, probably looking for a place on the narrow field to deploy.[77]

Meanwhile, the Texas Brigade advanced through the woods in line of battle. Shells crashed through the trees. Spent musket balls spattered the ground and ripped the foliage around the men. The brigade advanced through the woods at an oblique angle to the turnpike, causing the regiments to approach the road progressively from right to left.[78] The 1st Texas was in its usual place in the center of the line. To its right were the 4th and 5th Texas; to its left, the 18th Georgia and Hampton's Legion.[79] As the right of the brigade line neared the Dunker Church the 5th Texas formed a column and entered the Smoketown Road through the same gap in the fences that Law's men used.[80] The 1st Texas and the other regiments remained in line, passed to the left of the church, and climbed over the turnpike fences to get into the pasture.[81]

They were confronted head on with the terrible panorama of battle. In the field before them, Law's regiments were deploying into line. Beyond Law, bits and pieces of Jackson's shattered brigades stubbornly fell back before the Federal onslaught. Beyond Jackson's remnants were the long dark lines of the enemy, stretching across the pasture in front of the Cornfield and then along the front of the East Woods. At irregular intervals, stands of colors marked the centers of the many Federal regiments. The enemy lines were continuously punctuated by thousands of white smoky puffs from individual rifle shots, each adding to the haze that at moments obscured the field.[82] Artillery projectiles, fired by friend and foe, arched overhead and exploded in deadly blossoms of fire and smoke. Dead bodies and the writhing wounded of Lawton's and Jones' divisions sprinkled the fields everywhere. The sulfurous stench of burnt gunpowder and the roar of thousands of rifles, cannons, and voices heightened the impact of this grim spectacle upon the Texans.

Once the Texas Brigade was out of the woods, musket balls zipped through their line and shells shrieked in upon them.[83] The rifle fire was from Gibbon's 6th and 2nd Wisconsin and Phelps' New Yorkers, only 200 yards from the left of the brigade and bearing down on them.[84] Hampton's Legion and the 18th Georgia immediately returned Gibbon's fire about the same time that Law's Brigade

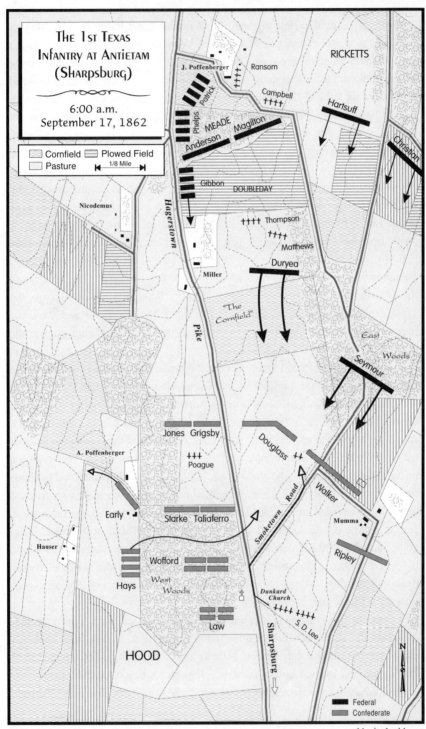

THE 1st TEXAS
INFANTRY AT ANTIETAM
(SHARPSBURG)

6:00 a.m.
September 17, 1862

Cornfield   Plowed Field
Pasture   ⊢ 1/8 Mile ⊣

RICKETTS

J. Poffenberger   Ransom

Patrick   Campbell ††††

Hartsuff

Phelps   MEADE   Magilton

Anderson

Christian

Gibbon   DOUBLEDAY

Nicodemus

Hagerstown

†††† Thompson
††††
Matthews

Miller

Duryea

"The
Cornfield"

Pike

East
Woods

Seymour

Jones Grigsby

Douglass ††

A. Poffenberger

††† Poague

Walker

Early

Starke Taliaferro

Smoketown Road

Mumma

Hauser

Wofford

Ripley

Hays

West
Woods

Dunkard
Church
†††† ††††

Law

S. D. Lee

HOOD

Sharpsburg

N

Federal
Confederate

Mark A. Moore

unleashed its first volley. Also, Starke's Brigade, and possibly other units from Jones' Division, had reformed and were advancing again west of the turnpike. The three Texas regiments were masked by Law's men and were unable to shoot. It didn't matter. The blue lines, already weakened from their fight for the Cornfield, were shattered without the help of Texas rifles. The Federals turned and ran from the pasture. Major Dawes of the 6th Wisconsin described the arrival of Hood's Division: "A long and steady line of rebel gray, unbroken by the fugitives who fly before us, comes sweeping down through the woods around the church. They raise the yell and fire. It is like a scythe running through our line. 'Now, save, who can.' It is a race for life that each man runs for the cornfield."[85]

From the pasture north of the Cornfield, Meade observed Doubleday's lines falling back. He ordered Anderson's and Magilton's brigades to deploy into line of battle along a rail fence about 30 yards beyond the northern edge of the Cornfield. There the Pennsylvanians laid down behind a low wall formed over the years by farmer Miller piling rocks under the fence.[86] Starting from the turnpike and running eastward were the 9th, 11th, 12th, 7th, 4th and 8th Pennsylvania Reserves.[87]

Colonel Wofford was behind the Legion and Georgians when they started firing at Gibbon's line on the plateau. Seeing the enemy line overlapping his flank and worried that his brigade would be surrounded if it continued to advance into the pasture, he ordered the Legion and 18th Georgia to change direction to the left oblique. Without slowing their fire, the South Carolinians and Georgians changed front to align their advance along the Hagerstown Turnpike and stepped off toward the retreating foe. Wofford then sent an order to the 1st Texas to move to its left to support the Legion and Georgians.[88] By the time the order got to Work, the three Texas regiments had already advanced 150 to 200 yards beyond the turnpike and were closing on Law's regiments in the pasture. When Colonel Work received Wofford's directive, he faced the 1st Texas to the left, forming a column of fours, and then led them at the double-quick back toward the Hagerstown Turnpike.[89]

After the 1st Texas moved off, the 4th and 5th Texas halted behind Law's line where they were ordered to lie down. A few minutes later, Law's brigade began its pursuit of the Federals, leaving behind a line of dead men.[90] Law's Mississippians and North Carolinians bore down on Coulter's shaken brigade in the Cornfield while the 4th Alabama, which had finally deployed into line of battle, advanced against Lyle's brigade in the East Woods. When Law advanced, the 4th and 5th Texas were left behind lying in the swale.

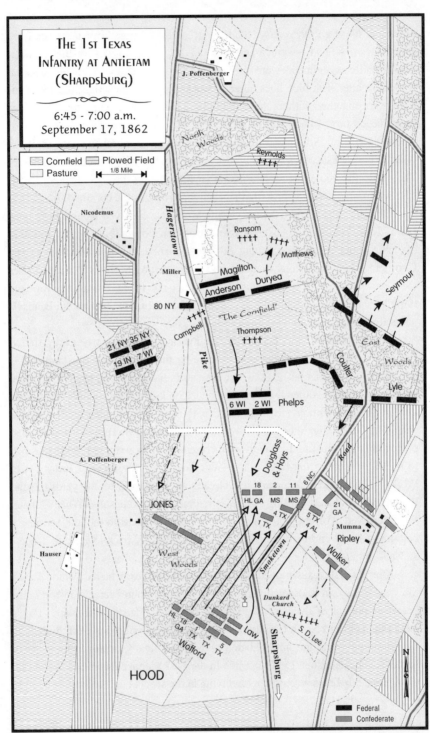

THE 1ST TEXAS
INFANTRY AT ANTIETAM
(SHARPSBURG)

6:45 - 7:00 a.m.
September 17, 1862

Cornfield   Plowed Field
Pasture |◄ 1/8 Mile ►|

J. Poffenberger

North
Woods

Reynolds
††††

Nicodemus

Ransom
††††   ††††

Matthews

Miller   Magilton   Duryea
           Anderson

80 NY
††††   "The Cornfield"

Campbell   Thompson
                     ††††

21 NY 35 NY
19 IN 7 WI   Coulter

Pike   East

                                            Woods
6 WI   2 WI   Phelps   Lyle

Seymour

A. Poffenberger
                    Douglass
                    & Hays

                    18   2   11   6 NC
JONES   HL GA MS MS   21
                        4 TX   GA
Hauser   1 TX   5 TX   Mumma
West   4 AL
Woods   Ripley
                    Smoketown
                                         Walker

                    Dunkard
HL 18 1 4 5   Church
GA TX TX TX TX   †††† ††††
         Law   S. D. Lee
Wofford   Sharpsburg

HOOD
                                    N

                              ■ Federal
                              ■ Confederate

Mark A. Moore

After double-quicking to the left about a hundred yards, Colonel Work formed his 1st Texas back into line facing north and ordered them forward. The color guard, with the Lone Star flag waving alongside the Army of Northern Virginia battle flag, advanced a few paces in front of the regiment and then the entire line stepped off after them. The grim Texans, perhaps jittery before, were calmly focused on the enemy ahead. "The command to forward dispels all fear," remembered Cpl. Pritchard, "and from the first volley all traces of that fear and dread are gone, all is lost in the excitement. Men who five minutes before were trembling and praying are now cool, collected and more than apt to be cursing. . . . The din and confusion of battle seem to drown all thoughts."[91]

The 1st Texas battle was about 160 feet long. The privates and corporals were in two ranks, the rear about 16 inches behind the front rank.[92] Two paces behind the rear rank a line of sergeants and lieutenants, known as file closers, supervised the men. From several paces behind the file closers the captains and first sergeants watched over their companies. Major Dale supervised the right wing of the regiment and Capt. John R. Woodward, a 30-year old doctor from Palestine, Texas and commander of Company G, took charge of the left wing.[93] Their places in the formation were 12 paces behind the centers of their respective wings. Colonel Work commanded them all from his post 30 paces behind the center of the regiment. The Texans advanced rapidly up the plateau and directly toward the corn. Soldiers in the middle of the line were continuously pushed right, and then left, and right again, as the men toward the ends of the line struggled to maintain their guide on the colors. File closers barked directions to maintain proper alignment. Captains and first sergeants bellowed encouragement to steady the men. Approaching the Cornfield, the Texans passed the position recently held by Douglass' Brigade, grimly marked by a row of dead Georgians.[94] Ahead of the 1st Texas, Hampton's Legion and the 18th Georgia pushed Gibbon and Phelps into the corn.

Advancing quickly, the 1st Texas caught up with their comrades at the edge of the Cornfield and took position on the right of the 18th Georgia. The three regiments then burst into the Cornfield with such impetuosity that "the corn blades rose like a whirlwind."[95] From hundreds of Confederate lips came the chilling rebel yell.[96] Some of the retreating Federals attempted a stand 50 or so yards into the corn, but Wofford's three regiments let loose a volley that shattered all resistance.[97] Many of the Carolinians and Georgians swarmed down the turnpike and fired between the plank rails of the fences on either side, ripping the flank of the fleeing infantry east of the road and Campbell's Battery west of the road.[98]

When the Federals in the Cornfield broke, Colonel Work was unable to restrain his Texans. They bolted after the fleeing Union soldiers, outpacing the Georgians and the Legion. Realizing his regiment was perilously exposed, Work sent Capt. Woodward to report to Wofford that the 1st Texas was driving the enemy but needed support. A few minutes later, Work sent Pvt. Amos Hanks of Company F with a similar request. Woodward made his report and returned to the regiment, but Hanks was shot before he reached Wofford.[99]

The Texans crashed through the tall cornstalks, driving the Badgers and New Yorkers out of the corn and pretty much out of the fight. Minie balls crackled through the stalks at every step and artillery shells exploded among them. A piece of shrapnel crushed Capt. Todd's foot, knocking the company commander out of the battle.[100] Pvt. John Wilson of Company K was luckier. He was hit under the arm by another shell fragment, but it did not break his skin.[101] Those who were not hit pressed on. "The fall of a comrade near (us) produces no perceptible effect," remembered Private Pritchard. "One, two, even three may fall in touch, but on (we) go conscious of but one thing and that is to conquer or die."[102] When the Texans were nearly through the Cornfield, Work received an order to halt, perhaps as a result of his earlier entreaty for support. Work screamed at his officers and men as they rushed ahead to the far edge of the corn. There Work was finally able to rein in his Texans just as Meade's Pennsylvania Reserves rose from behind the rock and rail fence thirty yards ahead and fired a volley into their faces.[103] At the same time, Ransom's battery blasted the Texans at nearly point-blank range from a hill a hundred yards behind the Federal infantry.[104] The Texans returned the fire, driving some of the Federal infantrymen away from the fence and forcing many of the gunners to quit their pieces.[105]

The impetuous charge of the 1st Texas left both flanks of the regiment in the air. To their left, the Legion and 18th Georgia had not kept pace because the 7th Wisconsin and 19th Indiana in the West Woods changed front from south to east and opened fire into the flank of the Carolinians and Georgians. Hampton's Legion was pinned down in the southwest corner of the Cornfield. To the right of the Legion, the 18th Georgia advanced a few yards farther into the corn, but Campbell's gunners opened on them with double rounds of canister, stopping them in their tracks. Returning the fire, the Georgians shot down many of the gunners, silencing some of the guns. But the fire from the remaining pieces, one of which was briefly served by General Gibbon, inflicted heavy losses.[106]

To the right of the 1st Texas, Law's 2nd and 11th Mississippi and 6th North Carolina drifted to the right as they drove Coulter's brigade through the Cornfield. A gap opened between Law and Wofford. Advancing to the far edge of the

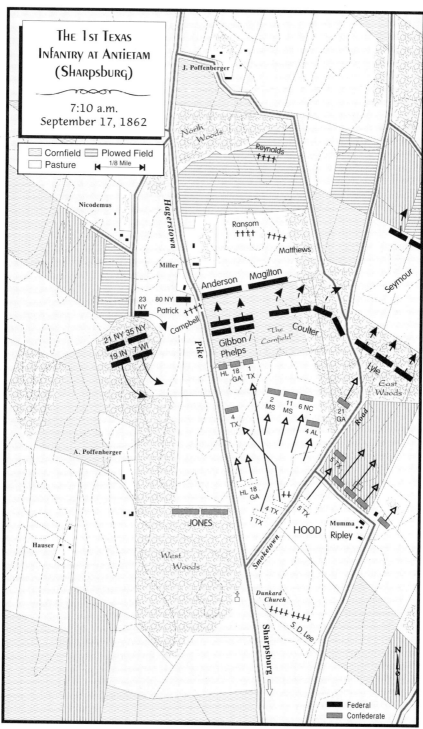

The 1st Texas
Infantry at Antietam
(Sharpsburg)

7:10 a.m.
September 17, 1862

Cornfield   Plowed Field
Pasture   1/8 Mile

J. Poffenberger

North Woods

Reynolds

Nicodemus

Hagerstown

Ransom

Matthews

Miller

Anderson   Magilton

Seymour

23 NY   80 NY
Patrick

Campbell

21 NY 35 NY
19 IN 7 WI

Gibbon / Phelps

"The Cornfield"

Coulter

Lyle

East Woods

HL 18 1
GA TX

2 11 6 NC
MS MS

Pike

21 GA

4 TX

4 AL

5 TX

A. Poffenberger

HL 18
GA

JONES

4 TX

5 TX

Mumma

1 TX

HOOD   Ripley

Hauser

West Woods

Smoketown

Dunkard Church

Sharpsburg

S.D. Lee

N

Federal
Confederate

Mark A. Moore

corn, Law's attack caught Magilton's brigade just as it was moving to support the Federals in the East Woods. Law routed Magilton's right and center regiments and opened a destructive fire on Ransom's and Matthews' batteries beyond.[107] This fire, added to that of the 1st Texas, chased off many of the Federal artillerymen.[108] Magilton's other two regiments held their ground long enough for Magilton to rally and for Meade to redirect Ransom's artillery fire. Together with the fire from remnants of other infantry commands in the area, Magilton and Ransom contained Law's advance to the northern edge of the Cornfield.

While directing the advance of his three left regiments, Wofford left the 4th and 5th Texas lying in the pasture. Hood was on the scene, however, and personally directed the Texas units to positions covering the flanks of his division. Hood ordered Captain Ike Turner, temporarily commanding the 5th Texas, to advance obliquely to the right to clear the Federals out of the East Woods.[109] Law's 4th Alabamans and the 21st Georgia of Walker's Brigade were already there fighting Lyle's Federals. Hood ordered Lt. Col. Carter's 4th Texas to the left of the division.[110] The 4th Texas double-quicked to the Hagerstown Pike so that the left of the regiment rested on the road. From there they advanced to the edge of the Cornfield, where they were hit by a murderous fire from the Federals on the other side of the turnpike. The 4th wheeled leftward to the turnpike fences from where they poured deadly volleys into the 7th Wisconsin.[111]

Hood's attack ground to a halt. On the left of his division, the 4th Texas, Hampton's Legion and 18th Georgia were unable to make headway against Doubleday's infantry and Campbell's gunners. In the center, the 1st Texas and Law's regiments slugged it out with Meade's Pennsylvanians and Hooker's artillerymen at the far edge of the Cornfield, but were unable to drive them. On the right of the division, the 5th Texas and the 4th Alabama, with help from the 21st Georgia, had driven the Federals through the East Woods, but they could go no farther.

It was the 1st Texas that faced the most severe fire. They stood practically toe to toe with their determined enemy, two lines of men bent on killing and maiming. Each line was seemingly a single writhing organism as soldiers twirled their rammers overhead to load their rifles, others primed and fired, and still others lurched backwards or slumped to the ground when bullets slammed into their bodies. To the Texans in the ranks the sound of battle was deafening: the boom of artillery; the loud reports of dozens of nearby rifles and the steady popping of thousands more distant; the explosions of shells and the whine and hiss of lead balls and steel fragments. Men whooped and yelled; others screamed to be heard by their comrades. File closers and company commanders bellowed

orders and encouragement until they were hoarse—or shot. Dead and dangerously wounded Texans lay among the living and unhurt. Walking wounded dribbled from the line. Like a funeral pall, thick clouds of smoke drifted over the corn
and at times obscured the sun.[112]

Jutting proudly above the cornstalks and waving defiantly in the breeze, the
1st Texas battle flags symbolized why the Texans were there, half a continent
from their homes, fighting over a miserable patch of corn. The colors marked the
center of the regiment, physically and emotionally; but they were also the center
of the enemy's lethal exertions. Colorbearers were shot down one after another:
John Hanson of Company L, James Day of Company M, Charles Kingsley of
Company L and then James K. Malone of Company A.[113]

Enemy fire sweeping the entire length of the regiment struck down many
Texans right and left. A rifle ball struck Capt. Richard W. Cotton of Company I
in the head. Company I's Orderly Sergeant, Russell Mitchell, was struck in the
head by a shell fragment.[114] "They were too strong for us, cutting us down like
grain before a cradle," wrote Cpl. O. T. Hanks of Company K. Hanks fired at the
enemy until he noticed a Northerner behind the fence, thirty yards away, on his
knees and peering between two fence rails placed on end. "I had a good gun and
drew directly at his breast," remembered Hanks. "I thought to myself, 'If we
whip I am going to see if I killed you.' I did not get to investigate. Just [as] I was
raising my gun to my face to fire again, a bullet. . .struck me in the left side, close
up under the arm, coming out under my shoulder blade near my back bone."
Hanks dropped his rifle and staggered back into the corn.[115]

The other Texas Brigade regiments fared little better. Across the turnpike, the
7th Wisconsin and 19th Indiana advanced to a limestone ledge that bisected the
cloverfield parallel to the road. The 21st and 35th New York regiments swung
into line behind the 7th Wisconsin while the 23rd New York fell into line next to
Campbell's battery.[116] Sgt. E. Scott Carson of the Hampton's Legion remembered that "it seemed the whole world was in arms against us. . . .Their new
bright flags were waving in every direction."[117] Another South Carolinian remembered a continuous sheet of flame along the Union lines.[118] Campbell's
artillerists blasted the Rebels along the turnpike, their shells blowing fence rails
into the air.[119] To Pvt. J. M. Polk of the 4th Texas, "the air was full of shot and
shell. . .it seemed almost impossible for a rat to live in such a place."[120] Another
4th Texan recalled that it was "the hottest place I ever saw on earth or want to see
hereafter. There were shot, shells, and Minie balls sweeping the face of the earth;
legs, arms, and other parts of human bodies were flying in the air like straw in a
whirlwind. The dogs of war were loose, and havoc was their cry."[121] Pvt. W.E.

Barry of the 4th Texas was in the turnpike and firing through the fence at the Federals in the clover field. "We were in extreme peril and our position was absolutely terrible to contemplate," he later wrote. Through the thick smoke, Barry saw to his right-rear the 1st Texas fighting in the Cornfield. "On one brief occasion," he said, "I saw the fragments of the legs of one poor [1st] Texan's body flying in the air, having been torn and dismembered by a shell." Of the soldiers of the 1st Texas he wrote: "These brave men were mowed down like the corn surrounding them."[122]

The 1st Texas hung on tenaciously at the far edge of the Cornfield. Colonel Work saw the Federals massed in the clover field to his left. He sent Adjutant J. Winkfield Shropshire back to Col. Wofford to report that the 1st Texas would have to retire unless it was supported. A few minutes later Work sent Pvt. Charles Hicks of Company F to repeat the request.[123] Hicks had just left Work when Maj. Dale, commanding the right wing of the regiment, rushed up to report that nearly every man in his wing was shot and that none would survive unless the regiment was withdrawn. "The roar all about us of nearby small arms and of artillery more distant was so deafening that the Major, in making his report, had to place his mouth to my ear," remembered Col. Work. "Just as he concluded and whilst we still were standing breast to breast, he with his right side and I with my left towards the front, he was stricken by a bullet, straightened, stiffened and fell backwards prone upon the ground, dead."[124]

The enemy fire intensified from the left and rear as the Federal regiments on the other side of the turnpike began to press forward from the limestone ledge. Just after Maj. Dale fell, Capt. Woodward, commanding the left wing of the regiment, reported to Col. Work that his wing too was badly shot up.[125] Work had seen enough. Without waiting for word from Wofford, he directed Capt. U. S. Connally of Company D to pull back the right wing and Capt. Woodward to pull back the left. In the center of the regiment, the colorbearers took but a few steps backward before one of them was shot and his flag fell to the ground. Work saw about a half dozen Texans rush over to raise the flag, one of whom did so and started toward the rear. Colonel Work himself headed toward the left of the regiment to get a better look at the enemy in the clover field and he soon lost sight of the colors.[126]

When the 1st Texas withdrew from the edge of the corn, the 9th, 11th and 12th Pennsylvania Reserves climbed over the rock and rail fence to follow.[127] But the Texans did not panic. They retreated slowly and deliberately while exchanging shots with the pursuing enemy. They answered the Yankee huzzas with their own Rebel yell.[128] Losses mounted with every step. Pvt. J. T. Evans of

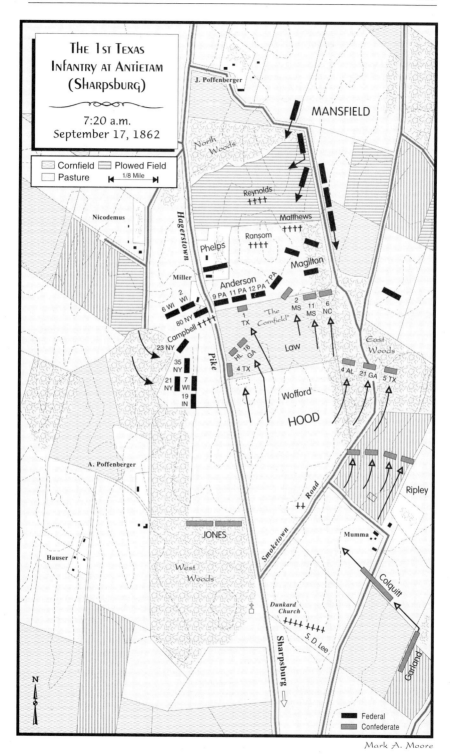

The 1st Texas
Infantry at Antietam
(Sharpsburg)

7:20 a.m.
September 17, 1862

Cornfield   Plowed Field
Pasture   1/8 Mile

Federal
Confederate

Mark A. Moore

Company M was shot through the hip and fell to the ground. Fearful that Evans would fall into the enemy's hands, Pvt. Bill Townes, himself wounded, picked up his disabled comrade and carried him to the rear.[129] Tom Samford of Company I was not as fortunate. No one noticed when he was shot through the thigh and he was left to the mercy of the enemy.[130]

Hood's line crumbled everywhere in the Cornfield. Along the turnpike the Texas Brigade regiments fell like dominoes when Patrick's New Yorkers and the 19th Indiana pressed up to the turnpike fences.[131] Colonel Ruff, who had already lost two-thirds of his Georgians, ordered his men to fall back to the pasture.[132] Lieutenant Colonel Gary of Hampton's Legion saw the Georgians retreating on his right and the Federals advancing on his left and ordered his handful of South Carolinians to quit the corn and take cover behind the crest of the plateau.[133] The retreating South Carolinians in turn uncovered the right flank of the 4th Texas, who were still in the turnpike contesting the advancing Federals from behind the fences. To escape, Lt. Col. Carter at first ordered his men to move by the left flank along the turnpike, but the enemy fire was so hot he quickly ordered them to fall back from the fence and to reform in the swale.[134] Colonel Wofford was in the swale conferring with one of Hood's staff officers when Ruff's, Gary's and Carter's shattered regiments tumbled back from the turnpike and Cornfield. Wofford ordered them to regroup in the West Woods.[135] The 4th Texas was still in some semblance of order and marched by the left flank down the swale and into the trees near the Dunker Church. Behind them, the South Carolinians and Georgians fell back slowly, some of them stopping to gather cartridges from the dead and to shoot at the Federals pressing up to the Hagerstown Turnpike.[136]

In the eastern half of the Cornfield, Law's Brigade tenaciously held its line for several minutes against the fire of Magilton's infantry and several Union batteries. But in the fields to the north, Law saw the dark masses of thousands of fresh Federal troops: General Mansfield's 7,200-man XII Corps moving up to bolster Hooker's attack. Law's line was also threatened on the left flank by Anderson's Pennsylvanians pursuing the 1st Texas into the Cornfield.[137] Unsupported, Law quickly withdrew his command from the Cornfield and joined the bulk of Wofford's men in their retreat to the West Woods.

The rapid withdrawal of Wofford and Law left the stubborn 1st Texas alone in the Cornfield. The Texans slowly fell back, shooting at the blue figures following them through the corn rows. At some point—it will never be known exactly where—the Pennsylvanians unleashed a devastating volley into the 1st Texas that shot down the two colorbearers and nearly a dozen other men around the colors. Private William Pritchard of Company I, the latest Texan to end up with the

Confederate battle flag, was shot in the face with buckshot. As he bent over grasping his face, a rifle ball struck him in the breast, penetrated his clothing and skin and ranged downwards, where it lodged in his belly.[138] Pritchard and his cherished banner fell among the bloody cornstalks. Private Blessing, the one who had taken "French leave" when the army crossed the Potomac, was standing near the last Texan to bear the Lone Star flag—his name now unknown—when the man and the flag fell to the ground. "My first impulse was to pick it up," Blessing remembered, "but then thought I could do more good shooting. . . .Very shortly I fell, shot through the leg and a buckshot in the hand. . . ." Blessing and Pritchard, both wounded, watched helplessly as the enemy rush forward and seized the Lone Star flag and the Army of Northern Virginia battle flag from among the dead and wounded Texans lying around them.[139]

The few survivors of the 1st Texas drifted back through the smoke and the corn, many of them oblivious to the fate of their colors. The 9th Pennsylvania, which had captured the colors, followed them.[140] The 11th and 12th Pennsylvania regiments were content with their gains and held their ground in the Cornfield. The 1st Texas fell back to the pasture where Colonel Work ordered the unit to halt. He asked someone near him about the colors so that the men could rally upon them and was mistakenly informed that the color guard had already left the Cornfield.[141] Work then noticed about 30 Confederates from another regiment rallied around a battle flag some thirty yards toward the turnpike and on higher ground. As his Texans emerged from the Cornfield one or two men at a time, Work ordered them to rally on the battle flag squad. While thus engaged, Captain Woodward ran to him and cried out, "The flags, the flags! Where are the flags? The bearers are shot down. . . ." Woodward then ran back into the corn to recover the colors, but after a few yards he came face to face with the 9th Pennsylvania. Woodward quickly retraced his steps and reported to Work that the colors were lost. By then the rallied Confederate squad had given way to the oncoming Federals and were fleeing toward the West Woods, taking with them those 1st Texans who had gone over to them.[142] With the enemy swarming up to the turnpike fences on his left and crashing through the corn in his front, Work ordered his remaining Texans, numbering only 17 men, to retreat.

But the direct route back to the West Woods was cut off. Patrick's New York regiments had charged to the turnpike fences and stopped, but the impetuous 19th Indiana had climbed the fences about 150 yards south of the Cornfield and were in the pasture between the 1st Texas and what was left of Hood's Division streaming into the trees around the Dunker Church.[143] Work looked around for another way out. To the southeast he saw a fence along the Smoketown Road and ordered his men to run for it.[144] The Texans ran across the swale and part way up the far slope before the Indianans, and possibly some of the 9th Pennsylvanians, opened fire on them. As Work recalled,

> Their bullets when striking the hillside ground raised puffs of dust just as in the beginning of a shower do large drops of rain on a dusty road. Strange to say, and Providentially, not a man of us received a wound. Capt. Woodward's canteen, swinging against his left side and hip, was shot through from back to front. The scabbard of my light dress sword was stricken in such a way as threw the lower end between my legs from in front and gave me a fall. Before arising I removed the belt from about my waist and upon regaining my feet carried it in my hand the balance of the way.
>
> Upon reaching the fence some crawled through between the bottom slab and the ground, some crawled through between slabs and others climbed and bounded over. To our relief and great joy we found that this fence stood from two to three feet (from the) side of an old road which from long usage and rain washing had worn and been cut down for a depth of from three to four feet leaving precipitous sides. To us this was a "casemate." To the right and left of where we reached it we found men of various commands to the number of probably sixty who, also, had taken refuge there. Many of these still had their rifles and cartridge boxes. In addition the base of the road was littered over with castaway rifles and cartridge boxes, cast away by other fugitives who had continued on in quest of greater safety. Thus there was the greatest plenty both of arms and ammunition.
>
> Whilst Capt. Woodward and myself became actively and sternly busy in requiring all of these other fugitives to take rifles and ammunition, "fall in" and open fire upon the advancing enemy, the members of the 1st Texas were pouring into . . . [the Union soldiers] a deadly and telling fire, every shot counting. All told, about seventy-five rifles were brought to bear and soon the Federals were not only repulsed but routed.[145]

Actually, Work had help in repulsing the aggressive Indianans, who had charged across the plateau to the edge of the swale when Work's riflemen fired on them from the Smoketown Road.[146] More intimidating to the Federals than Work's scratch command was the large brigade of Brig. Gen. Roswell Ripley entering the pasture to the right of Work's position. Ripley's Brigade had been stationed just south of the Mumma farm and when Hood launched his attack against Hooker the Georgians and North Carolinians advanced to the edge of the East Woods. Finding no enemy there, and perhaps aware of Hood's repulse, Ripley ordered his brigade into the pasture. Ripley's arrival proved timely for Colonel Work and most likely had much to do with stopping the Indianans and

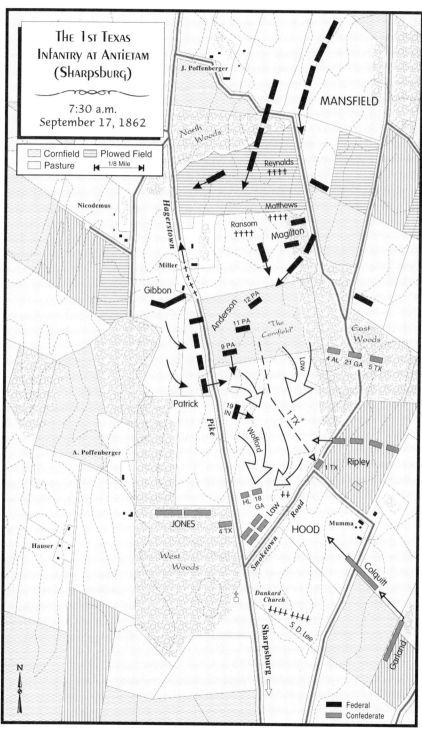

The 1st Texas
Infantry at Antietam
(Sharpsburg)

7:30 a.m.
September 17, 1862

Cornfield   Plowed Field
Pasture   1/8 Mile

Mark A. Moore

causing them to fall back to the turnpike where they rallied on Patrick's New Yorkers.[147] With the Indianans gone from their front, Colonel Work, his seventeen 1st Texas survivors and the other Confederates he had commandeered fell back from the Smoketown Road. They were soon spotted by Hood, who led them over to the West Woods.[148]

Ripley continued into the pasture. With help from Confederate flanking fire from the West Woods, Ripley's strong line drove the 19th Indiana and Patrick's New York regiments away from the turnpike fences and shot up the unsupported 9th Pennsylvania, which had emerged unsupported from the Cornfield in pursuit of the 1st Texas.[149] After the Pennsylvanians retreated, Ripley's regiments advanced to the edge of the trampled Cornfield where they linked with the 5th Texas and 4th Alabama of Hood's Division, still holding their own in the East Woods with the 21st Georgia. By that time, the commanders of the 11th and 12th Pennsylvania regiments, believing they were relieved by elements of Mansfield's rapidly approaching corps, had already ordered their regiments to retire from the Cornfield.[150]

"The battlefield was too terrible to behold. . . ."

It was about 7:30 a.m. when Colonel Work and the remnant of the 1st Texas Infantry re-entered the West Woods, just 30 minutes after they began their attack. Assembling among the trees were roughly 650 survivors from the seven regiments of Hood's Division that fought in the Cornfield.[151] While Ripley's Confederates ran off the last of Hooker's Federals, Hood reorganized his shattered division to hold the West Woods until reinforcements arrived. The 4th Texas, possibly because it was the least disorganized of the Texas Brigade regiments, was posted on the left of the Turnpike along the southern edge of the clover field. Colonel Wofford assembled the 18th Georgia, Hampton's Legion, Work's 1st Texas squad and remnants of other commands and deployed them as skirmishers on a wide front along the turnpike. General Law formed his Mississippi and North Carolina regiments into line of battle about 100 yards behind Wofford's skirmish line.[152] For the next hour, Hood's Division held the West Woods while three brigades of D. H. Hill's Division moved up from the Confederate center and fought Mansfield's Federal corps for possession of the Cornfield and the East Woods. Mansfield won, mauling Hill's brigades in the process and driving Hood's 5th Texas and 4th Alabama out of the East Woods. The 5th Texas retreated to the West Woods where they finally rejoined the Texas Brigade.

After driving off Hill, two brigades of Brig. Gen. George Sears Greene's division of Mansfield's Corps advanced into the pasture south of the Smoketown Road to within 200 yards of the West Woods. Out of ammunition, Hood's command put up a bold front by defiantly waving their battle flags at the enemy.[153] Then the 125th Pennsylvania, a large new regiment in Mansfield's Corps, crossed the pasture north of the Smoketown Road. Behind the Pennsylvanians, Maj. Gen. John Sedgewick's division of Maj. Gen. Edwin V. Sumner's II Corps spilled out of the East Woods to renew the attack on the Confederate left flank. Confronted by the enemy masses, Wofford and Law pulled back to a fence bordering the western edge of the West Woods.[154] There they met reinforcements: three brigades of Maj. Gen. Lafayette McLaw's Division, just arrived from Harpers Ferry. Also on hand were Early's Brigade, which had moved over from its supporting position near Nicodemus Hill, and Brig. Gen. G. T. Anderson's Brigade sent over from the Confederate right flank. As the fresh Confederate brigades crowded into the West Woods, Hood's Division was relieved to replenish its ammunition.

Hood led his division southward several hundred yards to an open field near the Piper farm where his men rested and drew ammunition.[155] While there, McLaws, Early and G.T. Anderson smashed Sedgewick's attacking division in the West Woods, ending the last Union threat of the day on the Confederate left flank. At the same time, the battle intensified in the Confederate center where the two remaining brigades under D. H. Hill defended a sunken road against two divisions from the Union II Corps. On the right flank, Maj. Gen. Ambrose Burnside's IX Corps frittered the morning away down by the lower bridge in front of Longstreet's troops.

At noon, Hood's Division was ordered back to the West Woods. They arrived just as Maj. Gen. John G. Walker's Division, shifted from the Confederate right by General Lee, collapsed the last Federal foothold west of the Hagerstown Turnpike. The Texans entered the woods and formed on the same ground they occupied just before their early morning attack.[156] The infantry fight on this flank was over and the West Woods were entirely in the hands of Confederate forces from McLaw's, Walker's, Lawton's and Hood's divisions. Meanwhile, in the center of General Lee's line, the Confederates had been driven out of the Sunken Road, but the Federals failed to follow up on their success against a paper-thin Southern line.

Throughout the afternoon, Hood's brigades held their positions in the West Woods under enemy artillery fire. Late in the day heavy firing was heard to the south where Burnside forced a crossing of Antietam Creek at the Lower Bridge and drove back elements of Longstreet's Corps nearly to Sharpsburg. In the nick of time, Maj. Gen. A. P. Hill's Light Division of Jackson's Corps arrived from Harpers Ferry and turned back Burnside's attack. The battle ended with the setting sun. At nightfall, Hood was ordered to move his division about a half mile to the right where they remained in line of battle throughout the night.[157]

General Lee decided to remain on the field the next day, September 18, in order to remove his wounded, rest his men and gain time to remove the captured ordnance and supplies from Harpers Ferry. Amazingly, with over 26,000 fresh troops at his disposal, McClellan failed to renew his attack against Lee's battered army. A truce was called to bring off the thousands of wounded lying between the lines. They were taken to field hospitals where they swamped the overworked surgeons. Some were luckier and avoided the miserable hospitals. Captain Todd of the 1st Texas, who had been wounded in the foot in the Cornfield, declined "the offer of the surgeon, Dr. Ewing, to cut off (my) foot." Rather than face the scalpel, Todd got into an ambulance and crossed the Potomac.[158]

During the truce one of Law's staff officers observed that "many from either side met in the space between the lines and while the dead and wounded were being cared for, chatted as pleasantly as though they had never done each other harm."[159] Many officers later commented on the ghastly appearance of the battle-field. Lieutenant Colonel Bragg of the 6th Wisconsin, himself wounded in the battle, described the scene where the Texan Brigade fought: "The battlefield was too terrible to behold without a shock. I never want to see another such. I counted eighty Rebels in one row along the fence in front of us, lying so thick you could step from one to the other, and this was only in one place. In others they lay in heaps, mowed down, and many of our brave boys with them. So it was every-where."[160]

That night, Lee's army left the battlefield and marched to the Potomac River crossing at Boteler's Ford. In the early morning hours of September 19th, the Texans crossed the Potomac to the melancholic strains of "Carry Me Back to Ole Virginny."[161] The most desperately wounded Confederates had to be left behind in the field hospitals and later fell into enemy hands. Twenty-three of them were from the 1st Texas, including privates Blessing and Hanks.[162]

In Virginia, the army marched south to the friendlier environs around Winchester, where it spent the next month recovering from the arduous campaign and the brutal day at Sharpsburg. While there, many of the men may have reflected upon the terrific battle they had survived. We will never know how most of them categorized the battle—win, loss, or draw—but perhaps Pvt. Watters Berryman of Company I spoke for many when he wrote home to his mother: "I can't say we were whipped, but we were overwhelmed."[163]

"No man knew save him who had fallen with them."

Confederate losses during the Sharpsburg Campaign were staggering. The army lost over 10,700 men killed, wounded and missing, which exceeded 30 percent of the number engaged.[164] Hood's Division lost 940 men, or 44 percent.[165] The Texas Brigade lost 548 men, nearly all killed and wounded, for a loss of 64.1 percent, the third highest loss for any Confederate brigade during the war.[166]

For the 1st Texas, the losses were even more appalling. It was the hardest hit regiment in the division in terms of total casualties and the hardest hit in the army as a proportion to the number of men in the regiment engaged. The loss percentage of the 1st Texas, 82.3 percent, was the highest loss proportional to numbers engaged of any regiment, North or South, during the entire war.[167] Forty-five 1st Texans were killed and 141 wounded—a total of 186 out of the 226 men and officers that went into the fight.[168] Twelve of the wounded died in the days and weeks following the battle, bringing the total killed to 57.[169] Only two regiments in Lee's army had more men killed outright that day and only five regiments had greater total losses in the entire campaign. The number of killed in the 1st Texas was more than all of the other regiments in the Texas Brigade combined, and the 1st Texas had nearly 80 more casualties than any other regiment in the brigade.[170] After the battle, company F had no one left to answer the roll call, Company A had one, and Company C had but two.[171]

Another loss to the 1st Texas, and a great one, was that of its colors, the Lone Star flag and the Army of Northern Virginia battle flag. The Texans had lost the symbols of their identity as a regiment and as a wartime community of devoted friends and family members. For some, the sense of loss was deep, as reflected in the battle report of Colonel Work:

> It is a source of mortification to state that, upon retiring from the engagement, our colors were not brought off. I can but feel that some degree of odium must attach under the most favorable circumstances, and although such are the circumstances surrounding the conduct of this regiment, *the loss of our flag will always remain a matter of sore and deep regret.* . . .No blame, I feel, should attach to the men or officers, all of whom fought heroically and well. There was no such conduct upon their part as abandoning or deserting their colors. They fought bravely, and unflinchingly faced a terrible hail of bullets and artillery until ordered by me to retire. The colors started back with them, and when they were lost no man knew save him who had fallen with them.[172]

On the morning of the battle, the 1st Texas colors were taken to General McClellan's headquarters under an escort. The escort passed a group of Confederate prisoners, among whom was Pvt. W. E. Barry of the 4th Texas, who had been captured in the Hagerstown Turnpike. Barry was standing in the road next to a Union major when the colors passed, an event he wrote about after the war. Even allowing for the sentimentality of long years gone by, perhaps Barry's words expressed the feelings most Texans had for their flags:

> While standing there I saw coming up the road from the battlefield some colors, with an escort. When they arrived the Major asked the Yankee with the colors where they got them. He said in the cornfield. He turned to me and inquired if I knew the colors. I told him they belonged to the First Texas Regiment, remarking at the time that where he got the flag there was many a dead Texan there. He said there were thirteen dead men lying on and around it when he found it. I asked him to hand it to me a moment, which he did. I took it in my hand, kissed it, and handed it back to him, tears blinding my eyes.[173]

Many 1st Texans were only slightly wounded and returned to the regiment during the month of October and succeeding weeks. Those footsore who had fallen out of the ranks during the campaign, as well as others who broke down on the long road from the Peninsula to the Potomac, also returned to the ranks soon after the battle. Later in the year, other Texans who had been seriously wounded on the Peninsula, at Manassas and at Sharpsburg also returned, including a few captured at Sharpsburg and later paroled.[174] Eventually, the regiment once again reached the numbers it carried into the Cornfield.

The 1st Texas remained in the Texas Brigade and Lee's army until the end of the war.[175] During that time, the 1st Texas fought on many fields and distinguished itself in the bloody battles at Gettysburg, Chickamauga and the Wilderness, where losses totaled another 95 killed and 261 wounded.[176] For the entire war, total combat casualties in the 1st Texas amounted to over 53 percent of the total enrollment of the regiment.[177] In a wartime letter to his mother, Pvt. Watters Berryman of Co. I wrote: "They always take the Texians to the hottest part of the field."[178]

So it was at Sharpsburg on September 17, 1862.

This Lone Star flag so faded now,
So worn by shot and shell,
Waved proudly once o'er gallant men
In the days when war was hell.

No foeman's hand e'er touched its folds
Till those who bore it fell
And died on Sharpsburg's bloody field
In the days when war was hell.

Rest, old flag, your mission's done;
Our sons will guard you well.
Their fathers loved you long ago
In the days when war was hell.

The Flag of the First Texas
—by Val Giles, 1907[179]

Notes

1. Harold B. Simpson, "Hood's Texas Brigade," *Valor: The Biennial Publication of Hood's Texas Brigade Association*, vol. 71 (1971), p. 5. The formation of the 1st Texas differed from the norm in both armies. Typically, independent companies were assembled in their home state and then organized into regiments before going to the front. The eager volunteers of the 1st Texas refused to wait for their formal organization and followed their leaders on what seemed the quickest path to war.

2. The 1st Texas was unique in the Army of Northern Virginia in that it was composed of twelve companies instead of the usual ten. Eleven of the companies were raised under Confederate troop levies of April 8 and 16, 1861, and the twelfth was recruited during the spring of 1862. Harold B. Simpson, *Hood's Texas Brigade: A Compendium* (Hillsboro, 1977), p.10; Harold B. Simpson, *Hood's Texas Brigade, Lee's Grenadier Guard* (Dallas, 1983, reprint; orig. pub. 1970), pp. 10-11.

3. Following the Seven Days battles General Lee reorganized his army into nine infantry divisions and two infantry corps. Technically, the corps were not legally established by the Confederate Congress until after the Sharpsburg Campaign. Lt. Gen. Thomas J. Jackson commanded the other corps.

4. Ezra J. Warner, *Generals in Gray* (Baton Rouge, 1959), p. 343.

5. Judge John W. Stevens, *Reminiscences of the Civil War* (Hillsboro, 1982, reprint; orig. pub. 1902), p. 66.

6. Robert K. Krick, *Lee's Colonels* (Dayton, 1984), p. 352.

7. Simpson, *Compendium*, p. 10. Rainey never returned to the regiment, but remained on the rolls as colonel until July 15, 1864. Because of this, Work, who deserved promotion to colonel, never received the title. (Krick, Lee's Colonels, p. 269)

8. Krick, *Lee's Colonels*, p. 94.

9. Simpson, *Compendium*, p. 11.

10. Samuel Thomas Blessing in *Reminiscences of the Boys in Gray, 1861-1865*, edited by Mamie Yeary (Dayton, 1986, reprint; orig. pub. 1912), p. 60.

11. Stevens, *Reminiscences*, p. 67; J.B. Polley, *Hood's Texas Brigade, Its Marches, Its Battles, Its Achievements* (Dayton, 1976, reprint; orig. pub. 1910), p. 115. W.R. Hamby, "Hood's Texas Brigade at Sharpsburg," *Confederate Veteran*, vol. 16 (1908), p. 19.

12. Watters Berryman to his mother, September 8, 1862, Texas-Confederate Collection, Confederate Research Center, Hillsboro, Texas. Material from the collection at the Confederate Research Center is hereinafter cited as CRC.

13. O.T. Hanks, *"History of Captain B.F. Benton's Company, 1861-1865,"* (unpublished manuscript, 1921), p. 20, CRC.

14. Ibid., p.20

15. Dr. John O. Scott, "Battle Flags of Hood's Texas Brigade," *Official Minutes of the Hood's Texas Brigade Monument Dedication and 39th Annual Reunion* (Houston, 1911), p. 349.

16. Val C. Giles, "The Flag of the First Texas, A. N. Virginia," *Confederate Veteran*, vol. 15, no. 9 (1907), p. 417.

17. Richard Rollins, *The Damned Red Flags of the Rebellion: The Capture of Confederate Battleflags at Gettysburg,* (Rank and File Publications: forthcoming).

18. General John B. Hood, *Advance and Retreat* (Seacacus, 1985, reprint; orig. pub. 1880), p. 39.

19. Polley, *Hood's Texas Brigade*, p. 114; Hood, *Advance and Retreat*, pp. 39-40; Stevens, *Reminiscences*, p. 69.

20. Hood, *Advance and Retreat*, pp. 40-41; Douglas S. Freeman, *Lee's Lieutenant's*, 3 vols. (New York, 1943), vol. 2, pp. 181-182.

21. Harold B. Simpson, ed., *Touched With Valor, The Civil War Papers of General Jerome B. Robertson* (Hillsboro, 1964), pp. 72-91. Robertson reported the casualties of the Texas regiments only.

22. The bridge at Shepherdstown was burned early in the war.

23. Hamby, "Hood's Texas Brigade at Sharpsburg," p. 19; W.E. Barry, "Dauntless Courage and Heroic Deeds," *Official Minutes of Hood's Texas Brigade Monument Dedication and 39th Annual Re-union* (Houston, 1911), p. 107.

24. Hood's report of the Battle of Sharpsburg, U.S. War Department, *The War of the Rebellion: The Official Records of the Union and Confederate Armies*, 128 vols. (Wash-

ington, D.C., 1880-1901), series I, vol. 19, pt.1, p. 922. Hereinafter cited as *OR* 19. All references are to series I unless otherwise noted.

25. James Longstreet, "The Invasion of Maryland," in Robert U. Johnson and Clarence C. Buel, eds., *Battles and Leaders of the Civil War,* 4 vols. (Secaucus, 1983, reprint), vol. 2 p. 667.

26. *OR* 19, p. 927.

27. *OR* 19, pp. 927, 929, 936-937; Hamby, "Hood's Texas Brigade," p. 19; Lt. Col. Philip A. Work, *The 1st Texas Regiment of the Texas Brigade of the Army of Northern Virginia at the Battles of Boonsboro Pass or Gap and Sharpsburg or Antietam, Maryland in September 1862,* (unpublished manuscript, 1907), pp. 2-3, CRC. Col. Work mistakenly merged the movement of Hood's Division on the afternoon of September 15th with the movement on the evening of September 16th (described herein).

28. George T. Todd, *First Texas Regiment* (Waco, 1963, reprint; orig. pub. 1909), p. 11.

29. Hood, *Advance and Retreat,* p. 41; Miles V. Smith, *Reminiscences of the Civil War* (unpublished manuscript, circa 1915), p. 20, CRC.

30. *OR* 19, p. 1007. General Jones assumed command of the division following the wounding of Gen. Taliaferro at Second Manassas; Taliaferro commanded the division after the death of Maj. Gen. Charles Winder at Cedar Mountain on August 9, 1862. During the Sharpsburg Campaign, Jones' Brigade was temporarily commanded by Capt. J.E. Penn and Taliaferro's Brigade was temporarily commanded by Col. James W. Jackson.

31. Ibid., p. 967. Lawton assumed command of the division following the wounding of Maj. Gen. Richard S. Ewell at Second Manassas. Colonel Douglas assumed temporary command of Lawton's Brigade while Lawton commanded the division. Colonel Walker temporarily commanded Brig. Gen. Isaac Trimble's Brigade after Trimble was wounded at Second Manassas.

32. Ibid., p. 844; Robert K. Krick, *Parker's Virginia Battery, C.S.A.* (Berryville, 1975), pp. 48-49.

33. *OR* 19, p. 1022.

34. Sgt. Austin C. Stearns, *Three Years with Company K,* edited by Arthur A. Kent (Rutherford, 1976), p. 125; Regimental History Commission, *History of the Third Pennsylvania Cavalry, Sixtieth Regiment Pennsylvania Volunteers in the American Civil War, 1861-1865* (Philadelphia, 1905), p. 120, hereinafter cited as *Third Pa. Cav.*

35. *Third Pa. Cav.* p. 122; *OR* 19, pp. 268-269, 937. The Regimental History Commission confused the Martin Line (mistakenly referred to as George Lyon) farm lane with the Samuel Poffenberger farm lane. It is not recorded when Law deployed his skirmishers, but it is likely they were put out soon after Hood moved his division to the Dunker Church area on the 15th.

36. *OR* 19, p. 937; Capt. Neill W. Ray, "Sixth Regiment," in *Histories of the Several Regiments and Battalions from North Carolina in the Great War, 1861-1865,* edited by Walter Clark (reprint, Wilmington, 1991, orig. pub. 1901), vol. 1, p. 307.

37. My interpretation of the movements of the Texas Brigade and Law are based on the assumption that the two brigades remained in about the same positions they had taken on the 15th, i.e., along the turnpike with Law on the left and the Texas Brigade on the right. I could find no evidence indicating the regiments did not remain in that order throughout the afternoon of the 15th and all day on the 16th. The movements on the evening of the 16th resulted in a reversal of the order of the two brigades, i.e., Law on the right of the Texas Brigade. Some post-war accounts (Hamby and Hood) describe the skirmish as if Hood's Division had been initially deployed in the order that they fought. I am assuming the writers either forgot about the original disposition of the brigades or they thought it unimportant to mention.

38. *OR* 19, pp. 845; Hood, *Advance and Retreat*, p. 42.

39. As is typical with Civil War battle accounts, virtually no two witnesses recorded the same time for a particular event. From the available sources, it can only be stated that the skirmish on the 16th started sometime between "sunset" and "just at dark." *OR* 19, pp. 927, 929, 936; Smith, *Reminiscences,* p. 20.

40. *OR* 19, pp. 269; *OR*, Series I, v. 51, pt. 1, Supplement, p. 153, hereinafter referred to as *OR* 51.

41. Hamby, "Hood's Texas Brigade," p. 19.

42. *OR* 51, pp. 149, 150, 153; Lt. Col. A.J. Warner, 10th Penn. Res., in "The Ordeal of Adoniram Judson Warner: His Minutes of South Mountain and Antietam," edited by James B. Casey, *Civil War History*, vol. 28 (1982), p. 221.

43. *OR* 51, pp. 150, 153, 155; *OR*, pp. 269, 273, 927; Work, *The 1st Texas at Sharpsburg,* p. 3. Meade deployed Lt. John G. Simpson's Battery A, Pennsylvania Light, on a ridge in rear of his division to counter Rhett's fire from the church.

44. *OR* 19, pp. 1007, 1009, 1012; Edward A. Moore, *The Story of a Cannoneer Under Stonewall Jackson* (Lynchburg, 1910), p. 147.

45. *OR* 19, pp. 927, 929, 937; Hood, *Advance and Retreat,* p. 42; Smith, *Reminiscences,* p. 20; John M. Priest, *Antietam: The Soldiers' Battle* (Shippensburg, PA, 1989), pp 14-22. Smith seems to have completely forgotten about the skirmish on the evening of the 16th. Priest offers a different interpretation of the movements of Hood's brigades.

46. *OR* 19, pp. 927, 936; Nicholas Pomeroy, *Memoirs of Nicholas Pomeroy, Co.A, 5th Texas Infantry,* (unpublished manuscript, circa 1915), p. 38, CRC. Pomeroy, who wrote his memoirs many years after the war, claimed that the 5th Texas charged through the woods and drove the enemy to the other side. Capt. Turner, commanding the 5th Texas, wrote in his official report that his regiment checked the enemy's advance with rifle fire and did not mention an advance into the woods. I accepted Capt. Turner's account.

47. *OR* 19, p. 937

48. Krick, *Parker's Virginia Battery,* p. 51.

49. "The Texans at Sharpsburg," *Confederate Veteran*, vol. 22 (1914), p. 555. This article was written by an anonymous member of the 4th Texas Infantry.

50. Work, *The 1st Texas at Sharpsburg,* p. 2; J. M. Gould to Capt. Wall (1st Texas), June 9, 1894, Antietam National Battlefield library, hereinafter referred to ANB.

51. Benjamin F. Cook, *History of the 12th Massachusetts Volunteers (Webster Regiment)* (Boston, 1882), pp. 71-72; J. M. Gould, letter, June 9, 1894, ANB. Capt. Ballenger is not mentioned by name by either Cook or Gould, but according to Simpson's *Compendium* (p. 84), Ballenger was the only 1st Texas captain captured at Sharpsburg.

52. *OR* 19, pp. 148, 927, 929, 939, 955, 967, 976. Confederate estimates of the time Jackson's men replaced Hood's varied between 9 o'clock and midnight.

53. Todd, *First Texas Regiment,* p. 11; Stevens, *Reminiscences,* p. 73; Pomeroy, *Memoirs,* p. 38; Hanks, *History of Captain Benton's Company,* p. 21.

54. *OR* 19, pp. 218, 975, 976; Moore, *Story of a Cannoneer,* p. 147.

55. Todd, *First Texas Regiment,* p. 11; Stevens, *Reminiscences,* p. 74; Smith, *Reminiscences,* p. 21; J.M. Polk, *The North and South American Review* (Austin, 1912) p. 14; *Confederate Veteran,* vol. 22 (1914), p. 555.

56. *OR* 19, p. 845; Krick, *Parker's Virginia Battery,* p. 52.

57. *OR* 19, pp. 223, 226-227.

58. Ibid., pp. 930, 936.

59. Ibid., pp. 968, 976; James V. Murfin, *The Gleam of Bayonets* (New York, 1965), p. 212. Federal battle reports do not specify the time of Hooker's attack. General Jubal Early and Col. James A. Walker of Jackson's Division reported the start of the Federal advance as sunrise. Official sunrise was 5:43 a.m.

60. *OR* 19, pp. 229, 262

61. *OR* 19, p. 845; Cope Map 2, ANB. The two guns were from Jordan's Battery.

62. Colonel Lyle assumed command of the brigade earlier in the morning after Colonel Christian succumbed to fear and departed the field.

63. Doubleday left one brigade behind as a reserve.

64. Overnight, two of Poague's three guns were replaced by two howitzers from Capt. C.J. Raines' Battery. Poague occupied two positions in the cloverfield and fired only a few rounds before retiring from the area. Cope Map 2 shows Capt. John B. Brockenbrough's battery in the cloverfield at this time, probably based on brief mentions in the official reports of Generals Jones and Jackson. I was unable to determine if Brockenbrough fired or when he retired. *OR* 19, p. 1008-1009, 1012; Cope Map 2, ANB.

65. *OR* 19, p. 244.

66. Ibid., p. 257.

67. Rufus R. Dawes, *Service with the Sixth Wisconsin Volunteers* (Dayton, 1984, reprint; orig. 1890), p. 90.

68. Ibid., p. 91.

69. Ibid., p. 227, 269; Cope Maps 3 and 4, ANB. Thompson advanced into the Cornfield to support Coulter's attack.

70. Dawes, *Service with the Sixth Wisconsin,* p. 91.

71. W.D. Pritchard, *Civil War Reminiscences* (unpublished manuscript, 1898), ANB. The manuscript has no page numbers.

72. Hood, *Advance and Retreat*, pp. 42-43; *OR* 19, pp. 930, 935, 937. Colonels Ruff and Carter stated that the order to advance came at 7 o'clock. Law estimated that the order came an hour and a half after the battle commenced. If Hooker's attack commenced at sunrise (5:43 a.m.), then Law's estimate was not far off.

73. Murfin, *Gleam of Bayonets*, p. 212.

74. This is my interpretation; the exact locations of Hood's brigades were not reported.

75. Hood stated in his official report that he "marched [his division] out on the field in line of battle," which suggests that both Law's Brigade and the Texas Brigade advanced through the woods in line. In *Advance and Retreat*, however, Hood described the advance as being by the right flank. It seems both accounts may have been half right. Law's official report stated that he deployed his brigade into line of battle *after* entering the open fields across the turnpike, which implies that his regiments were deployed in a column before entering the pasture. The official reports of Colonels Wofford, Gary, and Carter leave little doubt that the Texas Brigade was deployed in line of battle from the moment the advance commenced.

76. *OR* 19, p. 937.

77. Cope Map 3, ANB.

78. *OR* 19, pp. 932, 935; Autobiography of L. A. Daffan, in Katie Daffan, *My Father as I Remember Him*, United Daughters of the Confederacy publication, ca. 1906, p. 44.

79. *OR* 19, pp. 928, 932, 934-935.

80. W. T. Hill (5th Texas) to J. M. Gould, July 21, 1891, ANB.

81. Edward Stephen Welch to his parents, September 22, 1862, from Winchester, Va., Edward Stephen Welch Papers, Library of Congress. Welch was in the Hampton's Legion.

82. *OR* 19, p. 935; Hamby, "Hood's Texas Brigade," p. 19; Dawes, *Service with the Sixth Wisconsin*, p. 91. Dawes makes it clear that his men fired as they advanced.

83. *OR* 19, p. 935; Hamby, "Hood's Texas Brigade," p. 19; Pomeroy, *Memoirs*, p. 39.

84. *OR* 19, pp. 930, 931.

85. Dawes, *Service with the Sixth Wisconsin*, p. 91.

86. *OR* 51, pp. 148-150, 153, 155. J.M. Gould to Capt. Wall (1st Texas), June 7, 1894, ANB.

87. Cope maps 3 & 4, ANB.

88. *OR* 19, pp. 928, 930.

89. Ibid., pp 928, 932.

90. Ibid., pp. 935, 936; *Confederate Veteran*, vol. 22 (1914), p. 555. Carter reported that his regiment came up behind the 11th Mississippi. The 5th Texas may have been in the field south of the Smoketown Road.

91. Pritchard, *Civil War Reminiscences*.

92. The length of the battleline is based on 232 men present in the regiment, not including field grade officers. If about 72 were company officers and NCO's in the line of file closers, then the remaining 160 men, each two feet wide, in two ranks of 80 men each, would occupy a line 160 feet long. Sixteen inches between ranks was recommended for a battleline that is advancing (*Rifle and Light Infantry Tactics,* W.J. Hardee, published in 1861 by J.B. Lippincott and Co. of Philadelphia.)

93. Work, *The 1st Texas at Sharpsburg*, pp. 4-5; Krick, *Lee's Colonels*, p. 351. Woodward was mortally wounded at Gettysburg.

94. Daffan, *Autobiography*, p. 45.

95. Ibid.

96. Dawes, *Service with the Sixth Wisconsin,* p. 95.

97. *OR* 19, pp. 931, 932. Colonels Gary and Work reported that they engaged the enemy *in* the corn. Major Dawes of the 6th Wisconsin, however, did not mention in his memoirs a stand in the Cornfield. Most likely, the stand was made by just a portion of the retreating Federals. The retreating tide of Federal infantry also took Thompson's battery with them.

98. Lt. Col. E. S. Bragg to E.A. Carmen, Dec. 26, 1894, ANB. Campbell's four remaining guns joined Stewart's section near the Miller Barn at about the time Hood launched his attack.

99. *OR* 19, p. 932; Work, *The 1st Texas at Sharpsburg*, p. 4. Hanks lost his leg as a result of his wound.

100. Todd, *First Texas Regiment,* p. 11.

101. John Wilson, in Yeary, *Reminiscences of the Boys in Gray,* p. 808.

102. Pritchard, *Civil War Reminiscences.*

103. *OR* 19, pp. 932, 934; *OR, v. LI*, pp. 150-151, 154; Gould, letter, June 7, 1894, ANB. The 11th Pennsylvania was immediately in front of the 1st Texas.

104. *OR* 19, p. 932; Cope Map 4, ANB.

105. Ibid., p. 932.

106. Ibid., pp. 229, 928, 930; John Gibbon, *Personal Recollections of the Civil War* (Dayton, 1978, reprint; orig. pub. 1928), p. 83.

107. *OR* 19, pp. 269-270, 274; Sears, *Landscape Turned Red,* p. 200.

108. *OR* 19, p. 938; James Steptoe Johnston, letter, September 22, 1862, Mercer Green Steptoe Collection, Library of Congress. Oddly, in reporting on Law's attack, neither Law nor Hood remembered to mention advancing into or through the Cornfield.

109. *OR* 19, p. 936.

110. Ibid., pp. 929, 935.

111. Ibid., pp. 935, 258; Daffan, *Autobiography*, p. 45. Carter's official report does not jibe well with those of Colonels Gary and Ruff of the Hampton's Legion and the 18th Georgia. Carter said he encountered enemy fire in his front from the Cornfield as well from across the pike. But Gary and Ruff clearly indicated they were in the Cornfield next to the pike. It seems unlikely that Carter would have wheeled his regiment up to the turnpike fences if doing so would have exposed the right flank of his regiment to enemy

fire from out of the corn. Daffan's post-war account confuses the matter further. He remembered the charge of the 4th Texas as being "directly to the west" up to the turnpike fences.

112. Hanks, *History of Captain Benton's Company*, p. 21; Barry, "Dauntless Courage," p. 107; E. Scott Carson, "Hampton's Legion and Hood's Texas Brigade," *Confederate Veteran*, vol. 16 (1908), p. 342.

113. *OR* 19, p. 933.

114. Watters H. Berryman to his mother, September 22, 1862, from "Camp near Martinsburg, Va.," ANB. Capt. Cotton died on September 31, 1862. Sgt. Mitchell, who survived his wound, was the grandfather of *Gone with the Wind* author Margaret Mitchell (Simpson, *Compendium*, pp. 64, 69).

115. Hanks, *History of Captain Benton's Company*, pp. 21-22.

116. *OR* 19, pp. 244, 258; J. R. Putnam, "Patrick's Brigade," *National Tribune*, April 30, 1908.

117. Carson, "Hampton's Legion," p. 342.

118. Welch, letter, Sept. 22, 1862.

119. Ibid.; Dawes, *Service with the Sixth Wisconsin*, p. 91.

120. Polk, *North and South American Review*, p. 15.

121. *Confederate Veteran*, vol. 22 (1914), p. 555.

122. Barry, "Dauntless Courage," p. 107.

123. *OR* 19, p. 932; Work, *1st Texas at Sharpsburg*, p. 4.

124. Work, *1st Texas at Sharpsburg*, p. 5.

125. Ibid., p. 5.

126. *OR* 19, pp. 933-934. In his post-war manuscript Work stated that he personally withdrew the right wing of the regiment.

127. *OR* 51, pp. 151, 154-155.

128. *OR* 19, p. 933; Barry, "Dauntless Courage," p. 107.

129. D.H. Hamilton, *History of Company M, First Texas Infantry, Hood's Brigade* (Waco, 1962; orig. pub. 1925) pp. 23-24; Simpson, *Compendium*, p. 85.

130. F. Halsey Wigfall to Sen. L.T. Wigfall, October 4, 1862, from "Camp near Winchester, Va.", ANB.

131. Cope Map 4, ANB; *OR* 19, pp. 244, 258, 930; Dawes, *Service with the Sixth Wisconsin*, p. 92. The 7th Wisconsin was passed over by Patrick's line a few minutes earlier and did not advance to the pike. The regiment retired a short distance to the rear.

132. *OR* 19, p. 930.

133. Ibid., p. 931.

134. Ibid., p. 935.

135. Ibid., p. 928.

136. Welch, letter, September 22, 1862; James Steptoe Johnston, "A Reminiscence of Sharpsburg," *Southern Historical Society Papers*, vol. 8 (1880), p. 527.

137. Ray, "Sixth Regiment," p. 308; *OR* 19, p. 270.

138. Watters H. Berryman, letter, September 22, 1862.

139. Blessing, in Yeary, *Reminiscences of the Boys in Gray*, pp. 60-61. The scenario presented here for the loss of the 1st Texas colors is my interpretation based on official reports and several post-war accounts by 1st Texans and others, none of which contain a full eyewitness account of all of the events surrounding the loss of the colors. Scott, in "Battle Flags of Hood's Texas Brigade," p. 349, provides a second-hand account. See Barry, "Dauntless Courage," p.108, for the number of Texans found lying near the flags.

140. *OR* 51, p. 151, 154-155, 1042; *OR, v. XIX, pt. 2*, p. 729; 50th Congress, 1st Session, House of Representatives, Ex. Doc. No. 163, "Captured Battle Flags," pp. 19-20, nos. 103 and 110. Pvt. Samuel Johnson of Company G, 9th Pennsylvania Reserves, who was himself wounded in the Cornfield, was later awarded the Medal of Honor and a commission for capturing the flags (Military Service Records of Samuel Johnson, Co. G, 9th Penn. Res. Inf., National Archives, Washington D.C.) There were others who claimed the capture of the 1st Texas colors. After the war, Colonel Bragg of the 6th Wisconsin claimed that a man in his regiment captured the 1st Texas colors "during the last stand of the 6th," but that the flag was laid aside and later picked up by a soldier of the 80th New York (Lt. Col. E. S. Bragg to Col. E.A. Carmen, Dec. 24, 1894, ANB). The commander of the 80th New York, in his official report of the battle, claimed his regiment captured a Confederate battleflag in the Cornfield, but did not specify that it belonged to the 1st Texas (*OR* 19, pp. 246-7). If the 6th Wisconsin captured a flag that eventually ended up with the 80th New York, it is likely the flag was captured from a regiment in Lawton's Division when the 6th Wisconsin was in the pasture south of the Cornfield. After the war, Benjamin Cook of the 12th Massachusetts Infantry wrote a history of his unit in which he quoted another member of his regiment who claimed to have seen after the battle a 1st Texas flag captured by Hartsuff's brigade (Cook, *The Webster Regiment*, p. 73). The flag the soldier saw may have been one of the 1st Texas flags captured in the Cornfield, but it most certainly was not captured by any of the regiments in Hartsuff's brigade.

141. *OR* 19, p. 933.

142. Work, *The 1st Texas at Sharpsburg*, pp. 5-6.

143. *OR* 19, p. 251; Putnam, "Patrick's Brigade," *National Tribune*; Cope Map 5, ANB.

144. Work, *The 1st Texas at Sharpsburg*, p. 6.

145. Ibid., pp. 6-7.

146. *OR* 19, p. 251.

147. Ibid., p. 251; Cope Map 4, ANB; Sears, *Landscape Turned Red*, p. 205.

148. Work, *1st Texas at Sharpsburg*, pp. 7-8.

149. *OR* 19, pp. 251-252; *OR* 51, p. 151. The Confederate fire from the West Woods was most likely from fragments of Jones' and Lawton's divisions that had rallied.

150. *OR* 51, pp. 151, 154-5.

151. Work, *1st Texas Infantry*, p. 8; Johnston, "A Reminiscence," p. 528.

152. *OR* 19, pp. 928, 935, 938; Hamby, "Hood's Texas Brigade," p. 20; Work, *1st Texas Infantry*, p. 8; Johnston, "A Reminiscence," p. 528.

153. Hood, *Advance and Retreat*, p. 44; Hamby, "Hood's Texas Brigade," p. 20.

154. *OR* 19, p. 928; Carson, "Hampton's Legion," p. 342.

155. Cope Map 8, ANB.

156. *OR* 19, pp. 923, 938, 979; Hamby, "Hood's Texas Brigade," p. 20; *Confederate Veteran*, vol. 16 (1922), p. 555; Cope Map 10, ANB.

157. *OR* 19, pp. 923, 928, 938; Confederate Veteran, vol. 16 (1922), p. 555; Pomeroy, *Memoirs*, p. 43.

158. Todd, *First Texas Regiment*, p. 11.

159. Johnston, letter, September 22, 1862.

160. Lt. Col. E.S. Bragg to his wife, September 21, 1862, ANB.

161. *Confederate Veteran*, vol. 16 (1922), p. 555.

162. Simpson, *Compendium*, p. 535, Chart III.

163. Berryman, letter, September 22, 1862.

164. I have taken the average of the numbers reported in *Battles and Leaders*, vol. 2, p. 603, which were compiled from the *Official Records*, and the number reported in Sears, *Landscape Turned Red*, p. 296, which were taken from "History of the Antietam Campaign," Ezra A. Carman Papers, Library of Congress. The Confederate losses reported in Thomas L. Livermore's *Numbers and Losses in the Civil War in America: 1861-1865* (Millwood, KY, 1977, reprint; orig. pub. 1900) are most likely too high. For Union losses, which amounted to about 12,400, see *Battles and Leaders*, vol. 2, p. 600; Livermore, *Numbers and Losses*, p. 92; and William F. Fox, *Regimental Losses in the American Civil War* (Dayton, 1985, reprint; orig. pub. 1898) p. 541.

165. *OR* 19, p. 811.

166. Fox, *Regimental Losses*, p. 558.

167. Ibid., p. 556.

168. *OR* 19, p. 811. 1st Texas losses are from the official report of Surgeon Lafayette Guild, Medical Director of the Army of Northern Virginia. Col. Work officially reported losses of 182 out of 226 present. In a February 13, 1891 letter to Major Robert Burns, Work remembered losses of 132. In the same letter, Work also recalled that about 15 men were absent from the regiment at the time of the battle, which would mean that 211 were engaged in the battle rather than 226. Since Work's memory failed him in battle losses, I chose not to trust his memory completely as to total engaged. It can probably be proved that nearly every regiment went into battle with a few men more or less than officially reported.

169. Simpson, *Compendium*, p. 535, Chart III.

170. *OR* 19, pp. 810-13.

171. Simpson, *Compendium*, p. 532

172. *OR* 19, p. 933. Italics added.

173. Barry, "Dauntless Courage," p. 108.

174. Pvt. Blessing was paroled to his family's house in Maryland to recover from his wound, was exchanged later in the year and eventually rejoined the regiment (Blessing, in Yeary, p. 61). While in the hospital at Antietam, Pvt. Hanks saw Abraham Lincoln

during the President's visit to the Army of the Potomac. He was paroled shortly afterward, was later exchanged and rejoined the regiment (Hanks, *History of Captain Benton's Company*, pp. 23-24).

175. When Lee's army was reorganized in October 1862, the 18th Georgia and Hampton's Legion were transferred to other brigades and the 3rd Arkansas was assigned to the Texas Brigade. There were no other changes to the Texas Brigade during the war.

176. Simpson, *Compendium*, p. 535, Chart III.

177. Ibid., p. 533, Chart I.

178. Berryman, letter, September 22, 1862.

179. Giles, "The Flag of the First Texas," *Confederate Veteran*, vol.

". . .they stood amidst a shower of musketry for nearly 3 hours."

"A Dear Bought Name"

The 7th West Virginia Infantry's Assault on Bloody Lane

David W. Mellott

The 7th West Virginia Infantry is one of the great unknown regiments of the Civil War. Melodramatically self-styled the "Bloody Seventh" long before they had seen much real blood, the tough farmers comprising this overlooked unit fought in more battles and suffered more losses than any other regiment from West Virginia by the end of the Civil War. Little publicized and largely ignored, they compiled an excellent combat record that compares favorably with the more renowned regiments of the conflict.[1]

Some confusion surrounds the name of the regiment. Until the end of 1862, the 7th West Virginia was known variously as the "7th Regiment Virginia Volunteers," the "7th Regiment Virginia Infantry," the "7th Regiment Virginia Volunteer Infantry," the "7th Virginia Regiment," the "7th Virginia Infantry," the "Seventh Virginia Volunteers" or simply the "Seventh Virginia." Complicating the matter was the existence of a Confederate "7th Virginia" infantry regiment that served in the Army of Northern Virginia (and fought at Antietam). Misunderstanding engendered by the designation "7th Virginia" enhanced the danger to which the Union volunteers examined in this study were exposed, subjecting them on one occasion to "friendly" fire from their own troops. As a result, the regiment's name was officially changed to the "Seventh Union Virginia Volunteers" in December, 1862. With the advent of West Virginia statehood six months later in June 1863, the regiment became more commonly known as the "7th West Virginia." For the purpose of clarity, that is the name used in the present essay, although at the time of the Battle of Antietam, the regiment was called the "7th Virginia."[2]

Before the Battle of Antietam there was little to distinguish the 7th West Virginia. The men's first year of service was unremarkable and did not fully prepare them for the trial they would face in front of a sunken farm lane near Sharpsburg, Maryland on a warm September 17, 1862.

A distinguished-looking Morgantown politician by the name of James Evans organized the Seventh during the summer and fall of 1861 and at 51 years of age became its first colonel. Most of his recruits were (West) Virginians living in the counties of Preston, Monongalia, Marshall, Ohio, Tyler and Hardy who refused to follow the Commonwealth into secession and remained faithful to the Federal government. Several companies, however, were recruited in nearby Monroe County, Ohio, and Greene County, Pennsylvania. According to a post-war address by a former officer of the Seventh, these Ohioans and Pennsylvanians crossed the border to serve with the 7th West Virginia in furtherance of assurances of aid that had been given the Western Virginians to encourage their loyalty to the Union. In other words, by helping to ensure the fidelity of Western Virginia, the Seventh's Ohio and Pennsylvania soldiers hoped to establish a more secure buffer between their homes and families on the one hand and a rebellious Virginia on the other.[3]

The typical 7th West Virginia soldier was a 25-year-old farmer. At least 70% of the men who signed the rolls worked the land for a living. Most of the rest were men who today would be considered blue-collar workers: carpenters, mechanics, shoemakers, blacksmiths and coopers, to name a few. A handful were teachers, and two were professionals.[4]

Despite the prevailing Union sentiment in Western Virginia, the ranks of the Seventh filled slowly, and the regiment was not fully assembled until early 1862. This did not reflect a want of zeal among those Union men eligible for military service. To be sure, the initial rush of patriotic fervor at the outset of the war had subsided by the time the recruitment of the regiment began. The hill country of Western Virginia was sparsely settled, however, and this limited pool of manpower was reduced by those inhabitants of the border area who supported the Confederate cause. Of the remaining Union men, a number probably were reluctant to leave farm and family to the depredations of bushwhackers and armed secessionists who were routinely reported to be committing outrages on the loyal citizenry. A shortage of arms and equipment, competition from other regiments and the approach of cold weather late in the year also tended to dampen the influx of recruits to Colonel Evans' regiment.[5]

The 7th West Virginia's early service was confined to the backwaters of the war in Western Virginia. Contingents from the regiment took part in several

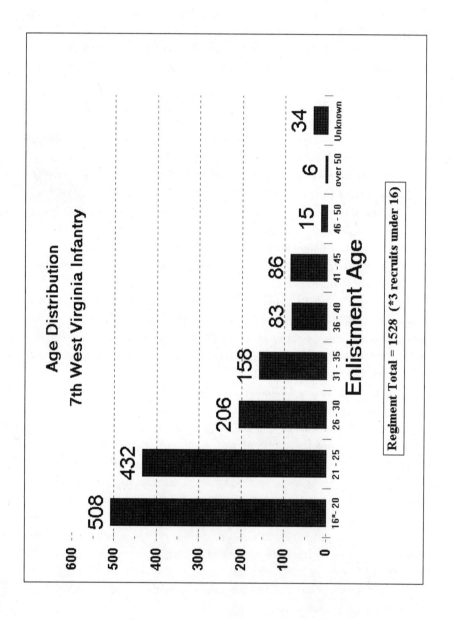

Age Distribution
7th West Virginia Infantry

Enlistment Age

Regiment Total = 1528 (*3 recruits under 16)

police actions designed to quell local unrest resulting from the area's conflicting political sympathies. During one of these expeditions, men from the Seventh gunned down the notorious Zach Cochran, a Confederate sympathizer and former sheriff of Taylor County. The regiment also served with the force assigned to protect the Baltimore and Ohio Railroad. The men participated in skirmishes at Romney, (West) Virginia on October 26, 1861 and Bloomery Gap, (West) Virginia on February 14, 1862, both aimed at driving the Confederates away from that important east-west artery.[6]

In April 1862, the soldiers of the 7th West Virginia took their first step toward a bigger arena, leaving behind the dull duty of guarding the railroad. Assigned to the division of Gen. James Shields, the regiment followed the main body of Shields' force up the Shenandoah Valley, vainly searching for the elusive "Stonewall" Jackson. When Jackson no longer appeared to be a threat, Shields' division was transferred to General McDowell's command at Fredericksburg as part of the buildup for the planned advance on Richmond. Suddenly Jackson re-appeared in the Valley, striking with fury and driving the Federals still there back across the Potomac River. Colonel Evans' men swiftly countermarched to the Valley and again found themselves pursuing the wily Confederate commander. Although a portion of Shields' force finally caught up with Jackson, it was repulsed near Port Republic. The men of the 7th West Virginia missed the fighting altogether and had the unenviable distinction of counting themselves among the thousands of Federal troops that Jackson had successfully held in the Valley and denied to the "On to Richmond" movement.[7]

With Jackson's Valley Campaign at an end, Shields' division was broken up, the West Virginians were transferred to the Army of the Potomac on the Peninsula. The Seventh, as part of Gen. Nathan Kimball's independent western brigade, which included the 4th and 8th Ohio Infantry and the 14th Indiana Infantry, arrived aboard the steamer *Georgia* at Harrison's Landing in early July, 1862, just after Malvern Hill had concluded the Seven Days' fighting. The Army of the Potomac was by far the largest assemblage of military manpower of which the 7th West Virginia yet had been a part. Moving to the front shortly after touching shore, Kimball's men skirmished with J. E. B. Stuart's horse artillery on Evlington Heights from where the Confederate cavalry commander had imprudently shelled McClellan's huddled army.[8]

Sweltering from the heat and plagued by clouds of flies, many of the Seventh's soldiers sickened during their stay on the Peninsula before McClellan withdrew his idle army from the unhealthy setting. A year and a half later, the 7th

West Virginia's Maj. Jonathan Lockwood wrote of the unit's miserable time at Harrison's Landing:

> Here we remained amid the unhealthy swamps of the peninsula using bad water and drinking the meanest kind of whiskey through the hot weather, nearly eaten up by flies by day and mosquitoes by night, here also that deadly enemy to the soldier in camp, chronic diarrhea, broke among us, carrying away many of our brave boys, rendering many more unfit for duty and to the present day the poison of it still lingers in the systems of many.[9]

This widespread illness would seriously weaken the 7th West Virginia for the upcoming Maryland Campaign.

Having evacuated the Peninsula, Kimball's brigade steamed northward toward the Washington defenses in August 1862. The 7th West Virginia took passage aboard the *Illinois*. If McClellan was not going to use his men to fight, President Lincoln reasoned that maybe Federal Gen. John Pope would, and so he ordered part of the Army of the Potomac attached to Pope's command. Kimball's men, however, only arrived in time to advance to the front and help cover the retreat of Pope's defeated Army of Virginia from the licking it had received at Second Bull Run. If the men of the 7th West Virginia were beginning to wonder about these Eastern armies, they left no record of it.[10]

Disposing of Pope enabled Gen. Robert E. Lee to speedily launch his offensive into Maryland during the first week of September. By invading, Lee aimed to encourage both the pro-Southern element of Maryland and the peace faction of the North, as well as relieve war-weary Virginia for awhile and better provision his troops off the bountiful Northern countryside. By winning a battle, Lee might even earn foreign recognition of the Confederacy.[11]

The 7th West Virginia and the rest of old Gen. Edwin "Bull" Sumner's II Corps, which were back under McClellan's control after their short-lived duty with Pope, took up a leisurely pursuit of the Confederates northwestward toward Frederick, Maryland. September 5 was a fine day for marching as Kimball's brigade, probably with some regret, stepped out onto the Frederick City Pike, leaving behind the brief comfort and safety afforded by their proximity to Washington. The brigade made 10 miles and entered camp in a peach orchard a mile and a half or so beyond Rockville at 10:00 that night.[12]

During the march into Maryland, several questions hovered among the men of the 7th West Virginia. Foremost was how they would perform in a major battle. The men were seasoned, but like many had not yet "seen the elephant" in a significant way beyond some skirmishes. They definitely would need good

Colonel Joseph Snider,
commander of the 7th West Virginia Infantry at the Battle of Antietam.

Loyal West Virginia from 1861 to 1865

leadership, but the campaign was beginning with several command and organizational changes that created uncertainty about that leadership and the fighting power of the brigade.

The most important change was that the 7th West Virginia received a new colonel heading into the impending collision with Lee's determined fighters. The previous month, while the West Virginians, Ohioans and Pennsylvanians of the regiment were falling prey to disease in their wretched camp at Harrison's Landing, Col. James Evans himself became so ill that he was unable to discharge his field duties and resigned his commission. He was replaced by another, younger Morgantown politician, the 35-year-old Joseph Snider, who was commissioned colonel on August 22 to rank from August 20. The oval-faced Snider was a Stephen Douglas Democrat, decidedly against secession, but he had no prior military experience. Whether Snider could provide the competent battlefield leadership his men would need remained to be seen.[13]

Shortly after Snider filled the vacant colonelcy, a new vacuum in the regimental leadership arose when Lt. Col. John G. Kelley, a son of Gen. Benjamin F. Kelley (commander of the Union Department of West Virginia) resigned effective September 10, 1862. Kelley's departure, which came less than two weeks after his 26th birthday, was for medical reasons and not due to a fit of pique over being passed over for colonel. He suffered from "typhoid pneumonia" contracted in the Cheat River Valley, and a leg injury sustained at Romney back in Western Virginia.[14]

At the brigade level, another unpromising development occurred when Kimball lost the services of one of his seasoned regiments, the 4th Ohio, during the march into Maryland because of epidemic sickness. The Buckeyes returned to Washington where their numerous sick could recuperate. The regiment was replaced by the 132d Pennsylvania Infantry, whose ranks were full of green nine-month volunteers. In the action looming ahead, the 7th West Virginia would find themselves fighting alongside these untried men who were an unknown quantity until they smelled powder.[15]

Further restructuring took place when Kimball's brigade was assigned to the newly-created Third Division of the II Corps. Kimball's men, denominated the "First Brigade," formed the nucleus of the new division commanded by Brig. Gen. William H. French. Known as "Old Blink Eye" for his distracting habit of constantly blinking, the red-faced and bad-tempered French was bald and bearded at 47 years of age. He had been classmates at West Point with Confederates Braxton Bragg, Jubal Early and John Pemberton. French fought against the Seminoles in Florida and later served in Mexico where he was brevetted captain and major for gallantry and meritorious conduct. When North and South split, French was on garrison duty in Texas, and in defiance of his Southern commanding officer, he successfully managed to extract his command from the Lone Star State.[16]

Practically the only constant in command as far as the 7th West Virginia was concerned was Brig. Gen. Nathan Kimball, who had led the brigade though the travails of the Valley and the Peninsula. He had been a doctor in civilian life back in Indiana. A veteran of the Mexican War in which he had served as a captain of volunteers, Kimball became colonel of the 14th Indiana on June 7, 1861 and served at Cheat Mountain in Western Virginia that fall. He commanded Shields' division at the battle of Kernstown in March, 1862, and was one of the few men who could say he had beaten "Stonewall" Jackson. Kimball's victory at Kernstown earned him a brigadier's star. Now 39 years of age, the general had something of a shaggy, wind-blown appearance with hair that swept up and back from the forehead and flared out over his protruding ears, wide, tired-looking eyes under heavy askew eyebrows and a broad nose above a full beard that hid the mouth.[17]

While the re-organizational shuffling was underway, McClellan, true to form, advanced cautiously through Maryland. On September 10, the 7th West Virginia marched only six miles toward Frederick. Proceeding via Clarksburg (Maryland), the West Virginians covered another 11 miles on September 11th. Twelve more miles on September 12 brought the regiment to Monocacy Junction in the charming valley of the Monocacy River, where the men encamped on ground that had been used very recently by a soldiers of the Army of Northern Virginia to slaughter beef. Although rain during the latter part of the day had quelled the suffocating dust along the line of march, it made for wet beds that night which were further fouled by the sickening stench of offal.[18]

On the morning of September 13, Kimball's men entered Frederick, festively draped everywhere with the national colors, and were enthusiastically greeted by the happy, handkerchief-waving townsfolk who a few days earlier saw the passing of the thousands of Confederate soldiers. Invigorated by the warm welcome, Kimball's men passed through and bivouacked half a mile beyond the town near the reservoir, just a few miles from the foot of Catoctin Mountain.[19]

Early the next morning, September 14, the Battle of South Mountain began as the plodding McClellan, invariably greeted by cheers from his men, tried to force Turner's and Crampton's Gaps to get at Lee's scattered army. The II Corps did not participate in this engagement, but came up to occupy a position in reserve. Breaking camp at daylight on the Sabbath, Kimball's men initially took the Hagerstown pike, but in order to remain concealed from the Confederates, they soon moved cross-country along with the rest of the II Corps through the fields on the right of the pike to the base of Catoctin Mountain, which was the first range of hills to the east of South Mountain. The day was fair and warm. As the morning's fighting for the South Mountain gaps wore on, Kimball's men and the II Corps zig-zagged up Catoctin Mountain. They climbed the wooded eastern slope along a bridle path, listening to the heavy thudding of artillery fire from beyond. After the winded men reached the top, they finally came within view of the action that up to that point they had only been able to hear. Then an odd thing happened. A temporary acoustical shadow muted the explosive sounds of the contest so that the spectators of Kimball's brigade could now see, but not hear, the fighting. Watching from the crest, they beheld a strangely silent tableau of the distant battle in the valley below and on the face of South Mountain where miniature troops and batteries swept to the assault amid curtains of smoke from cannon and musketry.

As the II Corps continued its advance toward the fighting, some of Kimball's brigade enjoyed the fruits of the land. They raided orchards of ripe apples and peaches along the line of march, and when a halt was called, the men were again fortunate to find themselves amidst a patch of potatoes, which they soon were cooking.

Within two miles of Turner's Gap, the II Corps formed a reserve battle line along a ridge and rested. Around sunset, the II Corps moved up to support West Virginia native Gen. Jesse Reno who had carried Fox's Gap on the left of Turner's Gap. As night fell, the fighting died out, but a brilliant moon bathed the corpses of the fallen in an eerie light. After midnight, having marched 10 miles for the day, the 7th West Virginia and the rest of Kimball's men finally entered a crowded and uncomfortable bivouac among the dead at the gap and rested on their arms while the stretcher bearers and ambulances worked through the night carrying away their grisly loads.[20]

On Monday, September 15, McClellan's native caution continued to hold the Army of the Potomac back. Instead of lunging forward and coming to grips with the pieces of Lee's divided command, McClellan advanced his army tentatively. Kimball's men rose at dawn, and after cleaning and inspecting arms and receiving 60 rounds of fresh ammunition, they struck out about 6:00 a.m. toward Boonsboro at the western foot of South Mountain. French's division followed Richardson's and Sedgwick's divisions of the II Corps through the gap, striding toward the boom of artillery fire at the front. Around noon, Kimball's men halted for a couple of hours, then came up on Richardson's left at Boonsboro.

The only live Confederates encountered by Kimball's men were either prisoners already or were among the wounded occupying some Boonsboro houses which had been appropriated by the Confederates for use as field hospitals. The Confederate rear guard had fallen back on Sharpsburg and as night fell II Corps pursued them southward down the Shepherdstown road. The hot day's march concluded after dark, a mile beyond Keedysville, where the men entered camp under cover of the reverse slope of a low ridge bordering Antietam Creek. After enjoying a cup of coffee, they slept on their arms again.[21]

French's division, compactly massed by brigades, mainly spent the day of September 16 under the relatively protected lee side of the ridge, while the Union artillery posted along the crest of the ridge sparred with the Confederate artillery occupying the high ground on the opposite side of the creek toward Sharpsburg. The right of Kimball's brigade rested on the pike near the middle bridge. Kimball's men, under orders to remain near their stacked arms, lied low, so to speak, throughout the day, talking, eating and gambling, while some curious souls snuck peeks at the artillery duel. Most sought to keep their minds off what promised to come, but as night closed in and the artillery fire died down, the camp became deathly still as the thoughts of the men turned inward. They were about to see the elephant.[22]

Under orders to remain quiet and not to light any fires so as to avoid disclosing their position, the men tried to rest in spite of gnawing anxiety and rain that fell during the night. Such sleep as they managed to get was short-lived. Kimball's men were quietly awakened early, and roll call was taken at 3:00 a. m. Still packed together with the other brigades of French's division, Kimball's men then waited expectantly in readiness as the tension mounted with the growing of dawn on what would become the bloodiest single day in American military history.

As soon as it became light enough to draw a bead on the enemy, Maj. Gen. Joe Hooker's I Corps on the right opened the Battle of Antietam by striking Lee's left. At 7:20 a.m., Sumner received orders to take II Corps across Antietam Creek and move to Hooker's support. About 10 minutes later, French's division, following Sedgwick's division of II Corps, was in motion to the right. Retracing their steps back to the vicinity of Keedysville, Kimball's brigade turned left and descended the eastern bank of the Antietam close to two miles from the prior night's camp. Crossing the waist-deep creek at one of the fords downstream of Pry's Mill and passing the Meyer spring, Kimball's soggy-footed men, constituting the right column of the division, neared the battlefield. According to the admittedly nervous soldier-historian of the 132d Pennsylvania, a "deafening pandemonium of cannonading, with shrieking and bursting shells, filled the air beyond," and volleys of musketry "sounded in the distance like the rapid pouring of shot upon a tinpan, or the tearing of heavy canvas, with slight pauses interspersed with single shots, or desultory shooting."[23]

Behind a screen of woods about a mile from the ford, French faced his division left in three successive lines of battle about 8:00 a. m. Weber's brigade, which had only served garrison duty, comprised the first line. Morris' brigade of green recruits made up the second, and Kimball's brigade of seasoned veterans and rookies formed the third line in the rear.

By this time, Sumner had lost control of II Corps. Impetuously leading Sedgwick's division headlong into action directly westward, Sumner outdistanced French's division, leaving "Old Blink Eye" on his own. By the time French's out-of-touch division formed in line of battle, its commander could only guess where Sedgwick's left was. Moving forward through the trees over rocky, broken ground, French's men veered southwest toward the Roulette farm buildings, only widening the gap on Sedgwick's unprotected left.

The clear, warm morning was about to become an inferno. Following 100 yards behind Morris' untried and undrilled brigade, Kimball's men had advanced three quarters of a mile when Weber in front first made contact with the Confederates. Weber's men cleaned the Confederates out of the area around the Roulette buildings, and the butternut-clad defenders tumbled back to higher ground.[24]

French ordered Kimball to pass Morris' raw brigade, which had become disorganized, and form at the front on Weber's left. Kimball rode along the line, consisting from right to left of the 14th Indiana, 8th Ohio, 132d Pennsylvania and 7th West Virginia, and told his men, "Now boys, we are going, and we'll stay with them all day if they want us to!" Kimball's men fixed bayonets and moved forward under fire.[25]

Depleted by illness, the 7th West Virginia only carried about 300 muskets into the fight. Seven companies were without captains, leaving their lieutenants in charge. Company C was commanded by Lt. James Swartz and Company K by Lt. Benjamin Shriver. Company D apparently could not even muster a lieutenant to direct the men and had to borrow Lt. F. M. Roberts of Company H.[26]

The advancing line was divided into two segments (or as Kimball termed them, "wings") by the Roulette farm lane. From this lane the 8th Ohio and 14th Indiana extended the line to the right and the 132d Pennsylvania and 7th West Virginia extended it to the left. The Roulette lane formed the stem of a crude capital "T" which up ahead was crossed by a sunken road held by the Confeder-

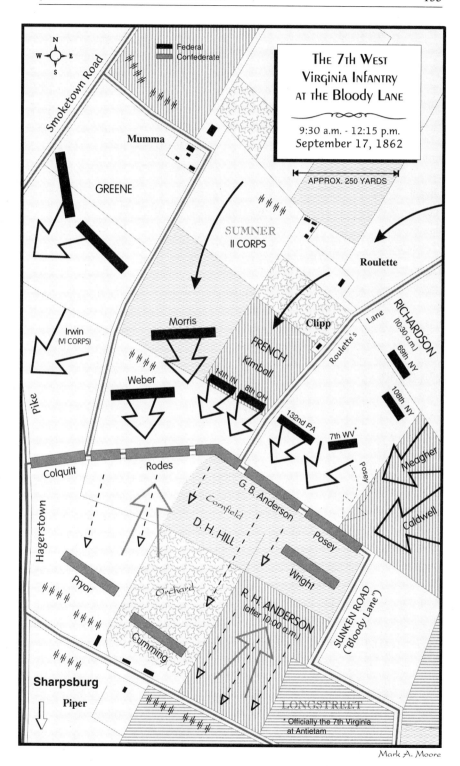

The 7th West Virginia Infantry at the Bloody Lane

9:30 a.m. - 12:15 p.m.
September 17, 1862

APPROX. 250 YARDS

Federal
Confederate

Smoketown Road

N
W · E
S

Mumma

GREENE

SUMNER
II CORPS

Roulette

Irwin
(VI CORPS)

Morris

Clipp

FRENCH
Kimball

Roulette's Lane

RICHARDSON
(10:30 a.m.)

69th NY

108th NY

Pike

Weber

14th IN   8th OH

132nd PA

7th WV*

Meagher

Colquitt

Rodes

G. B. Anderson

Posey

Caldwell

Hagerstown

Cornfield

D. H. HILL

Posey

Pryor

Orchard

Wright

SUNKEN ROAD
("Bloody Lane")

Cumming

R. H. ANDERSON
(after 10:00 a.m.)

Sharpsburg

Piper

LONGSTREET

*Officially the 7th Virginia
at Antietam

Mark A. Moore

ates. The sunken road, afterwards known as "Bloody Lane," lay just beyond the crest of the higher ground that rose on either side of the lane in front of the brigade. As Kimball's brigade advanced up the stem of the T, it approached the crest, its line roughly parallel with the Confederate position.[27]

Moving forward on the 7th West Virginia's right, the rookie soldiers of the 132d Pennsylvania were temporarily disconcerted by a sudden stinging attack from an unexpected quarter. The unlikely aggressors were a swarm of angry bees whose hives had been knocked over as the soldiers of the Keystone State advanced.[28] As the right of Kimball's line cleared the Roulette buildings and orchard, Kimball gave the order to charge. The brigade went forward at the double quick, unleashed a volley and won the crest of the rise in front of the sunken road. As Kimball's line reached the crest, they entered the gun sights of the Confederate defenders packed in the sunken road and the cornfield beyond. Suddenly, the Southern line erupted with a "terrific volley," as one soldier remembered it, aimed at Kimball's men who now found themselves in the midst of a flaming holocaust.[29]

Under "murderous fire," Kimball's brigade slammed to a stop less than 100 yards from the sunken road as killed and wounded men crumpled to the ground all along the line. On the brigade's left flank, the men of the 7th West Virginia were totally unprepared for the intensity, duration and horror of the carnage. Confederate lead quickly found the mark in all the regiment's companies. John Creak, Simon Keck, Isaac Hopkins, Rudolph Beck and James Gregory were all killed, and Clayton Baker, Charles Stetson, Aaron Davis, David Etline and George Hill were wounded. Corporal Jesse Hall fell dead as a ball tore through his bowels. George Groove and Hezekiah Shepherd were each shot in the side and died shortly afterward. Corporal Joseph Conaway received a bullet in the hip and Cpl. John Bible took one in the abdomen, both wounds mortal. Major Lockwood "saw the poor fellows mowed down like grass before the scythe."[30]

The 7th West Virginia's colors drew heavy fire from the Confederate rifle-men. The color bearer, perhaps Ens. Oliver Perkins of Company C, was shot, and the flag fell to the ground, but was promptly raised, only to fall again when the second bearer was hit. Once more the colors were lifted and were shot down again along with their third bearer of the day. Determined hands quickly snatched the flag up one more time, and although at least 20 balls ripped through the cloth and the spear of the staff was shot away, the flag continued to fly throughout the firefight.[31]

The 7th West Virginia's field officers on horseback also made inviting targets. Colonel Snider rode back and forth along the line telling his men to "give them hail, boys." The colonel sustained two slight wounds and had his horse killed under him. The poor animal took from three to five balls, while a book in the colonel's saddlebag stopped yet another. Likewise, Maj. Jonathan Lockwood "incessantly rode up and down the whole line cheering his men." At one point he received a volley from four Confederates. Three balls passed through and killed his mount and one punched a hole in his canteen, spilling all its applejack, but the major escaped injury.

Major Jonathan Lockwood, who later in the war would command the regiment. (From a painting.)

Courtesy of Gary Rider, Moundsville, WV

The company officers on foot fared worse. Of the three captains who entered the fight, Capt. D. C. M. Shell of Company I was killed and the other two were wounded, including Capt. Henry Lazier of Company E who received a ball in the thigh. Lieutenants Shriver and Swartz also died leading their companies, K and C, respectively. Swartz was shot through the bowels and neck. Among the injured were Lt. Samuel Kraus of Company B, severely wounded, Lt. John Fleahman of Company G, shot in the head, and Lt. John Garoy of Company I, mortally wounded.[32]

Although Kimball's casualties were high, the Confederates also were paying a steep price. On the 7th West Virginia's front, a brigade of North Carolinians commanded by G. B. Anderson of D. H. Hill's division fiercely defended the sunken road with their lives. Amidst their mounting dead, the bloodied survivors raised a white flag, which caused Snider's men to slacken their fire. This lull in the fighting was mirrored along Kimball's line as white handkerchiefs fluttered from the sunken road in several places. These makeshift flags of truce soon disappeared, however, as Confederate reinforcements from R. H. Anderson's division arrived after 10:00 a. m., and the killing resumed.

One fresh Confederate line, probably Featherston's Brigade under Col. Carnot Posey, poured into the sunken road and spilled forward, overlapping and menacing Kimball's left flank. Kimball parried this thrust by extending the 7th West Virginia and 132d Pennsylvania further to the left and partially refusing or swinging his left wing back. The 7th West Virginia's officers shouted the orders to change front over the numbing roar of combat as their regiment took more casualties. Confederate riflemen killed both William McBeth and Franklin Founds with shots through the "boddy" and dropped Abram Hays dead, shooting him through the "brest," as the poor-spelling regimental clerk later reported. Flying metal indiscriminately struck privates James Harper in the thigh, Mathias Helmick in the abdomen, Francis Lynch in the thigh, Henry Jones in the arm and leg, and Sgt. Abner Johnson in the thigh, seriously wounding them all, Jones mortally. About this time, the Irish Brigade of Richardson's division, coming up on Kimball's left, counterattacked and together with the hard-pressed West Virginians and Pennsylvanians soon drove the Confederates back. The 8th Ohio hurried the retreating Confederates along by directing an oblique fire to the left.[33]

In the confusion of the 7th West Virginia's shifting back to refuse Kimball's left wing, Private Jefferson Dye apparently believed that his regiment had been relieved and had retired from the field. He and Simon Main, both Pennsylvanians of Company F, their battle blood up, decided to stay put and stubbornly fought alongside the Irish Brigade for another hour. Dye used up all of his ammunition, then refilled his cartridge box from the box of a wounded comrade of Company H lying nearby. After exhausting his ammunition again, Dye rejoined his regiment. Years later, Dye felt that he and Main, who later lost both his legs and his life at Gettysburg, deserved medals for their conduct and applied to the president for one. The commander-in-chief referred the matter to the War Department, where Dye's application was shelved.[34]

As the contest's second hour wore to a close, the 7th West Virginia's already fearful toll of killed and wounded grew larger. The significant number of men who were shot in the head is probably reflective of the fact that they fought from a kneeling or prone position just behind the crest, attempting to expose as little of the body as possible. The lives of Benjamin Bartlett, Ens. Oliver Perkins, John Adams, John Amos, Cpl. William Cohn, Clarkson Haught, Warren Joy, Cpl. Samuel Kellar, John McKinley, and James Pool ended in front of Bloody Lane when bullets pierced their brains. Although Lt. John Fleahman, Cornelius Blackburn, Amos Moral, and Job Shell were more fortunate in that they lived to tell about it, all had close calls, suffering wounds to their heads.[35]

The musket fire was furious on both sides as the slugfest continued to rage along Kimball's line. Clouds of acrid powder smoke hung in the still, hot air, blackening faces, burning eyes and throats and making accurate shooting more difficult. One member of the 8th Ohio naively thought that crickets were making the grass around him tremble until he realized that Confederate minie balls were responsible. More destructive missiles tore through flesh in the 7th West Virginia. Sergeant Emory Leichter was wounded in the ankle and Richard Bingman in the hand. George Coffield was killed by a shot through the breast. John Sutter and Michael Martin were both mortally wounded, Martin in the leg. Daniel Mallow was hit in the shoulder, Henry Mungold and Isaac Summerfield in the hand, and Sgt. John C. Shell in the thigh. The losses appalled Kimball who muttered as he passed behind his ravaged line, "God save my poor boys!"[36]

The considerably thinned ranks of Kimball's brigade tenaciously clung to their position as a third hour of savage fighting passed. Although the soldiers ran low on ammunition and their guns became fouled, they took what they needed from the fallen. While officers gathered the cartridge boxes of the dead and wounded, the men scavenged useable weapons from the many scattered about the ground.[37]

Meanwhile, bedlam reigned in the sunken road. Casualties among the officers had disrupted the Confederate command. Regiments had been jammed into the lane and were hopelessly mixed together. Suddenly, the Confederate resistance collapsed. On the right, what was left of Anderson's command gave way before the enfilading fire of Caldwell's brigade of Richardson's division, and on the left Gen. Robert Rodes' Confederate infantrymen retired due to a misunderstanding of orders. Smelling blood, so to speak, Kimball's men "raised a savage yell," and pursuant to orders, charged Bloody Lane. Describing what happened, an officer of the 14th Indiana wrote his mother that "the men yelled like demons and fought like infuriated mad men, the Rebels at last broke and ran like sheep from the squad that was left of our brigade."[38]

The victory, if it could be called that at such cost, was short-lived as a new Confederate force of about 925 men now appeared in the cornfield on Kimball's right, imperiling that flank. Kimball swung the 8th Ohio and 14th Indiana back at a right angle to his main line and drove off the threat with help from a portion of Caldwell's brigade coming over from the left and Irwin's brigade of VI Corps which came up on the right and pushed into the Confederate left rear.[39]

Finally, around a quarter or a half past noon, the dazed survivors of Kimball's shattered brigade, out of ammunition, were pulled back behind the Roulette barn which served as a field hospital. The men got water and ammunition and then redeployed on low ground to the right, facing the cornfield in support of a Federal battery 200 yards behind them. For a time, counterbattery fire from the Confederate side fell short, wounding some of Kimball's men and making them restless. Kimball steadied the troops by mounting his horse and riding back and forth along the line, shouting, "Stand firm, trust in God, and do your duty." The men laid there for the remainder of the day in relative safety.[40]

The next morning, the 7th West Virginia's Joshua Rice, who had been sick and was assigned to the brigade wagons during the battle, hunted out his comrades. His diary entry gives a description of what he saw:

> I viewed the Battol Field [sic] the next morning Sept 18 and saw the offel [sic] Slaughter of men such a sight I never want to see a gan [sic] after looking around for a long time I found the Brigade and one glance at them showed me that many of them was gon [sic] after spending an hour I went to the Hospitol [sic] and saw the woonded [sic]. I then returned to Boons Burow [sic]about 4 miles where the wagons was left.[41]

Kimball's losses were enormous. The brigade officially lost 121 killed, 510 wounded and eight captured or missing, for an aggregate of 639 casualties. At great cost, the brigade, like a rock, had held its position under a hot fire for several grueling hours. A tearful French conveyed to Kimball's men the fitting *nom de guerre* General Sumner had bestowed on the unit—the "Gibraltar Brigade."[42] Like the rest of the brigade, the 7th West Virginia had been hit hard. The official tally was 29 killed and 116 wounded, for a total loss of 145. This represented a casualty rate of 48%. At least 21 of the 7th West Virginia's wounded subsequently died, raising the number of those who lost their lives as a result of the battle to at least 50.[43]

Company A lost three men killed in action, and according to Sgt. James Murdock, "nearly every one in the company was more or less wounded." Murdock counted himself lucky. Only slightly wounded in the leg, he found a half dozen or more bullet holes in his blouse.[44] Captain Solomon Spangler had led the 40 men of Company G into action that day. Fifteen of the "Rough and Ready Guards" were wounded. The most seriously injured were Michael Martin, who underwent amputation of a leg, and Smith Dailey, who was dangerously wounded in the face by a ball that had passed through both cheeks. Captain Spangler proudly wrote home that "[t]he 'Rough and Ready Guards' and the 'Graysville Wildcats' behaved nobly during the engagement, and fully sustained the reputation of Old Monroe [County, Ohio]. We cannot too highly recommend the determined bravery of the entire Regiment, as they stood amidst a shower of musketry for nearly 3 hours."[45]

The "Graysville Wildcats" referred to Capt. Isaac Fisher's Company D which had the worst of it in the 7th West Virginia. Fisher took 44 men into the battle and came out with 17. Twenty-seven men were casualties from the attack on Bloody Lane, including a father and son. The father, Benjamin Coss, survived, but lost his son John, who died from a shot to the neck. "[F]ighting like heroes," a dozen of Fisher's men were killed or mortally wounded and would never see their families in Ohio again. Nevertheless, Fisher was gratified, writing "[t]he Seventh [West] Va. Regiment in the above engagement, has shown that she is made up of the right kind of material to stand without flinching, notwithstanding the heavy volleys of musketry that was forced into her ranks."[46]

When word of these losses reached the folks back home in Ohio, the grief-stricken Graysville community which had sent Fisher's company to the field held a memorial service. They gathered at the Baptist church on the evening of Saturday, November 1, 1862, to remember their fallen friends, sons, brothers and husbands in song. The verses were composed by the musical duo of John W. Edington, a former second lieutenant of Fisher's company who had resigned well before Antietam, and a Miss Nancy Hamilton. Although this pair groped clumsily for the rhymes and meter of "Monroe Boys," they were at least well-meaning, as evinced by this sampling:

We left our own dear native state
And all its soldiers too
But all its rebels we do hate
For they're not loyal and true

Chorus

They left their own dear native homes
Their wives and parents dear
For in a rebel land to rome
Where no loved ones are near

* * *

Alas sad news now dims our joys
Though the stars and stripes still wave
Some of Capt. fishers noble boys
Are now laid in their graves
Chorus

* * *

In the state of Maryland
This battle hard was fought
That broke our gallant Graysville band
We morn to tell their lot

Chorus

* * *

But we hope to meet again
When this sad warfares oer
We hope to meet on jordens plain
Where battles are no more[47]

Beyond the immediate and permanent loss of those killed were the disabled men who dribbled out of the regiment over the ensuing months, unable to return to service. A case in point was Joseph Phillips of Company F. He was shot in the left side of the neck, the bullet exiting the opposite shoulder. The private was treated in a field hospital until September 27, then was moved to Satterlee Hospital in Philadelphia. His discharge came on November 28, 1862. Although the wound had healed, the 30-year-old's left arm was entirely paralyzed and part of his vision was gone.[48] Another example was J. M. Linhart of Company H Shot in the left forearm, a surgeon removed Linhart's arm between the elbow and the hand. The private was discharged on December 13, 1862 and later pensioned, the stump entirely healed.[49]

These cases were symptomatic of the dramatic increase in the number of discharges in the 7th West Virginia due to disability from sickness and wounds following Antietam. During the nine-month period of January through September, 1862, the regiment had averaged close to six discharges per month. The two peak months, which account for 10 discharges each, were May, following the fruitless rigors of chasing "Stonewall" Jackson, and July, when the regiment camped on the disease-ridden lowlands of the Peninsula. In contrast, the average rate of discharges per month tripled to nearly 18 during the last quarter of 1862, surely due in large measure to Antietam. In October alone the regiment appears to have lost 22 men discharged for medical reasons.[50]

The effects of the battle would be felt in the 7th West Virginia for the rest of the war. On the negative side, the large losses would never be fully replaced. This would contribute to the regiment's eventual consolidation and re-designation as a battalion following Gettysburg. In the positive column, however, the men had gained valuable experience and had "proven" themselves. They had learned the benefit of cover and would use it to their advantage three months later in the battle of Fredericksburg. In that engagement, Kimball's brigade led the doomed Federal assault on the impregnable stone wall at the foot of Marye's Heights. After first crossing ground which the noted Confederate artillerist E. P. Alexander had boasted "[a] chicken could not live on. . .when we open on it," the men of the 7th West Virginia managed to shield themselves behind a small undulation of ground and several buildings on the outskirts of town in front of the Confederate position. This pushed the casualty rate down: officially, three killed, 31 wounded and three missing, or roughly 20%—less than half of those suffered at Antietam.[51]

Meanwhile, the aftermath of Antietam left a lasting impression on the men of the 7th West Virginia who survived. Jonathan Lockwood, who won promotion from major to lieutenant colonel of the regiment a month after the battle, later recalled that "[a]fter the battle we encamped on the field of blood and carnage amidst the dying and the dead, alleviating the wants of the former and burying the latter. Truly it was a time long to be remembered."[52] Sergeant Murdock observed fresh troops pile up the corpses "black as any Negro you ever saw" for burial. One dead man in particular caught Murdock's attention. The deceased was firmly holding a deck of cards over his face, having vainly tried to toss them away before death overtook him. Other fallen men were found "in every conceivable shape" grasping ramrods, photographs of loved ones and Bibles.[53] With apparent satisfaction, Capt. Spangler noted that "[s]ince being over the battle field, we are of the opinion that the enemy have lost three to our one."[54]

The Battle of Antietam was only the first of many battles to come for the 7th West Virginia. Five days after the fight, Kimball's brigade marched to Harper's Ferry and encamped on Bolivar Heights back of the town. They rested and regrouped there until the end of October before resuming field operations with the Army of the Potomac. Over the course of the rest of the war the 7th West Virginia went on to fight with II Corps in every major engagement of the eastern theatre. At Chancellorsville a countercharge by the Seventh and a portion of Col. Samuel S. Carroll's (formerly Kimball's) brigade helped delay the Confederate advance on the Chancellor House crossroads. At Gettysburg—fought less than two weeks after West Virginia was granted acceptance into the Union as the 35th state—another countercharge by Carroll's brigade on the second day of the battle helped save a Union battery on East Cemetery Hill. The regiment was in the thick of the fighting in each of these battles and acquitted itself with distinction.

Combat, hardship and disease took their toll. By early September 1863, the regiment had sustained such losses that the skeletal remnants were consolidated into a battalion of four companies. The supernumerary officers were mustered out, including Col. Snider, still recuperating from wounds, whose supporters had failed in their efforts to get President Lincoln to name him a brigadier general. Regardless of their exposures and suffering, a majority of the men re-enlisted for another three years in early January 1864.[55]

These veterans voluntarily delayed leaving on their re-enlistment furloughs in order to participate in a diversionary attack at Morton's Ford, Virginia in February. Immediately after the affair, They departed for Wheeling and home. After returning from their furloughs in the spring of 1864 flush with 120 new recruits, the men of the Seventh marched and fought with U. S. Grant in the Overland Campaign against Lee. They went on to participate in the fighting surrounding the investment of Petersburg, including the disaster at Ream's Station on August 25, 1864. Despite this defeat, the men of the 7th West Virginia, reputed as crack shots, were rewarded with the coveted sixteen-shot, lever-action Henry repeating rifle, the precursor of the Winchester. This was a rare honor, since no more then 1,731 of the prized repeaters were purchased by the Federal government during the war.[56] After Lee's surrender at Appomattox, the 7th West Virginia marched in the Grand Review in Washington. The men were mustered-out of service in early July, 1865.[57]

Of all their hard fighting during the Civil War, the Battle of Antietam marked the 7th West Virginia's emergence as a premier combat unit. Referring to the brigade's sobriquet "Gibraltar Brigade," Lieut. Col. Lockwood called it "a dear bought name." The same could have been said for the "Bloody Seventh."[58]

Notes

1. "The Seventh Va. Regiment," *Wheeling Intelligencer,* February 1, 1862; William F. Fox, *Regimental Losses in the American Civil War 1861-1865* (1889; reprint, Dayton, 1985), p. 490.

2. Lieutenant Colonel Jonathan H. Lockwood to editors, December 31, 1862, *Wheeling Intelligencer,* January 19, 1863; David F. Riggs, *7th Virginia Infantry,* 2d ed. (Lynchburg, VA, H. E. Howard, Inc., 1982), p. 16.

3. Samuel T. Wiley, *History of Monongalia County, West Virginia* (Kingwood, WV, 1883), pp. 527-528 (courtesy of Thomas E. Mellott); *Annual Report of the Adjutant General of the State of West Virginia for the Year Ending December 31, 1864*

(Wheeling: John F. M'Dermot, 1865), p. 226; "Seventh Regiment West Virginia Volunteer Infantry History," regimental roster, West Virginia Division of Culture and History, Charleston, W. Va. (hereinafter cited as "7th West Virginia roster"); L. K. Evans, *Pioneer History of Greene County, Pennsylvania* (1941; reprint, Waynesburg, Pa.: Greene County Historical Society, 1969), p. 169.

4. 7th West Virginia roster. The antebellum occupational breakdown of the 7th follows: 695 farmers, 14 carpenters, 12 mechanics, 10 shoemakers, 7 blacksmiths, 6 coopers, 5 teachers, 4 masons, 4 millers, 3 miners, 3 tailors, 2 boatmen, 2 molders, 2 tinners, and 2 wagonmakers. Other occupations represented (one each) include: boatmaker, butcher, chairmaker, clerk, cigarmaker, clothier, engineer, glasscutter, gunsmith, jockey, lawyer, painter, pilot, plasterer, printer, saddler, silversmith, student, surgeon, wagoner and watchmaker.

5. Ibid; *Report of Adjutant General,* pp. 191-226; Frederick H. Dyer, *A Compendium of the War of the Rebellion* (1908; reprint, Dayton, 1978), pp. 11, 39, 1655-1666; *Wheeling Intelligencer,* July-December 1861; J. G. Randall and David Donald, *The Civil War and Reconstruction,* rev. 2d ed. (Boston, 1969), pp. 239-240; Katherine O'Brien, "The Seventh West Virginia Volunteer Infantry 1861 - 1865" (Master's thesis, West Virginia University, 1965), pp. 12-13, 30-31; John S. Carlile to Abraham Lincoln, 8 July 1861, U. S. War Department, *The War of the Rebellion: The Official Records of the Union and Confederate Armies,* 128 vols. (Washington, DC, 1890-1901), series III, vol. 1, pp. 323-324 (hereinafter cited as *OR,* all further references to series I unless otherwise noted).

6. "The Expedition to Worthington," *Wheeling Intelligencer,* September 4, 1861; "The Notorious Zach Cochran Killed," *Wheeling Intelligencer,* September 24, 1861; *Report of Adjutant General,* p. 226; Gen. Benjamin F. Kelley's report, October 28, 1861, *OR* 5, pp. 378-380; Gen. Frederick W. Lander's report, February 14, 1862, *OR* 5, pp. 405-406.

7. Lieutenant Colonel Jonathan H. Lockwood to Adj. Gen. F. P. Pierpont, January 1, 1864, West Virginia Division of Culture and History, Charleston, W. Va.; *Report of Adjutant General,* p. 227; Gen. Nathan Kimball, "Fighting Jackson at Kernstown," in Robert U. Johnson and Clarence C. Buel, eds., *Battles and Leaders of the Civil War,* 4 vols. (1884-89; reprint, Secaucus,, n. d.), vol. 2, pp. 302, 308-313; William Kepler, *History of the Fourth Regiment Ohio Volunteer Infantry* (1886; reprint, Huntington, WV, 1992), pp. 63, 67-69, 203-204; Gen. Nathaniel P. Banks to Secy. Edwin M. Stanton, 27 April 1862, *OR* 12, pt. 3, p. 110; Capt. James E. Murdock, "Preston in the Rebellion," *Preston County (West Virginia) Journal,* August 30, 1883; Gen. Nathaniel P. Banks to Secy. Edwin M. Stanton, April 30, 1862, *OR* 12, pt. 3, pp. 118-119; Secy. Edwin M. Stanton to Gen. Nathaniel P. Banks, May 1, 1862, *OR* 12, pt. 3, p. 122; Gen. Irvin McDowell to Secy. Edwin M. Stanton, May 2, 1862, *OR* 12, pt. 3, p. 124; Dyer, *Compendium,* p. 347; James M. McPherson, *Battle Cry of Freedom,* (New York, 1988), pp. 457-458; Franklin Sawyer, *A Military History of the 8th Regiment Ohio Vol. Inf'y,* ed.

Geo. A. Groot (Cleveland, 1881), pp. 50, 53; Gen. James Shields' report, June 13, 1862, *OR* 12, pt. 1, pp. 684-685; Gen. James Shields' report, n. d., *OR* 12, pt. 1, pp. 687-688.

8. Lieutenant Colonel Lockwood to Adj. Gen. Pierpont, January 1, 1864; *Report of Adjutant General,* p. 227; Douglas Southall Freeman, *Lee's Lieutenants,* 3 vols. (New York, 1942), vol. 1, pp. 640-641.

9. Lieutenant Colonel Lockwood to Adj. Gen. Pierpont, January 1, 1864.

10. Lieutenant Colonel Lockwood to Adj. Gen. Pierpont, January 1, 1864; *Report of Adjutant General,* p. 227.

11. Stephen W. Sears, *Landscape Turned Red* (New York, 1983), pp. 64-68.

12. 7th West Virginia regimental return for September, 1862, National Archives and Records Administration, Washington, D. C. (hereinafter cited as "regimental return for September, 1862"); *Report of Adjutant General,* p. 227; Kepler, *Fourth Ohio,* pp. 79, 206; Sawyer, *8th Ohio,* p. 69; Thomas Francis Galwey, *The Valiant Hours,* ed. W. S. Nye (Harrisburg, 1961), p. 33; Francis A. Walker, *History of the Second Army Corps in the Army of the Potomac* (1887; reprint, Gaithersburg, MD., n. d.), p. 92.

13. 7th West Virginia roster; Wiley, *Monongalia County,* pp. 528, 531. Evans resigned August 2, 1862.

14. 7th West Virginia roster; Lt. Col. John G. Kelley's pension records, National Archives and Records Administration, Washington, D. C. (Information courtesy of Mark Haselberger.)

15. Kepler, *Fourth Ohio,* pp. 79, 206; Sawyer, *8th Ohio,* pp. 69-70; Frederick L. Hitchcock, *War from the Inside* (1904; reprint, Alexandria,VA, 1985), pp. 17-18.

16. Dyer, *Compendium,* pp. 292, 294; Organization of the Army of the Potomac, 14-17 September 1862, *OR* 19, pt. 1, p. 173; Hitchcock, *War from the Inside,* p. 39; Walker, *Second Army Corps,* pp. 87, 97-98; Ezra J. Warner, *Generals in Blue* (Baton Rouge,1964), pp. 161-162; Sears, *Landscape Turned Red,* p. 237. According to Dyer, the Third Division of the II Corps was organized September 10, 1862, and Kimball's brigade was designated the First Brigade of the Third Division on September 12, 1862.

17. Warner, *Generals in Blue,* pp. 267-268.

18. Regimental return for September, 1862; Hitchcock, *War from the Inside,* pp. 36-37, 40-41; Sawyer, *8th Ohio,* pp. 70-71; Galwey, *Valiant Hours,* p. 34; Nancy Niblack Baxter, *Gallant Fourteenth,* 2d hardcover ed. (Indianapolis., 1991), p. 97 (see William Houghton to his mother, September 20,1862). The dates and distances of the several stages of the advance to Frederick, as related by the above-referenced regimental return, Sawyer, Galwey and Hitchcock, cannot be definitively reconciled until September 12, 1862, when the brigade occupied Monocacy Junction. The dates and marching distances recorded in the 7th West Virginia regimental return for September, 1862 are followed here.

19. Regimental return for September, 1862; Sawyer, *8th Ohio,* p. 71; Galwey, *Valiant Hours,* p. 35; Hitchcock, *War from the Inside,* p. 43; Walker, *Second Army Corps,* pp. 93-94.

20. Regimental return for September, 1862; Sawyer, *8th Ohio,* pp. 72-74; Galwey, *Valiant Hours,* pp. 35-36; Hitchcock, *War from the Inside,* pp. 46-47; Walker, *Second Army Corps,* p. 95.

21. Sawyer, *8th Ohio,* p. 74; Galwey, *Valiant Hours,* pp. 36-37; Hitchcock, *War from the Inside,* pp. 47-50; Walker, *Second Army Corps,* p. 96.

22. Sawyer, *8th Ohio,* pp. 75-76; Galwey, *Valiant Hours,* pp. 37-38; Hitchcock, *War from the Inside,* pp. 51-54.

23. Hitchcock, *War from the Inside,* pp. 56-57.

24. Sawyer, *8th Ohio,* pp. 76-77; Galwey, *Valiant Hours,* pp. 38-40; Hitchcock, *War from the Inside,* pp. 55-59; Gen. Nathan Kimball's report, September 18, 1862, *OR* 19, pt. 1, pp. 326-327; Gen. William French's report, 20 September 1862, *OR* 19, pt. 1, pp. 323-324; Walker, *Second Army Corps,* pp. 100-101; Sears, *Landscape Turned Red,* pp. 221-222, 237.

25. Galwey, *Valiant Hours,* p. 40; Gen. Kimball's report, *OR* 19, pt. 1, p. 327; Gen. French's report, *OR* 19, pt. 1, p. 324; Sawyer, *8th Ohio,* pp. 77-78.

26. Captain Isaac Fisher to editor, September 19, 1862, *Woodsfield (Ohio) Spirit of Democracy,* October 1, 1862 (courtesy of Mark Haselberger); Capt. Solomon Spangler letter, September 20, 1860 [*sic*—1862], *Woodsfield (Ohio) Spirit of Democracy,* October 1, 1862 (courtesy of Mark Haselberger); Company D record of guns delivered and received, 7th West Virginia regimental books, National Archives and Records Administration, Washington, D. C., microfilm frame 0642; O'Brien, "Seventh West Virginia," p. 66. Spangler, *supra,* writes that the regiment entered the battle with about 300 men. Although this figure seems low, it is probably not far off the mark. Spangler notes that his Company G went into action with 40 men, while Fisher reports that Company D took 44 into the engagement. If Spangler's total of 300 for the regiment is correct, then the remaining eight companies would have averaged only 27 men. This combat strength would compare with 320 officers and men engaged for the 14th Indiana on the opposite end of Kimball's line (14th Indiana memorial at Bloody Lane, Antietam National Battlefield). The out-of-action 4th Ohio had less than 200 men fit for duty around this time (Kepler, *Fourth Ohio,* p. 82). O'Brien, *supra,* writes that "[t]he Seventh had gone into battle with four hundred sixty-four men present for duty. . . ." However, deductions must be made for those who were present, but not fit for duty, and those who were detailed on non-combat duty. General Kimball's report, *OR* 19, pt. 1, p. 327. (At Shepherd College's George Tyler Moore Center for the Study of the Civil War, the Civil War Soldiers Database was queried to determine the number of soldiers listed as "present" during September - October 1862. [Men who were killed, wounded, missing, etc. as a result of the Battle of Antietam were considered to be "present".] The query listed 433 men present, 328 absent, and 21 on detached service. There was no record for 126 men. There is no way to determine, however, exactly how many of the 433 men listed as present during this time frame actually fought at Antietam.)

28. Sears, *Landscape Turned Red,* pp. 239-240; John M. Priest, *Antietam: The Soldiers' Battle* (Shippensburg, PA, 1989; reprint, New York, 1993), p. 146.

29. Sawyer, *8th Ohio,* p. 78; Gen. Kimball's report, *OR* 19, pt. 1, p. 327; Hitchcock, *War from the Inside,* p. 59.

30. General Kimball's report, *OR* 19, pt. 1, p. 327; 7th West Virginia roster; Registers of Deaths of Companies D and I, 7th West Virginia regimental books, National Archives and Records Administration, Washington, D. C., microfilm frames 0065, 0168; Lt. Col. Jonathan H. Lockwood to editors, 12 November 1862, *Wheeling Intelligencer,* November 18, 1862.

31. Colonel Joseph Snider's report, September 20, 1862, *OR* 19, pt. 1, p. 332; *Report of Adjutant General,* pp. 197, 227; Register of Deaths of Company C, 7th West Virginia regimental books, National Archives and Records Administration, Washington, D. C., microfilm frame 0033; Lieut. Col. Lockwood to editors, *Wheeling Intelligencer,* November 18, 1862 (in which Lockwood states the flag was pierced 25 times by musket balls); Lieut. Col. Lockwood to Adj. Gen. Pierpont, January 1, 1864.

32. Lieutenant Colonel Lockwood to Adjutant General Pierpont, January 1, 1864; *Report of Adjutant General,* p. 227; Capt. James E. Murdock, "Preston in the Rebellion," *Preston County (West Virginia) Journal,* September 13, 1883; Abraham Lincoln, memorandum concerning Joseph Snider, March 9, 1863, The Abraham Lincoln Association, *The Collected Works of Abraham Lincoln,* ed. Roy P. Basler, History Book Club ed. (New Brunswick, N J, 1953), vol. 6, p. 130; Wiley, *Monongalia County,* p. 532; Capt. Spangler letter, *Woodsfield (Ohio) Spirit of Democracy,* October 1, 1862; Capt. Fisher to editor, *Woodsfield (Ohio) Spirit of Democracy,* October 1, 1862; manuscript account of Lt. Col. Jonathan H. Lockwood, n. d., copy in possession of the author (courtesy of Gary L. Rider); 7th West Virginia roster; Registers of Deaths of Companies C, K and I, 7th West Virginia regimental books, National Archives and Records Administration, microfilm frames 0033, 0168; Gibson Lamb Cranmer, ed., *History of Wheeling City and Ohio County, West Virginia and Representative Citizens* (Chicago, 1902), pp. 517, 769.

33. 7th West Virginia roster; Registers of Deaths of Companies C and I, 7th West Virginia regimental books, National Archives and Records Administration, Washington, D. C., microfilm frames 0033, 0168; Sawyer, *8th Ohio,* p. 78; Galwey, *Valiant Hours,* p. 43; Hitchcock, *War from the Inside,* pp. 62-63; Col. Snider's report, *OR* 19, pt. 1, p. 332; Gen. Kimball's report, *OR* 19, pt. 1, p. 327; Capt. A. M. Feltus' report, September 22, 1862, *OR* 19, pt. 1, p. 884; Gen. Thomas Francis Meagher's report, September 30, 1862, *OR* 19, pt. 1, pp. 293-295; Gen. George B. McClellan's report, *OR* 19, pt. 1, p. 58. Note that Sears, *Landscape Turned Red,* pp. 243-244, differs from the writer's interpretation that Meagher repulsed Posey, but Sears' map at p. 233 and Priest, *The Soldiers' Battle,* p. 160, support the writer's view.

34. Jefferson Dye to Ed (Liebune?), April 13, 1895, copy in possession of the writer (courtesy of Elizabeth and J. Robert Rice). If the letter to the president was written around this time, then it was directed to Grover Cleveland, who served his second (non-consecutive) term as the chief executive from March 4, 1893 to March 3, 1897.

35. Galwey, *Valiant Hours,* p. 43; Hitchcock, *War from the Inside,* p. 59; Registers of Deaths of Companies C and D, 7th West Virginia regimental books, National Archives and Records Administration, Washington, D. C., microfilm frames 0033, 0065; 7th West Virginia roster.

36. Galwey, *Valiant Hours,* p. 42; Hitchcock, *War from the Inside,* p. 61; 7th West Virginia roster; Registers of Deaths of Companies C and H, 7th West Virginia regimental books, National Archives and Records Administration, Washington, D. C., microfilm frame 0033; Surgeon to Mrs. Michael Martin, October 16, 1862, Michael Martin's pension records, National Archives, Washington, D. C. According to the latter, Michael Martin's wound resulted in the amputation of his thigh. He initially did well, but then "was taken with a heavy chill, which followed him daily until he sank in death" at eleven in the morning on October 16, 1862 at Smoketown Hospital.

37. Sawyer, *8th Ohio,* p. 79; Galwey, *Valiant Hours,* p. 43; Hitchcock, *War from the Inside,* p. 62; 8th Ohio's monument at Bloody Lane, Antietam National Battlefield.

38. Galwey, *Valiant Hours,* p. 44; William Houghton to his mother, 20 September 1862, as quoted in Baxter, *Gallant Fourteenth,* p. 100; Hitchcock, *War from the Inside,* p. 63; Gen. Kimball's report, *OR* 19, pt. 1, p. 327; Col. Francis Barlow's report, September 22, 1862, *OR* 19, pt. 1, p. 289; Gen. John C. Caldwell's report, September 24, 1862, *OR* 19, pt. 1, p. 285; Gen. McClellan's report, *OR* 19, pt. 1, p. 59; Col. R. T. Bennett's report, December 6, 1862, *OR* 19, pt. 1, pp. 1047-1048; Capt. A. J. Griffith's report, 1862, *OR* 19, pt. 1, p. 1050; Maj. W. W. Sillers' report, 13 October 1862, *OR* 19, pt. 1, p. 1051; Sears, *Landscape Turned Red,* pp. 244-247.

39. General Kimball's report, *OR* 19, pt. 1, p. 327; Galwey, *Valiant Hours,* pp. 44-45; Sears, *Landscape Turned Red,* pp. 247-250; Priest, *The Soldiers' Battle,* pp. 196-197, 199, 201.

40. Sawyer, *8th Ohio,* p. 81; Galwey, *Valiant Hours,* pp. 45-46; Hitchcock, *War from the Inside,* pp. 64, 68.

41. Joshua Rice transcribed diary, September 18, 1862, copy in possession of the author (courtesy of Elizabeth and J. Robert Rice).

42. Galwey, *Valiant Hours,* p. 45; Hitchcock, *War from the Inside,* p. 63; 14th Indiana's monument at Bloody Lane, Antietam National Battlefield; Return of Casualties, *OR* 19, pt. 1, p. 193; 7th West Virginia roster; Registers of Deaths of Companies B, C, H, K, D, F and I, 7th West Virginia regimental books, National Archives and Records Administration, Washington, D. C., microfilm frames 0005, 0033, 0065, 0127, 0168.

43. Return of Casualties, *OR* 19, pt. 1, p. 193; Captain Spangler letter, *Woodsfield (Ohio) Spirit of Democracy* October 1, 1862; 7th West Virginia roster; Registers of Deaths of Companies B, C, H, K, D, F and I, 7th West Virginia regimental books, National Archives and Records Administration, Washington, DC, microfilm frames 0005, 0033, 0065, 0127, 0168. The casualty figures for the brigade and the 7th West Virginia recorded in the previously-cited Rice diary for September 17, 1862 correspond exactly with the official numbers. Both Lieutenant Colonel Lockwood to Adjutant General Pierpont, 1 January 1864, and *Report of Adjutant General,* p. 227, give 30 killed and

129 wounded. Spangler, *supra,* indicates 29 killed and 112 wounded. O'Brien, "Seventh West Virginia," p. 66, says a count of the muster rolls shows 56 who were killed or died of their wounds.

44. Murdock, "Preston in the Rebellion," *Preston County (West Virginia) Journal,* September 13, 1883; 7th West Virginia roster.

45. Captain Spangler letter, *Woodsfield (Ohio) Spirit of Democracy,* 1 October 1862 (bracketed material added).

46. 7th West Virginia roster; Register of Deaths of Company D and Company D record of guns delivered and received, 7th West Virginia regimental books, National Archives and Records Administration, Washington, D. C., microfilm frames 0065, 0642 (the latter noting the loss of 27 Austrian rifles at Antietam); Captain Fisher to editor, *Woodsfield (Ohio) Spirit of Democracy,* 1 October 1862.

47. John W. Edington and Nancy Hamilton, "Monroe Boys," typed copy of original manuscript donated by Denzil Gates in 1975 to the Monroe County Historical Society, Woodsfield, Ohio.

48. *The Medical and Surgical History of the Civil War,* (Wilmington, NC,1991), vol. 8, p. 411.

49. Ibid, vol. 10, p. 981.

50. 7th West Virginia roster. Figures include the number of discharges remaining after excluding soldiers discharged for the purpose of re-enlisting in the regular army. These non-re-enlistment discharges are presumed to represent men discharged for medical reasons. However, some of these men are listed as being discharged for unknown reasons, and they may have been discharged in order to re-enlist in the regular service.

51. General James Longstreet, "The Battle of Fredericksburg," in Robert U. Johnson and Clarence C. Buel, eds., *Battles and Leaders of the Civil War,* 4 vols. (New York, 1884-89), vol. 3, p. 79; Return of Casualties, *OR* 21, p. 131.

52. Lieutenant Colonel Lockwood to Adjutant General Pierpont, January 1, 1864; 7th West Virginia roster.

53. Capt. James E. Murdock, "Preston in the Rebellion," *Preston County (West Virginia) Journal,* September 20, 1883.

54. Captain Spangler letter, *Woodsfield (Ohio) Spirit of Democracy,* October 1, 1862.

55. *Report of Adjutant General,* pp. 214-226, 228; 7th West Virginia roster; Lincoln Association, *Collected Works of Lincoln,* vol. 6, p. 130.

56. Captain James E. Murdock, "Preston in the Rebellion," *Preston County (West Virginia) Journal,* December 13, 1883; *Report of Adjutant General,* p. 229; Mark M. Boatner, III, *The Civil War Dictionary,* 1st Vintage Civil War Library ed. (New York, 1991), p. 397.

57. Captain James E. Murdock, "Preston in the Rebellion," *Preston County [West Virginia] Journal,* 17 July 1884; 7th West Virginia roster.

58. Lieutenant Colonel Lockwood to editors, *Wheeling Intelligencer,* November 18, 1862.

Book Reviews

Raphael Semmes and the Alabama, by Spencer C. Tucker and *Cottonclads! The Battle of Galveston and the Defense of the Texas Coast*, by Donald S. Frazier (Ryan Place Publishers, Inc., 2525 Arapahoe Ave., Suite E4-231, Boulder, CO 80302-6720) 1996. Contents, appendixes, b & w photos. 110 pp. and 144 pp. Paperback. $11.95.

One might ask what these two books, one about the Battle of Galveston on the Texas Gulf Coast and a second about the famed Confederate raider, have in common. The link, of course, is the *C. S. S. Alabama.* During the twenty-one month career of Raphael Semmes and this notorious commerce raider, the Rebel vessel met the United States Navy in battle only twice. The more famous encounter was in June 1864 when, as the Alabama's career came to a dramatic end in the English Channel, the cruiser was sunk by the *U. S. S. Kearsarge.* But before that fatal encounter on the French coast, the Alabama had embarrassed the U.S. Navy by defeating the *U. S. S. Hatteras* off Galveston. While both of these works focus on naval operations, the Alabama is the only connection between the two, other than having a common publisher and being part of the "Civil War Campaigns and Commanders" series. The object of this series is to produce short, yet scholarly, books that will appeal to a wide audience. For this reason, there are no notes or bibliography, although each volume includes suggestions for further reading.

Spencer C. Tucker, an authority on naval history in the years before the Civil War, begins his book with a description of privateers, privately owned volunteer cruisers that sold their prizes for profit. Tucker points out that Americans used them in the American Revolution and the War of 1812. At the beginning of the Civil War, the Confederacy had some initial success with privateers, but difficulties arose as European nations declared neutrality and fewer ports welcomed the Confederates and their captured vessels. Secretary of the Navy Stephen R. Mallory decided that the Confederacy needed government owned and financed commerce raiders specially designed for preying on enemy commerce. To procure these ships he turned to England, and the man authorized as purchasing agent was James D. Bulloch, who Tucker correctly describes as the "most effective Confederate agent abroad" (p. 31). Bulloch, a fourteen-year veteran of the U. S. Navy (and incidentally half-brother to Teddy Roosevelt's Georgia-born mother), was captain of a New York mail steamer when he offered his services to the Confederacy. By working around the British Neutrality Proclamation and the Foreign Enlistment Act of 1819, he contracted for several ships. Six Confederate cruisers would be built in England, including the most famous, the Alabama.

Bulloch slipped the vessel out of England just before the British government planned to intervene, and on August 24, while in international waters, the new captain, Raphael Semmes, ran up the Rebel flag and, to the tune of "Dixie," christened his cruiser the *Alabama*. Thus began an odyssey that would span 75,000 miles and almost two years.

During the Civil War, the Alabama and other Confederate commerce raiders destroyed almost 260 Union merchant ships, the Alabama accounting for nearly a quarter of that total. Over four years of war, more than 700 U. S. ships transferred to foreign registry to avoid flying the American flag and thus being a target. Twenty-five Union warships searched for the raiders, at a cost t of over $7 million, but it was the *U. S .S. Kearsarge* that finally trapped the cruiser in the harbor at Cherbourg. There, when Semmes tried to escape, the *Alabama's* colorful career ended.

Semmes had only engaged a Union naval vessel once before, but on that previous occasion his victory had cost the U. S. Government $160,000. This Federal disaster, which occurred off the Texas coast, forms part of the story told by Donald S. Frazier in his book, *Cottonclads!* Not only does Frazier cover the Battle of Galveston, but he also discusses major operations along the four hundred miles of the Texas coast.

By late 1862, the prospect of a successful Union citadel on the Texas coast seemed a possibility when Galveston fell to federal forces. But John B. Magruder, transferred from Virginia to Texas to take command, had other ideas. He planned to retake Galveston, and not having ironclads at his disposal, used Texas cotton bales to substitute for armor. In spite of his unconventional "cottonclads," Magruder succeeded in retaking Galveston on January 1, 1863, a disaster that Union Admiral David Farragut called "the most melancholy affair ever recorded in the history of our gallant navy" (p. 93).

Adding to the Union woes, it was scarcely over a week later when the Alabama appeared in the Gulf of Mexico. Thinking the mysterious vessel was a blockade runner, the *U. S. S. Hatteras* approached only to realize that it had run upon the famed raider. After the *Alabama* opened fire, the Union vessel sank in just minutes, leaving 118 survivors for Semmes to rescue. This was the only time during the entire war that a U.S. Navy warship was destroyed by a Confederate raider.

Besides minor operations up and down the Texas coast, the only other major naval engagement was at Sabine Pass on September 8, 1863, when the Union Navy tried again to plant the American flag on Texas soil. Two Union ships ran aground, and the Confederates took over 300 prisoners and inflicted 70 casualties. Lincoln was horrified, and stock prices fell in New York. "After the loss of seven warships in nine months," concludes Frazier, "Texas had become a dangerous place for the U. S. Navy" (p. 112).

Both volumes are welcome additions to the Ryan Place series. Although the story of the *Alabama* forms part of Rebel folklore, Tucker has written a concise narrative of the raider's career, including an appendix that lists the ships taken by both the *Alabama* and the *Sumter* (the first Confederate commerce raider, also commanded by Semmes). Frazier's story is not as widely-known, but it adds to our understanding of the Union effort to control the Southern coast. Both books are readable and scholarly accounts of important events in the naval history of the Civil War.

Anne J. Bailey   University of Arkansas

Custer, by Jeffry D. Wert (Simon & Schuster, Simon and Schuster Bldg., 1230 Avenue of the Americas, New York, N.Y. 10020), 1996. Notes bibliography, index, black & white photos. 462 pp. HC. $27.50

There is a frequently reproduced 1982 watercolor by artist Stoney Compton which shows George Armstrong Custer surrounded by Indians titled, "That's the way it was, June 25, 1876." The author of this Custer biography, Jeffry D. Wert, attempts to overcome that common image of Custer and the "last stand" perception held by most Americans by writing a comprehensive volume that describes Custer's style and leadership characteristics in superb detail and provides abundant information about his early education, his experiences at West Point leading to his graduation as last in the class of 1862, as well as the engagements and battles in which he participated during the Civil War, including Gettysburg, Haw's Shop, Trevilian Station, Winchester, Cedar Creek, Waynesborough, and Appomattox. Wert also targets Custer's post-Civil War years and his love for Libbia Bacon Custer. The final two chapters are an outstanding chronicle of the events preceding the Battle of the Little Big Horn and the end of Custer's life.

Wert's basic text is 322 pages of easy reading, the balance covering 1,155 footnotes, 465 references, a 20-page index, and 16 pages of photos. The author has included the most recently researched facts and documentation about Custer and the latest archeological data. His style is exciting, informative and non-judgmental. He brings historical evidence to the reader in a well organized and accurate fashion, provides timely chains of events, and occasionally reconstructs what must have happened but does not force his reader to agree with him. Wert tells of Custer's leadership methods and procedures as seen and evaluated by staff and subordinates at various times in his military career; of Custer's possible motivation; his horsemanship and cavalry officer skills; and his relationships with other officers, both junior and senior. He also discusses the complexities and controversies that many other writers have attributed to Custer's life.

For all of the positive qualities of this outstanding biography, and through no fault of the author, this *Custer* still can not answer satisfactorily many questions that continue to puzzle Custer scholars, including: (1) why was the "Boy General" so flamboyant? Wert's reader does become more knowledgeable about the possible causes of that flamboyancy; (2) was Custer ever unfaithful to Libbie? Probably, the author concludes, but he neither condemns or defends Custer's ethics or morality; (3) and what flawed Custer's judgment so badly that he led the 7th Cavalry to its defeat at the Battle of the Little Big Horn? After reading chapters 18 and 19, the reader has a better understanding of some of the causes for Custer's actions. Wert's readers also become more empathetic to Custer the individual, in the process discovering trivia and developing better insight into the historical events of 1839 through 1876.

Custer's life probably brought added meaning to the concept of "manifest destiny" as it applied to his personal philosophy. In a letter to Libbie after one of his Civil War engagements, Custer wrote, "Never have I failed to command [sic] myself to God's keeping. . .asking Him to forgive my past sins, to watch over me in danger. . .and to receive me if I fell. . . .After having done so, all anxiety for myself, here or hereafter, is dispelled. I feel that my destiny is in the hands of the Almighty, This belief, more than any other fact or reason, makes me brave and fearless as I am" (p. 152).

Under James K. Polk, eleventh president of the United States, the policy of "manifiest destiny" to expand westward and south- ward toward annexation of Texas, California & Oregon probably did create in Custer's psyche his personal doctrine of manifest destiny. The national mind set became a personal one that carried him through numerous conflicts and near-death experiences and contributed enormously to the successes he met prior to Little Big Horn. Perhaps Custer was more a tactician than a strategist, and that was the major reason for his final defeat. Jeffry D. Wert lets his reader draw his own conclusion.

This book should be on every Custer buff's library shelf, for two reasons: first, it is a well crafted, historically accurate and and well documented; and second, it is a delight to read.

Jerry Benson

Lufkin, Texas

Alexander Neil and the Last Shenandoah Valley Campaign, edited by Richard R. Duncan (White Mane Publishing Co., Inc. P.O. Box 152, Shippensburg, PA 17257) 1996. Contents, epilogue, appendix, endnotes, bibliography, index, b & w photos. 140 pp. HC. $19.95.

Letters written by soldiers have formed the basis for several insightful studies of the Civil War military experience written in the past decade. In *Embattled Courage: The Experience of Combat in the American Civil War* (1987), Gerald F. Linderman used published letters and diaries to support his argument that soldiers initially attempted to understand the war through notions of courage and duty. They became disillusioned when they realized that their early notions of bravery could not account for success and failure on the battlefield. Reid Mitchell also notes a transformation process among Civil War soldiers in *The Vacant Chair: The Northern Soldier Leaves Home* (1993). He argues that many nineteenth-century Americans tried to make sense of the Civil War transformation from civilian to soldier by linking it with the passage of boys into manhood; boys who enlisted in 1861 returned home as men. James M. McPherson's *What They Fought For 1861-1865* (1994) presents the argument that many Civil War soldiers were acutely aware of the issues at stake in the war and were generally concerned about them. McPherson notes that the themes of liberty and republicanism formed the ideological center of the cause for which each side fought. The provocative themes of these three studies show that the letters and diaries of the war's common soldiers can contain a wealth of information concerning the more current debates in Civil War historiography.

Alexander Neil was one of many letter-writing soldiers. Born in Ohio, Neil studied at Ohio Wesleyan University and graduated from the Cincinnati College of Medicine and Surgery in 1863. Wishing to avoid the draft at home, he accepted a surgeon's commission and served with the 12th West Virginia until the unit mustered out in June 1865.

Richard R. Duncan has compiled and edited sixty of Alexander Neil's letters written during the final struggle for control of the Shenandoah Valley. Unfortunately, Alexander Neil and the *Last Shenandoah Valley Campaign* adds few new insights to differentiate it from the many other published collections of Civil War soldiers' letters. Readers will learn little about the experiences of Civil War surgeons from Alexander Neil. His letters reveal that his duties included packing supplies, attending to sick soldiers, establishing temporary hospitals and directing ambulances on the battlefield. Occasionally he provides the insight that distinguishes classic accounts from more common collections of letters. Recalling the evening after the Battle of Piedmont, he paints a chilling scene of a surgeon's duties on a battlefield:

> How heart rending to hear the groans & shrieks of dying men as we went over the battlefield that night with torches, hunting up the wounded. Rebs and Union lay side by side, praying loud & fervently to God to have mercy on them, and when they saw a man with a green sash on [insignia of the ambulance detail], scores of them would beg at the same time for him to help them, but the Surgeon cannot do very-much on the field, except to administer a little cordial occasionally or ligate a bleeding artery & see that they are carefully handled by the stretcher-bearers (pp. 34-35)

Unfortunately, Neil refrained from describing the duties and special concerns of the medical corps. Usually, he reported mundane matters. A typical battle report reads, "I must lay down on the ground & sleep as it is getting late, & I was up all last night with the wounded" (p. 52). Neil admits that he was unable to capture the details of his military experience. "I see a great many things to write about every day," he noted. "(B)ut really I have not the time nor is this any place to concentrate one's thoughts on any thing" (p. 61).

While remaining silent about many important details of his medical experience, Neil offers a useful analysis of Southern morale. After the Battle of New Market he admits, "The people of this valley are all jubilant over this disaster to our arms and were tickled almost out of their senses at seeing us on our way back" (p. 32) However, by the time the federals took Lexington, civilian morale had plummeted: "The Rebs look down in the mouth and desperate. Woe unto us if we fail into their hands" (p. 37). Neil's observations add credence to the arguments presented in Gabor S. Boritt, *Why the Confederacy Lost* (1992), which suggested that civilian morale remained contingent on Confederate military success. As Neil shows, Southern civilians in the Valley remained hopeful even in the fall of 1864.

Neil does provide some enlightening discussions in his correspondence. In a pair of letters written in May 1864 he offers a detailed account of the condition of Winchester and later questions the policy of the "tyrant" David Hunter. During the fall of 1864 he offers a brief commentary on the soldiers' support of Abraham Lincoln. He writes, "[w]e are much encouraged by our recent successes in the South and our soldiers are still more strongly in favor of the re-election of 'Honest Abe" (p. 63).

To some extent, Neil's letters reflect the arguments of Linderman and Mitchell mentioned earlier. Apparently the war served as a transformation process for Neil. After a year of service he wrote, "I have already. . .had more experience than some of the oldest practitioners in civil practice and particularly in the branch of operative Surgery have had a fine experience" (p. 52). The war transformed Neil from an inexperienced medical school graduate to a tested surgeon. It seems that he became a hardened soldier as well. After the battle of Cedar Creek he traversed the field. "To go over the battlefield the next day after the battle was a great, but common sight to me," he reported, "as it was the 10th battle I have been in this summer & fall" (p. 73). Unfortunately, he does not dwell on either transformation process. Neil's observations about courage shed light on Linderman's argument; it seems that Neil never becomes convinced that personal bravery did not play a critical role on the battlefield. In the spring of 1864 he still valued heroic personal courage. When discussing a South Carolina regiment at New Market, he noted, "Braver men never lived, and though our men occasionally flinched and wavered, they never flinched for one moment" (p. 29). Neil's observations suggest that the importance of the notion of courage varied among individual soldiers. Neil does not reflect on his motivations for fighting. Thus, his letters neither support nor refute McPherson's assertions.

The quality of Richard. R. Duncan's editing varies, but unlike Neil's letters it generally provides the necessary details. In fact, the general reader may find some endnotes excessively detailed but this should not pose a problem for most readers. Duncan effectively cites important battles, locations and personalities, but on other issues remains disturbingly silent. While most readers would not be interested in a detailed family history, some notation about family situations would add to their understanding of Neil's experience. Neil's concern about his brother James runs through the selected correspondence. James is apparently ill, and continued correspondence suggests that he has a mental illness that endangers himself and his family. Neil urges his parents to send James to the "Infirmary," apparently a mental institution. He tells his parents that "no one could think hard of it as Every body knows full well the state of affairs" (p. 78). Everyone, that is, except the modern reader, for Duncan does not comment on James's illness or the family's reaction to it. References to cousins and uncles whom Neil visits are missing. Early in the selected correspondence Neil mentioned an incident in which a Cumberland, Maryland, citizen shot a member of his regiment, but this is the only information the reader receives because of Neil's taciturn style and a lack of documentation.

Duncan's introduction and epilogue effectively discuss the events surrounding the final Shenandoah Valley campaign and Alexander Neil's personal experience during those times. The scope of the work is curious but revealing; it is apparent from the introduction and epilogue that Neil was writing before and after the last Shenandoah Valley campaign but Duncan only includes letters from 1864 in his work. Duncan's selectivity makes for a wise editorial policy, but also suggests the average quality of his source material.

Alexander Neil and the Last Shenandoah Valley Campaign does not provide significant insight into the experience of Civil War surgeons. Relatively little in Neil's correspondence enables it to stand out from the many other published collections of Civil War letters. At times spotty but generally adequate, the editing of the work does not greatly add to the collection's limited appeal. Students of the Valley Campaign of 1864 will find parts of Neil's correspondence interesting, but the general reader interested in the experience of Civil War surgeons or vivid personal accounts of the war would be wise to seek out other published accounts before consulting the Neil correspondence.

Jonathan M. Berkey   The Pennsylvania State University

Black Confederates and Afro-Yankees in Civil War Virginia, by Ervin L. Jordan, Jr. (University Press of Virginia, Box 3508, Charlottesville, VA 22903-0608) 1995. Notes, black and white photographs, bibliography, index. 447 pp. Paperback. $18.95.

This volume considers the treatment of slaves and free blacks in Virginia during the Civil War, as well as their responses to new conditions and possibilities created by that conflict. The author is a curator with faculty status in the University or Virginia Library who earlier had written two books about the Civil War in Virginia. The first half of the volume focuses on the status of bondsmen and free blacks in antebellum and wartime Virginia. A prologue notes black roles in and reactions to John Brown's 1859 Harper's Ferry raid. The large numbers and uneven distribution of slaves and free blacks in Virginia are described. Yet contradictions seem to exist between the narrative and the tables concerning the growth of these groups in the state's population. Attention is also devoted to the Lemmon legal case that freed Virginia slaves taken to New York.

The lives of bondsmen in rural areas are the theme of the opening chapter. Clothing, food, music, and work are considered, along with white overseers and black drivers, slave sales and prices, the role of female slaves, and the hiring of bondsmen. Urban and Industrial slaves provide the focus for the second chapter, with more emphasis on wartime. Owned, hired and impressed bondsmen labored in iron foundries, on rail and water transportation, in hospitals, on construction of fortifications and roads, and in a variety of other factories and businesses. The Confederate and state governments employed several thousand slave laborers during the war. Yet Jordan's estimate that "nearly 180,000 Afro-Virginians toiled as logistical support for Confederate Virginia" (p. 67) seems high since that would have been one-third of the state's African-American population including women and children.

Escaped slaves before and during the war are the next focus for the author. As the war increased the opportunities for escape, the number of runaways grew by 1863 to about 38,000. That figure raises a question about the author's estimate that "slave runaways had a 90 percent chance of recapture" (p. 79). They left by foot and by boat to the Union lines along the coast and in northern and western Virginia. In Union contraband camps the escaped slaves met receptions that ranged from helpful to hostile. The impact of conflict on the health, housing, education and religion of slaves and free blacks also receives attention. Those hired to labor for the Confederacy often suffered greater dangers and death rates. Ironically, northern companies provided slave insurance for owners even after 1861. Some illegal schools for blacks existed before the war and the number grew in Union occupied regions. Black churches also increased in number and openness during the conflict. The pressures on black families are explored, including white male attention to slave women that led to 40 percent of free blacks and 15 percent of the bondsmen in Virginia being mixed in ancestry. The concept of Virginia as a slave "breeding state" (p. 121) is mentioned but not fully clarified. While prostitution and rape involving black and white women and men are noted, the author concludes that "black women were the victims of the majority of the war's rapes" (p. 133).

White racial views, Confederate and Union, as well as efforts by Virginians to retain control of slaves during the war are considered in some detail. Negative views of black Virginians appeared most clearly in terminology and in minstrel shows. Despite mixed treatment by Union soldiers, slaves often aided the escapes by Federal prisoners of war. Virginia tightened its legal controls over black Americans during the war, while the use of whippings, executions and threats of sale increased to 'limit aid for the Union cause. Nevertheless, slaves and free blacks especially in towns avoided or resisted punishment. Black Americans also became victims of white and black crime. The discussion of slave resistance seems unclear or contradictory in a few places.

Military historians will focus on the second half of this volume because it emphasizes the various aspects of black service with Civil War armies. Personal servants of Confederates, and some Union officers, are considered because they went with owners or employers into military units where the blacks cooked, washed and treated wounds. In Confederate reminiscences, personal servants appeared as faithful or humorous figures, although some used those connections to later gain pensions or to aid their postwar black communities. Other servants escaped during the war. Jordan estimates between twenty and thirty servants for each regiment in the Confederate Army of Northern Virginia during 1863.

The 58,000 free blacks in Virginia receive attention since they showed considerable ability in maintaining their status despite legal discrimination and even efforts to reenslave them. Both men and women owned property and operated businesses. With a growing need for labor, the Virginia government impressed free blacks to construct entrenchments. Early In the war some free blacks gave public support to the Confederacy, probably to protect their status. Yet by 1864 black delegates from Union held areas attended a national black convention In New York. Scattered reports of slaves as Confederate soldiers often seem to be based on rumors or memoirs that are not fully confirmed or analyzed. A few personal servants did become spies. Yet it is worth noting that most reports of black Confederates were dated before the emancipation proclamation. Even then the statement that "numerous black Virginians were enthusiastic about fighting Yankees" (p. 224) seems open to debate.

The author is on firmer ground describing the growing Confederate Interest during 1864 and 1865 in offering freedom to individual slaves if they enlisted for military service. Despite opposition from some government leaders and editors, the Confederate Congress acted in March 1865 and officers began to recruit a few companies of black troops. Two brief instances of combat seem to have occurred before the surrender of the Confederate armies. Yet suggestions that earlier "mobilization might have tipped the scales of fate in favor of the Confederacy" (p. 247) and about "the potential paralysis of segments of the Union war effort due to Northern blacks being viewed as a fifth column" (p. 251) appear rather unlikely.

Finally, the author focuses on the impact of emancipation in wartime Virginia. The proclamation did not include Unionist areas in the state, especially the region that became West Virginia, yet there black Americans could celebrate the new cause. White Virginians generally feared slave revolt, although a few freed their bondsmen. Officially 5,700 black Virginians joined the Union army in Federal occupied areas, but the author counts eight black regiments, two cavalry and six infantry, as well as an artillery battery raised In the state. Those units may have included an even larger number of soldiers. Black Virginians also served in regiments from other states and in the United States Navy. Despite facing some discrimination in the Federal military, they fought well in battles during 1864-1865, winning six Congressional Medals of Honor.Confederates killed unarmed black prisoners and enslaved others on several occasions, which caused black troops to carry off their wounded if possible and to retaliate in some instances. A number of blacks including women acted as spies or scouts for the Union army. Some Virginia slaveholders tried to retain control of their slaves into the summer of 1865. Yet black Virginians quickly began to hold meetings that expressed their hopes for full citizenship following the war.

This study reflects impressive research in a vast array of manuscripts as well as printed sources. It builds upon the work of Ira Berlin, James Brewer, Robert Durden and earlier generations of black historians, but goes beyond their scope and conclusions. The writing style generally is clear, although a few passages seem vague or contradictory. While the analysis usually appears sound, there will be debate about same conclusions such as those noted earlier. Greater use of slavery studies by historians such as John Blasslngame and Eugene Genovese who offer psychological models might have proved helpful on some topics. Despite some limitations, however, this is a valuable volume that offers important new information and insights on black Americans in the Civil War.

Alwyn Barr   Texas Tech University

Sumter is Avenged!, by Herbert M. Schiller (White Mane Publishing Co., Inc., P.O. Box 152, Shippensburg, PA 17257) 1996. Illustrations, maps., endnotes, bibliography, index. 201 pp. HC. $29.95.

Winfield Scott's Anaconda Plan, designed to strangle the Confederacy via a naval blockade, relied on Union forces achieving control over the Southern coastline by controlling certain key ports. Some ports were necessary logistical bases, while others were needed to deny their use by blockade runners. Forts along the eastern seaboard became increasingly important since they often determined who could travel near the coast. Constructed in the years preceding the Civil War at the mouth of the Savannah River, Fort Pulaski was crucial to both sides. Southern leaders had to keep the fort in order to maintain the flow of supplies into Savannah and therefore into the rest of Georgia and north Florida. Union leaders needed to take it in order to silence the fort's guns and reduce the Southern ability to break the blockade. *Sumter is Avenged!* describes the fight for the fort, the effect of rifling on siege warfare, and the difficulties of Union interservice coordination.

Like other forts of its type built in the mid-1800s, Fort Pulaski was a huge, pentagonal, masonry fortification; it possessed a large number and variety of guns arranged along the perimeter to protect Savannah and also defend the coastline. The fort was built on an island barely large enough to support it. The islands surrounding it were little more than marshes, and most actually disappeared during high tide. The adverse topography ensured that any land attacks would have to come from nearly a mile away, and the fort's designers felt comfortable that the walls would be more than sufficient to withstand a barrage of smoothbore cannon fire from that distance. Secure in the fort's invulnerability from land attack, Confederate commanders pulled forces within the fort's walls since the fort provided better protection from naval gunfire. However, this gave the Union military essentially uncontested use of the neighboring islands. The Union siege commander, Brigadier General Quincy Gillmore, selected the largest and most substantial island neighboring the fort, Tybee Island, to be the site of Union artillery. Gillmore also decided to incorporate three of the relatively new and untested rifled cannon batteries into the Union artillery force, the first use of rifled cannon during siege warfare. Rifling meant not only an increased lethality that had a devastating effect on the fort's brickwork, but also that the cannons could be effective from much farther away than Confederate officers imagined. During less than two days of bombardment Gillmore's artillerists destroyed much of the fort's southeastern wall, but also struck the fort's magazine and threatened to blow up the fort and its inhabitants. The fort commander, Colonel Charles Olmstead, tried to return fire but was unsuccessful, largely due to Gillmore's intelligent artillery placement and entrenchment. Unable to leave because of the artillery fire and the Union Navy, but also faced with the extermination of his men, Olmstead surrendered Fort Pulaski on April 11, 1862.

Arranged chronologically, Schiller's work aims at combining traditional battle history, technological history, and analysis of military leadership of both sides. He begins by providing background information on the fort's construction in the years preceding the war, then presents a well-organized narrative detailing the formation of the Union plan to attack the fort and the siege and eventual surrender of the fort. The battle history recounting the course of the siege is quite detailed, and Schiller makes extensive use of diaries and letters of both Confederate and Union officials.

In addition to presenting a history of the siege of Fort Pulaski, Schiller evaluates the effect of rifled cannon on siege warfare and on warfare in general. He concludes that rifled cannon had as profound an impact on warfare as the use of iron on the *Monitor* and *Virginia*; and served to render useless masonry forts such as Fort Pulaski. Unfortunately, in the desire to emphasize technology's impact on siege warfare, Schiller goes into tremendous detail on not only the number and type of cannon used by both sides, but also the inner workings of each piece, the angles of fire used, and a host of other technological tidbits that tend to clutter the narrative. Schiller uses terminology that artillery enthusiasts will find familiar but that the casual reader may find confusing. Fortunately, Schiller includes an indispensable Appendix at the end of the work detailing the evolution of rifled artillery. All readers, even those familiar with the specifications of Civil War artillery, should read the Appendix before reading the book, if for no other reason than to become familiar with the terminology used in the body of the work.

The third goal of the work, the analysis of military leadership, is adequate, although at times overshadowed by the technical explanations. Schiller focuses attention especially to the difficulties in the Union military of establishing interservice cooperation. Exemplary of this was the original plan to take Savannah and use the port as one of the logistical bases for the naval blockade, a plan that eventually fell through because the Army and Navy could not agree on the correct course of action. Schiller proposes that the difficulties in bureaucracy and the infighting among the Union Army for promotions and credit for success indicate problems encountered in other operations, but the generalization is not developed thoroughly. In addition, and despite the title, the reader gets little information to demonstrate that Union forces felt a deep desire to reduce Fort Pulaski to exact revenge for Fort Sumter, and Schiller does not establish emotional resentment towards the Confederacy.

Overall, the work provides an interesting insight into the devastating effect that rifled cannon had on the previous ideas of siege warfare, but Schiller's belief in its "revolutionary" effect is not proven. Masonry forts continued to be built, despite the supposed lessons learned from the example of Fort Pulaski. In addition, the Union Army did not immediately incorporate rifled cannon into all their artillery batteries, which either indicates a lack of understanding on their part, or a lack of conviction that rifled artillery was as revolutionary as Schiller purports. Schiller provides some insight into the personalities of the commanding officers on both sides, but does not devote enough attention to the human side of the siege. At times the combatants take a back seat to the battle narrative and the technological explanations. Despite these misgivings, *Sumter Is Avenged!* is useful in understanding the complex nature of siege warfare during the Civil War.

William Bridges   University of Nebraska-Lincoln

Army Life of an Illinois Soldier, by Charles W. Wills (Southern Illinois University Press, P.O. Box 3697, Carbondale, IL 62902-3697) 1996. Foreword, introduction. 385 pp. Paperback. $14.95.

This work was privately published in a limited edition in 1906. Included were the letters and diary which the soldier, Charles Wills, sent to his sister. She transcribed the material, apparently with few changes or omissions. In any event, the originals are now unavailable for comparison.

Because of the nature of Wills' service, his writings are well worth reprinting. Wills enlisted at the war's start as a private in the 8th Illinois for three months. After campaigning in Missouri, he received from an acquaintance in his hometown of Canton, Illinois, a lieutenant's commission as a battalion adjutant in the 7th Illinois Cavalry. While his unit's service along the Mississippi was relatively inactive, he described many less known actions, including an especially good account of the naval battle near Island Number Ten. When War Department orders eliminated battalion adjutants, Wills returned home to raise a company for the 103rd Illinois and received a captaincy. After participating on the fringes of the Chattanooga campaign, Wills's company played an active role in Sherman's Georgia operations and in the subsequent marches through the Carolinas. For 1864-1865, he kept a detailed, day-by-day record. Near the war's end he was promoted to major. This book is useful for the histories of all of Wills regiments but especially for that of the 103rd Illinois.

Because Wills received some college training, he wrote with literacy and style well above average. A critical, indeed cynical observer, he did not overlook the faults of either commanders or members of the rank and file. The unmarried Wills showed considerable interest in the women whom he met and was fairly candid in the views on them that he expressed to his sister. Throughoutthere is a negative tone; thus, in considering the possibility of a Southern invasion of Illinois, he opined, "About the worst feature of the case would be Southern officers sparking our girls as we do theirs now and the worst is, there is no doubt the girls would take to it kindly, for they do here, and I'm satisfied there is no difference in the feminines of the two sections, except that ours do not say 'thar' and 'whar.'" He went on to inquire, "How'd you like to see a 'Captain St. Clair de Monstachir' with C.S.A. on his buttons making calls in Canton? I'11 bet ten to one he could enjoy himself in that burg" (p. 76). Whatever his doubts about Northern women, Wills was yet more stern toward their Confederate sisters, especially the "regular snuff-dipping, swearing Southern women of the low, white-trash family" (p. 195). After the end of the fighting, he was even more indignant at North Carolina women. "At three different places there were groups of very healthy looking young ladies, well dressed, by the roadside, waving their handkerchiefs at us, and one told the boys she wished them to come back after they were mustered out, 'for you have killed all our young men off. . . .I venture that these same women coaxed their beaux off to war, and now that 'Yank' is ahead, they shake their handkerchiefs at us and cry,'bully Yanks.' The devil take them and he'll be sure to do it" (P. 375).

On other subjects the war modified Wills' outlooks. Having started the war uninterested in the emancipation of slaves, by 1863 he not only accepted it but favored the raising of black troops and even briefly considered seeking a commission in such a unit. Yet he continued to express white supremacist thoughts and to meet blacks mainly as unpaid servants. When he encountered a quadroon educated at Oberlin, he acknowledged, "A negro lady is something of a novelty, and if I did not conduct myself exactly right in her presence, I think I am somewhat excusable. . . ." Cp. 195).

Wills occasionally had the opportunity to observe leading people such as "Mrs. General Grant" whom he described as "a model lady. She has seen not over thirty years, medium size, healthy blonde complexion, brown hair, blue eyes (cross-eyed) and has a pretty hand. She dresses very plainly. . . .Believe her worthy of the general" (p. 187). Far more of his comments were on the pains and pleasures of camp life. Of the former bugs were a bane. Early on he said, "If you'd multiply all the bugs say by 10,000, you'd have something near the number that visit me nightly. They are of all sizes less than a door knob, and the shapes and colors are innumerable" (p. 111). Near war's end he asked, "You have heard of woodticks? The man who don't catch his pint a day is in awful luck" (p. 373). By then although he welcomed peace, he like many a civilian turned-officer had come to enjoy army life.

Wills' postwar career was partly political and likely to interest students of Louisiana history. One of his colonels had been William Pitt Kellogg, who President Abraham Lincoln appointed Collector of Customs at New Orleans. Kellogg, who had married Wills' sister (the addressee of these letters), supplied his brother-in-law with a job at the Customshouse. As Kellogg went on to become a controversial Louisiana "Carpetbag" governor and United States senator, Wills secured from another old friend from the 103rd Illinois a position as deputy collector of internal revenue. He also bought, together with Kellogg, a sugar plantation near Jeanerette, where he died. He was buried in Illinois, however.

Most of these facts are from the well-researched new Foreword written by John Y. Simon. Unfortunately, either by his choice or that of the publisher, he did not turn his editorial talent to the body of the book, which appears to have been reproduced from the original by photo offset. Thus unless readers remember to refer back to the Foreword, they are likely to be confused by several misdated and hence seriously misplaced letters. They will also lack identifications for many people, great or obscure, and for literary references. Especially serious in a book which refers to some military operations not well known, even to those well read on the Civil War is the absence of background information to explain them.

Despite the missing editorial matter, many readers are likely to value the inherent worth of Wills's well-written, often insightful writings. At its price the book is a bargain worth snapping up.

Frank L. Byrne   Kent State University

"Kill-Cavalry"—Sherman's Merchant of Terror by Samuel J. Martin (Associated University Press, 440 Forsgate Dr., Cranbury, NJ 08512) 1996. Epilogue, notes, bibliography, index, illustrations. 325 pp. HC. $48.50.

Civil War historiography is replete with biographies of Confederate cavalrymen that evoke larger-than-life images of their subjects. With the exception of the flamboyant George Custer and the steady Phil Sheridan, however, studies of Union cavalrymen represent a largely ignored facet of Civil War writing. In *"Kill-Cavalry"—Sherman's Merchant of Terror*, Samuel J. Martin attempts to correct this oversight with a biography of General Hugh Judson Kilpatrick. Martin concedes that Kilpatrick was "an anti-hero" (p. 12), whose life essentially became a series of frustrated attempts to fulfill an ambitious plan of becoming a soldier, then governor of New Jersey, and finally president of the United States. Although he did not achieve his life plan Kilpatrick played an important role in the evolutionary process that ultimately brought the Union cavalry to equality with the southern cavaliers. While many might call him despicable, none could ever proclaim him dull.

Kilpatrick began his Civil War career in 1861 as captain of Company H, 5th New York Infantry. He participated with the zouave infantrymen at Big Bethel and became the first Union officer to be wounded in the war. Kilpatrick used his sudden popularity to recruit soldiers for a cavalry regiment and became lieutenant colonel of the 2nd New York Cavalry. In July 1862, Kilpatrick distinguished himself by conducting three raids in two weeks. When Joseph Hooker took command of the Army of the Potomac and reorganized its cavalry, he placed Kilpatrick in charge of a brigade. Kilpatrick participated in Stoneman's Raid and destroyed a vast amount of public property, including two steam trains, two wagon trains, two ferries, a depot and a bridge. During the Gettysburg campaign, Kilpatrick's insufficient tactical skills served to limit his part in the Battle of Brandy Station and he wasted over 300 men in reckless charges at Aldie that failed to break through Jeb Stuart's cavalry screen to determine the whereabouts of Lee's army. Nevertheless, President Lincoln commissioned him a brigadier general at the age of twenty-seven.

In the fall of 1863, General Geprge G. Meade appointed Kilpatrick to command a division. Kilpatrick displayed a marked inability to control his subordinates and suffered an ignominious defeat at what became known as the "Buckland Races." In an attempt to restore his reputation, Kilpatrick led a raid into Richmond to free the 11,600 Union prisoners confined in and around the city, but he refused to charge the weakly defended garrison and the mission failed. To complicate matters, Col. Ulric Dahlgren had been killed leading a detachment of Kilpatrick's men, and the Confederates found papers on him exhorting the destruction of Richmond and the assassination of President Jefferson Davis and his cabinet. Kilpatrick had now become a pariah, and U. S. Grant eagerly transferred him to William T. Sherman's army. Sherman accepted his new cavalryman with some trepidation—"I know Kilpatrick is a hell of a damned fool" (p. 193)—but the match soon became amicable. Kilpatrick was in his element enforcing Sherman's doctrine to "make Georgia howl" (p. 192). During Sherman's March to the Sea and Carolina campaigns, he conducted himself with wanton abandon, committed numerous atrocities, bedded women of ill repute, and suffered decisive defeats. After the war, Kilpatrick received a major general's commission and accepted a position as ambassador to Chile, where he met and married his second wife, Louisa. He twice ran for governor of New Jersey, but a scandalous affair with a married prostitute and his checkered war record ruined all chances at nomination. Throughout the 1870s, he won public acclaim lecturing on the Civil War, and a genius for farming earned him a substantial income. A third attempt at a political career led to second term as diplomat to Chile, where Kilpatrick died of a kidney ailment in 1881.

Martin portrays Kilpatrick as "an egotistical, lying, sadistic, philandering, thieving miscreant whose lofty reputation had been gained by words, not deeds" (p. 12). Martin describes Kilpatrick as "more often contemptible than commendable" (p. 12) and finds much to contend with in Kilpatrick's life. As a West Point cadet he disliked the air of superiority displayed by the Southern students and engaged in numerous fistfights. Thus, young Judson began to show what Martin believes was "a sadistic urge that would reach unconscionable levels during the Civil War" (p. 17). As a soldier Kilpatrick proved adept at small cavalry raids but displayed numerous character flaws that hindered his battlefield performance and created animosity in his superiors. He embellished his official reports to incredulous proportions to pacify his enormous ego and fanatical ambition. He reacted rashly and struck out blindly against adversaries and showed little compunction about ordering his men to certain death in needless headlong charges. A major defect about which he kept no pretensions was womanizing, and he was often found performing "sack duty and horizontal drill" (p. 62) with white whores, escaped slaves, and a Chinese girl when he should have been in battle. Worst of all, however, Kilpatrick used his authority to fill his wallet at the expense of the Union army and the Southern populace. While conducting forays into the Confederacy, he seized horses, mules, and tobacco from private citizens, labeled it "contraband," and had army sutlers sell it and return the profitsto him. Union officials investigated Kilpatrick and his command and arrested the general, but due to a shortage of good officers within the Federal cavalry an army court cleared him of all charges.

"Kill-Cavalry "—Sherman's Merchant of Terror is a chronicle of the events in Kilpatrick's life; it is not an in-depth biography. Martin addresses Kilpatrick's antebellum years in just six pages and provides little insight into the general's personality during his formative years. He focuses most of his criticism on Kilpatrick's moral character and attributes the majority of Kilpatrick's later actions to intense ambition. Kilpatrick's obsession with women and fame does not explain why he stole, lacked tactical skills, and committed abominable acts against Southern civilians. The use of additional primary source material would have added considerably to the narrative and overall examination of Kilpatrick's life. According to the bibliography, Martin consulted only six manuscript repositories and failed to reference unpublished documents left by Kilpatrick's former soldiers. Likewise, the author neglected the M.O.L.L.U.S. Papers that contain four articles written by Kilpatrick's veterans on the Atlanta campaign alone, and although he utilized George King's dissertation on Kilpatrick, Martin did not use that author's excellent article published in 1973 which critically analyzes Kilpatrick's odious behavior.

Another major failing of the book is its odd organization. The narrative is interrupted a quarter of the way through (chapter six) and at the end of every chapter to interpose the author's conclusions on Kilpatrick's moral deficiencies and actions, all of which would have been better applied in a final chapter. Martin devotes an entire epilogue (five pages) to a detailed description of the lives of Kilpatrick's descendants that could have been aptly summarized in a few short paragraphs. There is no List of Illustrations, even though there are thirty-nine maps and twenty-three photographs interspersed throughout the book. Although the maps are abundant, they lack sufficient detail. For example, the map on page 51 does not show the Confederate cavalry position, and maps on pages 130, 158, 195, 202, 210, and 220 do not outline the marching routes for which they are labeled.

The book is generally well written, but Martin expends an inordinate amount of space needlessly detailing events in which Kilpatrick played no part. Descriptions of the 1862 Kentucky campaign, Jackson's Valley campaign in 1862, and the Chattanooga campaign contribute nothing to an understanding of Kilpatrick but rather give the impression of a padded narrative. In addition, the book's title is deceiving. To be sure, Kilpatrick carried Sherman's idea of total warfare to an extreme, but he served just one year under Sherman. Kilpatrick spent three years in the Eastern Theatre and earned the sobriquet "Kill-Cavalry" there. Consequently, only one-third of the book is devoted to Kilpatrick's service under Sherman.

This concise chronicle of Kilpatrick's military and political careers should provide an adequate introduction for the neophyte Civil War reader, but it suffers from too many critical shortcomings to prove satisfactory for students and scholars. Lacking an in-depth analysis of its subject and containing a disjointed narrative, the book appears hastily researched and padded with unnecessary information. It lacks the breadth of scholarship that normally graces books in this price range. As a leading figure in two theaters of the war and a major proponent of unlimited warfare, Kilpatrick deserves further examination and awaits a well-researched, scholarly biography.

Christopher S. Dwyer   Newtane, New York

More Generals in Gray, by Bruce S. Allardice (Louisiana State University Press, Baton Rouge, LA 70803) 1995. Bibliograghy. 300 pp. HC. $29.95.

Military historians pursuing information about a particular Confederate general usually consult Ewa Warner's *Generals in Gray: Lives of the Confederate Commanders* or Mark M. Boatner's *Civil War Dictionary*. The latter two sources provide adequate information about regularly appointed generals, but offer either few or no facts about the many Confederates who served as generals without the benefit of an official appointment from President Jefferson Davis and later approval by the Confederate Congress. Bruce S. Allardice's work seeks to fill this information gap with brief articles about 137 men who served as generals without presidential appointments and Congressional confirmation. Allardice's preface explains how Confederate law defined a general, the procedure for appointments and confirmation to the rank of general, and the criteria Allardice developed to select the men for examination in his book. The 137 men discussed in this work include soldiers that Lieutenant General Edmund Kirby Smith, commander of the Trans-Mississippi Department promoted to the rank of general, men that the *Official Records* shows as assigned to a general's rank, those viewed by contemporaries as generals though there is no official documentation of their appointment, generals in "one of the state armies organized in 1861" (p. 12), state militia generals who led their troops in a campaign, or one of five men (including Henry Kyd Douglas) that modern works often mention as generals but were "only occasionally called general by contemporaries" (p.12). The body of the work consists of short articles about these "other" Confederate generals arranged alphabetically by surname. Most of the articles are between one page and one and a half pages in length and contain valuable information such as birth data, names of parents, prewar career, war service, postwar career (if any), and an evaluation of the soldier's claim to the rank of general. Following each article is a helpful short bibliography of sources. Louisiana State University Press will include photographs for 108 men in the finished text, but this reviewer was unable to comment on photographic quality since L. S. U. included no photographs in the advance uncorrected proof review copy.

The variety of people discussed in this work and the colorful lives of many of them, encourages the reader to browse. William Bartee Wade, for example, shot seven occupation soldiers in 1866 before being wounded and carried to a local hotel. Three days later, soldiers removed the recuperating Wade from his bed and murdered him by throwing him out of an upper story window. John Robert Baylor of Texas possessed a "ferocious temper" (p. 33), and secretive Colton Greene of Missouri hid most facts about his antebellum life. Several entries detail the lives of men who compiled impressive combat records. These notables include Raphael Semmes, the famed commander of the *C. S. S. Alabama*, James Hagan who survived three wounds as he led his troops through the campaigns of the Army of Tennessee, and Meriwether "Jeff" Thompson, the famed "Swamp Fox" of the Trans-Mississippi. In addition, Allardice provides articles about Jeffrey E. Forrest, a fine officer and a younger brother of Lieutenant General Nathan Bedford Forrest, and George Washington Rains who constructed the impressive gunpowder factory in Augusta, Georgia.

Following the body of the work is an appendix and a bibliography. The appendix consists of brief entries about 135 additional men whose claims as general are less reliable. Many of these footnoted entries refer to state militia officers or men who simply assumed the title of general after the war. Allardice's bibliography reveals the impressive depth of research necessary to compile this book. Allardice effectively used many primary sources such as burial records, city directories, compiled service records, court records, family papers, genealogies, and newspapers to write about his often elusive subjects.

More Generals in Gray is a fine, well-organized, well-researched work that presents information about many men who contributed significantly to the Confederate war effort. This work includes articles about generals from all theaters of the war, but those who served in the western theater or the Trans-Mississippi theater are particularly well represented. *More Generals in Gray* belongs on your

Civil War reference shelf as a worthy companion volume to Ezra Warner's *Generals in Gray.*

M. Jane Johansson   Pryer, OK

The Returned Battle Flags (Rank & File Publications, 1926 South Pacific Coast Hwy Suite 228, Redondo Beach, CA 90277) 1995. Color illustrations. Paperback. $25.00.

This work is a reprint of a souvenir publication by the Cotton Belt Route Railway given in 1905 to confederate veterans attending the United Confederate Veterans reunion in Louisville, Kentucky. An exceedingly rare publication, the surviving originals are expensive collector items and to most researchers, were, until now, unavailable. The new printing adds only a useful and informative preface by historian Richard Rollins.

The Returned Battle Flags was the first published documentation of a large group of Confederate Civil War Flags. Illustrated with the detail only artists of the period could provide, the flags are seen with ah the tears, bullet holes, and frayed edges with which they ended their war service. Although all the illustrations are presented with only a single shade of red, white, and blue with yellow, orange, and other tints absent, the seventy-four illustrations of torn and battered banners give mute testimony to the ravages of war and the spirit that led men to follow these flags to glory.

Not intended to be a comprehensive history, the text merely documents the approximately 500 flags returned by the Department of War to the Southern states with some attempt to identify units when possible. Many of these flags were captured during or after savage fighting. Many varieties of Confederate battle flags are present, and as the types were not labeled until much later in the twentieth century, the reader must refer to other works to identify them accurately, a pleasant challenge.

Of special interest is the number of first and second national types clearly associated with combat units. In 1905 it was still well known, although not well-known today, that Confederate troops, depending on many factors, carried several basic types of battle flags including the national types. In addition to the first two nationals, the sharp eye can note not only state nags but also variants of some of the regimental pattern flags. Flags of the Army of Tennessee such as the Johnston 1864 battle flag so well known today, the Hardee, the Department of Alabama battle flag, as well as Army of Northern Virginia types such as the twelve-starred cotton issue, second bunting, third bunting, and later issues, are illustrated. The importance of this publication is not lessened because some common battle flag types, such as the pink-bordered Bragg, the Van Dorn crescent moon and stars, and the blue Polk with its red St. George's Cross, are not illustrated.

Of special interest is the "record of flags captured by Union troops" which documents the numerical designation number of each of the 542 flags so noted. Most of the flags documented in this work survive today in public collections with the stenciled "capture numbers" still remaining. This reprint is a useful tool when visiting these collections or orienting these flags with particular battles.

In and of itself the book *is* history. Contemporary with this work the United Confederate Veterans established and decreed one generic "battle flag" (late-war Army of Northern Virginia fourth-bunting issue) for symbolic purposes and the effects of that decree remain with us today. Perhaps there would have been less misinterpretation and misuse of Confederate heraldry in this century if this publication had been better known.

In several ways, *The Returned Battle Flags* is a splash in the face, refreshingly free of modern bias, cynicism, and slickness. It stands alone, and as such is a useful and necessary reference for the historian, vexillogist, and anyone who seeks historical truth. Although the back cover departs from the rest of the work in featuring stylistic/inspirational renditions of the first national (the *real* Stars and Bars), the second national (Stainless Banner), the third national (which was only issued to a few units at the end of the war), and a rectangular generic battle flag, the front cover with its illustration of five actual furled battle flags—two "Johnston 1864s" and three blue and white "Hardees"—provide the reader with an insight into the circumstances of the real Confederate soldier. A glance shows that the flag poles are merely hand trimmed saplings, not the manufactured and polished staffs of today. Those flags and crude poles best describe this work: rough and unpolished—but absolutely honest. It is a must for the Confederate historian.

Alan K. Sumrall   Livingston, Texas

Software Review

Antietam: Battleground 5. (TalonSoft, Inc., P.O. Box 632, Forest Hill, MD 21050 [www.Talonsoft.com.] $44.95).

While we rarely review software titles in *Civil War Regiments*, we believe the first class regimental level simulations produced by TalonSoft deserve the attention of our readers. The recent release of *Antietam* seemed particularly appropriate given the theme of this issue.

Antietam offers some 25 different scenarios, including the entire September 17, 1862 battle, smaller actions, such as the fight at Burnside's Bridge, and virtually everything else in between. In addition, various scenarios for South Mountain are also included. The multitude of options include either the traditional two-dimensional hexagon board format with unit counters, or a stunning 3-D miniatures-style wargame—complete with complex and realistic terrain features. Graphic options allow players to choose between three views: a close or "normal" view; a "zoom out" mode for a greater sweep of the field; or an entire battlefield shot. Period music and small video clips—keyed to the action on screen—can be enjoyed during the game or turned off, as the player may wish.

The method of play is also myriad. Games can be played alone against the computer (Artificial Intelligence, or simply AI), against another "live" body with the "Hot-Seat" mode, via E-Mail, or head-to-head over a modem. A list of the scenarios with a brief description of each game, including several "what if" variants, offer a banquet of choices from which an enthusiast may feast. The difficulty of play can be easily manipulated (in favor of one player or the other), and a wide variety of other options are available as well (including Fog-of War, which limits what you know and see, consequently making the game more realistic and enjoyable). Players can also choose to command only certain units by giving orders to subordinate officers and allowing the computer to interpret them. If military voyeurism is more your style, simply set both sides on AI and watch the computer battle it out.

Troops are designated in unit boxes which display the specific unit, its strength, armament, fatigue, formation, movement allowance, facing, and so forth. As TalonSoft advertises, movement is as simple as pointing and clicking. We found every aspect of the game to be smoothly and seamlessly meshed.

Whether you are an experienced gamer or a novice playing for the first time, you will find *Antietam* a serious challenge. The dramatically improved AI incorporated into this, the fifth release in TalonSoft's "Battleground" series, enables the computer to be a capable opponent when you play against it solitaire. Too many computer games that we have played solitaire in the past were disappointments. Even if the game was interesting, the visual elements attractive, and the historical detail well presented, the computer simply wasn't a very good opponent. In fact, the computer was often just plain stupid; it is usually too passive and does not respond quickly or well to attacks or unusual moves.

Not so with *Antietam*. The computer proved to be surprisingly aggressive, and successfully recaptured a key crossroads which was an important objective hex for victory conditions. In fact, the computer and Dana Lombardy slugged it out over this location for quite a while, with the vital hex changing hands several times. The computer pushed Dana's troops when they became disrupted (disordered or disorganized), maneuvered to hit his line on the flank, and charged whenever it could gain a definite advantage.

The South Mountain scenario was played three times in preparation for this review (computer as Confederate, reviewers as Federals). The Federals gradually gained a superiority in numbers as more troops continued to arrive in this 38 turn game (each daylight, dawn, or dusk turn represents 20 minutes; night turns each represent an hour of real time). The first two games were played without using the Fog of War option. FoW hides enemy units that in reality could not be seen by your units, and also hides their fatigue condition (fatigue is a unit's combat fatigue status and not its actual physical weariness from marching, etc.), unit designation and quality. It also provides only an estimate as to the unit's size. We discovered that using FoW tends to make players much more cautious—especially against such a vigorous opponent as the computer. The particulars of a given unit are revealed when enemy units come into adjacent contact. It is worth noting that the FoW kicks in again if and when the units separate. As a caveat, we hasten to add that there is still no substitute to playing another person. Computers cannot (yet) replicate human intuition and complex counter-strategies. Modem play, however, makes it simple to find a willing gamer, and TalonSoft offers a discussion group on its web page which makes it easy to find opponents.

Although major Union victories were achieved in each of the three South Mountain games, it took much longer using FoW. This mode of play significantly increases the enjoyment and makes each scenario a more realistic simulation of the dilemmas faced by historical Civil War commanders who weren't quite sure where the enemy was or his actual strength.

After learning the nuances of moving and fighting (and with FoW), it took about four hours to play 29 of the 38 turns (approximately 8 minutes per turn) the third time the South Mountain scenario was undertaken. This day-long simulation was intentionally selected so that we could take advantage of the extra turns and plethora of units in order to become familiar with the best ways to move, attack, defend and rally. Once you learn how to play, using FoW in a scenario in which the computer has the advantage (such as taking the Union side in the short, 8-turn "Carnage in the Cornfield" scenario), can be an excellent challenge. Be prepared to be defeated by AI!

As mentioned earlier, one of the nice things about TalonSoft's series of wargames is that you can also play against a real opponent using a modem and phone line, or play by E-Mail. There is also a way to play against a person in the same room or building using a "null-modem" connection directly between the two computers. However, one of the primary reasons both reviewers find computer games appealing is the flexibility they offer: we can play the game at our convenience. In the past, the low quality of the computer's AI was a deterrent to playing the same game more than once or twice. TalonSoft's improved AI greatly enhances replay value.

The scale of *Antietam* is 125 yards per hex. Most infantry and cavalry units are regiments with actual historical strengths to the nearest 25 men. Artillery units are batteries with the exact number of guns by type (rifles or smoothbores, with howitzers having a shorter range than Napoleons). Individual brigade, division, corps and army leaders are provided, each man rated by two factors: command value (which helps keep units subordinate to him from becoming disrupted in combat), and leadership value (which helps a disrupted or routed unit to recover). Artillery has a fixed amount of ammunition for both sides in each scenario, but infantry units can re-supply from wagons if they become low on ammunition (and if you do not lose them to enemy raids into your rear areas!)

As a game, *Antietam* is a lot of fun. It can also be used to introduce someone to Civil War history that might not be interested in reading a book on the subject. One of the most intriguing aspects of playing historical games is that they allow you to explore "what if" questions, which are often inappropriate in a scholarly book or journal article. Speculating whether an attack directed in another direction would have made a difference in a particular battle is simply an unprovable mental exercise in a written publication. In contrast, playing a game with excellent historical detail and accuracy of terrain can allow a player to actually explore alternative strategies and outcomes.

We do have a few criticisms of the game, primarily from an historian's perspective. Firing over your own or enemy units is permitted for both artillery and infantry fire. The computer's AI may need this edge to stay competitive, but Dana simply refused to do this even though he could have. Although there are historical examples of artillery firing over the heads of friendly troops, these occasions were not common and were usually performed under exceptional circumstances—and not as a matter of combat doctrine.

In melee situations, where units charge and attempt to capture an enemy-held position, sending in a leader with the assault troops gives the attacker an additional benefit. However, any leader gives the same benefit, whether it is Ambrose Burnside vs John Gibbon, or D. H. Hill vs. Roswell Ripley. In addition, you can risk anyone—including George McClellan or Robert E. Lee—in as many melees as you want (the computer lost Longstreet in just such an attack).

In a recent round of updates, TalonSoft addressed this problem by punishing a player for losing a high-ranking officer. If a leader is killed (or wounded or captured), he's always replaced by a "lower rung" leader (army replaced by corps, corps replaced by a divisional leader, etc). Losing a high-quality corp or army leader can actually have great repercussions on your army's entire command and control stucture, as his replacement (and that replacement's replacement, etc) is rarely as good as the one he replaced. Furthermore, one of the new optional rules added in the latest round of updates provides casualty points for eliminated officers. The points awarded are based on the sum of that leader's Command and Leadership ratings, multiplied by his "rank" (brigade leaders x1; division leaders x2; corps leaders x3; army leader x4). Thus, losing Robert E. Lee, who might boast a "C & L" rating of 6 and 6 could cost you 48 victory points!

These are minor quibbles compared to the basic soundness of the historical research and good-looking graphic presentation of TalonSoft's latest wargame. Besides, the game doesn't force you to throw McClellan personally into an attack (although Dana found the idea tempting). If you have been curious about trying a Civil War computer game, there is no better way to start than with TalonSoft's *Antietam.*

Reviewed by Dana Lombardy and Theodore P. Savas

INDEX

"One of The Most Daring of Men"

The LIFE
of
CONFEDERATE GENERAL
William Tatum Wofford

by Gerald J. Smith

First Full Length Biography

General Robert E. Lee called Wofford "One of The Most Daring of Men" and Lee had good reason to know since he had commanded Wofford and his Georgians at the great battles of Second Manassas, Sharpsburg, Chancellorsville and Gettysburg. Every War Between The States enthusiast has heard of Hood's Texas Brigade but - until now - Wofford and his Georgians who served shoulder to shoulder with the Texans have been forgotten. Georgia Professor and Historian Gerald J. Smith vividly brings to life the career of this worthy gentleman who served his state and country from the battlefields of Mexico to the most famous battles of The Civil War and through the bitter struggles of reconstruction. There are also some surprising but well-documented new interpretations of crucial events and personalities in The Army of Northern Virginia. Paperback, 255 pages, photos, maps, index, footnotes, bibliography. Send $16.95 . . .

to

Southern Heritage Press

4035 Emerald Drive
Murfreesboro, TN 37130

Sharpsburg Heritage Festival

Where History Comes Alive!

September 13-14, 1997
Along Main Street in Sharpsburg, Md.

- ❖ Walking Tours of Historic Sharpsburg
- ❖ Free Concerts of Civil War Music
- ❖ Civil War Events and Living History
- ❖ "How to Trace Your Civil War Ancestor"
- ❖ Workshops and Lectures
- ❖ Barn Dance
- ❖ Heirloom Quilts, Antiques, Collectibles
- ❖ Crafts & Food

. . . and more! Plus special events on the Antietam National Battlefield.

The Festival includes a day dedicated to the remembrance of Civil War ancestors. Festival visitors, descendants of those who fought in the war and descendants of those were freed by the war will become honorary citizens of Sharpsburg at noon on Sunday. Our newest citizens will be welcomed in a ceremony complete with citizenship papers.

Call 1-800-228-STAY for more information.

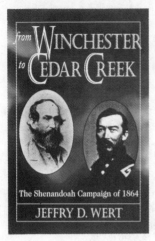

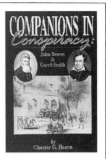

CAPITAL NAVY:

The Men, Ships and Operations of the James River Squadron, by John M. Coski,

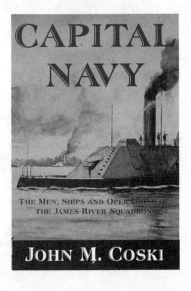

Finally, a rich and fully documented history of the important service rendered by the men and ships of the James River Squadron, whose role in defense of Richmond shaped the course of the Civil War in Virginia. Dr. John M. Coski, the historian with The Museum of the Confederacy, has spent years mining manuscript collections for unpublished letters, journals, diaries and reports. Basing his study on these primary source materials, many of which have never been used before, Coski has weaved a compelling account of Richmond's development into the naval capital of the South, and how her citizens, politicians and military establishment crafted, against heavy odds, the most powerful naval squadron to sail under the Confederate banner.

Capital Navy's fast-paced narrative carries the reader from the May 15, 1862 Battle of Drewry's Bluff, where the Rebels repulsed a powerful Federal naval thrust just a handful of miles below Richmond, through the stunning climactic battle sequences in Trent's Reach in January 1865. The face-to-face engagement with the Federal monitor *Onondaga* in Trent's Reach crushed Southern hopes for a naval victory in Virginia. Less than three months later, the James River Squadron hastened its own end with gunpowder and Southern torches, extinguishing forever the Confederacy's only "capital navy."

Sandwiched between Drewry's Bluff and Trent's Reach were the grueling years of torpedo and mine warfare that immobilized the vast resources of the United States Navy. *Capital Navy* introduces students of the Civil War to the officers, sailors and civilians that designed, built and launched the mammoth ironclads, and provides a detailed examination of Richmond's two river-based shipyards. In addition to offering exhaustive coverage of the careers of the iron warships, Coski sheds considerable light on the heretofore overlooked service rendered by the gallant wooden ships that fought alongside their more famous iron sisters, discusses the Confederate Naval Academy and its training facilities, the James River submarine mystery, and much more. The Civil War in Virginia cannot be fully understood without reading this book.

Specifications: Six maps by Mark A. Moore, 13 original blueprint-style drawings detailing every ironclad of the James River Squadron, 77 photographs and illus., many previously unpublished; End notes, appendices, biblio., index, 50-lb. acid-free paper, d.j., cloth, 343pp. ISBN 1-882810-03-1. $29.95 ($4.00 shipping)

"The research and writing is balanced, exciting, and timely. . . .Savas Woodbury has scored another major coup with *Capital Navy!*"

Edwin C. Bearss,
noted Civil War author and former Chief Historian for the National Park Service

---

Savas Publishing Company
1475 S. Bascom Ave., Suite 204, Campbell, CA 95008